TONY WADDINGTON

TONY WADDINGTON
DIRECTOR OF A WORKING MAN'S BALLET
JOHN LEONARD

First published by Pitch Publishing, 2018

Pitch Publishing
A2 Yeoman Gate
Yeoman Way
Worthing
Sussex
BN13 3QZ
www.pitchpublishing.co.uk
info@pitchpublishing.co.uk

© 2018, John Leonard

Every effort has been made to trace the copyright. Any oversight will be rectified in future editions at the earliest opportunity by the publisher.

All rights reserved. No part of this book may be reproduced, sold or utilised in any form or transmitted in any form or by any means, electronic or mechanical, including photocopying, recording or by any information storage and retrieval system, without prior permission in writing from the Publisher.

A CIP catalogue record is available for this book from the British Library.

ISBN 978-1-78531-423-0

Typesetting and origination by Pitch Publishing
Printed and bound in India by Replika Press Pvt. Ltd.

Contents

Introduction 7

1. Firing up the Potters 13
2. Waddington's Wall 26
3. An Old Man from the Sea 39
4. Winning Promotion 54
5. Centennial Celebrations 70
6. Banks of England 83
7. Team Spirit 93
8. Outgunned in the Cup 108
9. History Makers 123
10. The Man in a White Coat 145
11. The Crash 156
12. A Footballing Bromance 169
13. Title Challengers 181
14. The Roof Caves In 207
15. Taxi for 'Waddo' 227
16. Legendary Status 237

Select Bibliography 255

Introduction

A MAN with the appearance and manner of an urbane 1950s bank manager may hardly fit the stereotype of a hard-nosed football manager. Unlikely to be automatically viewed as the candidate most likely to reinvigorate chiselled old professional players, inspire aspiring footballers to fulfil their dreams, and receive the adulation of generations of fans. Yet Tony Waddington, or 'Waddo' as he was affectionately known to fans and players alike at Stoke City Football Club, was such a man; the director of what he termed 'a working man's ballet'.

In looking back on the work of this director of 'a working man's ballet', I chart how Waddington revived and transformed the fortunes of an ailing football club. On joining Stoke City in the 1950s, the club was yo-yoing in the nether regions of the Football League's Second Division, one bemoaning its luck after coming close to winning major honours just after the Second World War.

Stoke City was going nowhere as a football club, apart from further down the Football League pyramid and possibly even out of business. Waddington, through patience and footballing guile and the help of one or two friendly directors, changed its fortunes, returning to the top tier of English football, winning a major trophy and ultimately challenging, though failing, to win the league title.

To do so, he needed allies, like-minded people, both among those with the purse strings sitting in the directors' box and those recruited to go out on to the football pitch. Here's the story of how he sought out hardened old professional players, conjuring up among them an old wizard to work his magic.

This particular sorcerer was, of course, Stanley Matthews, a legend of the game who controversially walked out of Stoke City in the 1940s just six weeks before a title-challenging season ended in bitter failure. How and why Matthews was brought back to the club as the fans' messiah with all forgiven is a mark of the genius of Waddington. Theoretically, it made no sense bringing back a player in his dotage. Yet for 'Waddo' this was the coup of the century, making to him not just football sense but in what was possibly something of a gamble an absolute public relations masterstroke. Stoke City's current chairman, Peter Coates, describes the signing of Stanley Matthews as 'inspirational'.

Waddington always had an eye for public relations stunts in gradually rebuilding his football club. Stoke City and its fans had a manager publicly lacking the gruff and combative nature of the great Scottish managerial duo of Liverpool's Bill Shankly and Manchester United's Matt Busby, nor their resources. He did not have the flamboyance of his provincial rival Brian Clough, nor his eccentricities.

But Waddington, as many of his peers would come to recognise, possessed a quiet steely determination to succeed, not just for himself and the football club, but just as importantly for its fans and for all the people of the Potteries.

As Stoke's current chairman insists, 'In an old industrial area football means such a lot to people.' Waddington instinctively recognised this to be the case. For him it was almost a mission; a revival in a working-class district with the population craving for footballing success, looking to celebrate its place on the national and, indeed, the international stage. Tony Waddington ensured his working man's ballet would be playing to packed houses at a ground once left near deserted by Potteries football fans.

How did he coin his favourite term, 'a working man's ballet'? It was born out of evangelical zeal. He wanted to sell his love of the game of association football to an American audience, so Waddington used the phrase on a mid-1960s tour of the United States. He thought it helpful to write a booklet explaining the laws of the game for sceptical US sports fans and reasoned the description would 'appeal to the aesthetic tastes of the American public'. As a noble and visionary move it failed. 'We found it difficult to educate spectators on the niceties of our game, when they had been brought up on a diet of scoring points or making home runs in their national sports,' Waddington grumbled. He may have been disappointed with the reaction of American sports fans but back home in the UK his mantra of a 'working man's ballet' stuck.

As an evangelist for the game, he had few equals. On the more basic matter of being a tactician, critics questioned whether he was on a par with his vaunted managerial peers. Yet even some of those naysayers recognised in Waddington's case this hardly seemed to matter. He just simply had enough confidence in his chosen players to give them the freedom to go out and perform. In selecting those players most of his peers knew no better judge of who might or might not make a good footballer. Here was a man, among the first to talk about playing football the 'right way', pure uninhibited football, a joy for his performers to play and easy on the eye for fans.

Yet in moulding his teams there was something of a contradiction. Waddo had a philosophy of pure football but it was based, first, on stopping the opposition team from playing so his own team, at least his flair players, were able to perform with freedom. For all the neat moves his midfielders and forwards might weave together it came from being delivered the ball by uncompromising defenders, euphemistically termed 'Waddington's Wall'.

At first he relied on chiselled professionals in defence, recruiting the likes of Wolverhampton Wanderers' legendary Eddie Clamp and Eddie Stuart. His wall was then provided by a quartet of young local lads, John March, Denis Smith, Alan Bloor and Mike Pejic. They provided Waddington with his percussion as he directed his working man's ballet.

After taking over Stoke City while still in his early 30s, he essentially built three teams. The first was to get them out of the Second Division and into the First Division, what now would be termed the Premier League. The next consolidated the club's position at the top table of English football and eventually challenged for trophies, winning the League Cup in 1972. It wasn't enough for 'Waddo', who finally began building a team to challenge for, and ultimately agonisingly lose out on winning, the Football League title. If anything only financial misfortune prevented him from doing so at Stoke City.

Once a gale had wrecked one of the wooden stands at Stoke's Victoria Ground, the board of directors decided the only way to pay for the damage was to sell Waddington's best players. His captain, Jimmy Greenhoff, went to Manchester United. His midfield playmaker, Alan Hudson, returned to London to play for Arsenal. Once local recruit Mike Pejic was sold to Everton, Waddington contemplated overseeing the humility of a relegation season. Instead, he quit.

One or two of his players felt he was forced to go. If so, why didn't the Stoke directors keep faith in him and his players? Why did they no longer believe playing success may no longer end in trophies and riches for the club? All of this will be explored.

'Waddo' was a manager loved by his players, adored by his fans. Some ex-players believed the people of the Potteries underestimated what Tony Waddington had done for them and their football club, especially those chanting 'Waddington out!' as the club headed for relegation in the late 1970s. Actually, those questioning the level of appreciation of the work of this director of 'a working man's ballet' were wrong.

Stoke fans, even those airing their frustrations as the club struggled and hurling abuse from the terraces, always admired Waddington. They hold him in the greatest esteem. They recognise he rebuilt their football club, turned it into a recognisable sporting institution, one temporarily wrecked by a gale one 70s winter's night. Indeed the club itself, now owned by lifelong fans the Coates family, certainly recognise his achievements. As an example, Tony Waddington Place leads as a roadway to Stoke City's bet365 stadium, a ground complete with the Waddington Suite in its main stand.

Angela Smith, chair of the Stoke Supporters' Council told me, 'To many people of a youthful age, football only started with the advent of the Premier League. Had Tony Waddington managed in this time, his success, given the focus on the game with 24 hours sports broadcasting and social media,, would be the subject of discussion on a regular basis.'

She added, ' I often wonder how a 'Waddo' team , the team of the 70's or the team that won promotion back to the old First Division would fare in the modern day league. One thing is certain, they would not lack class, because Mr Tony Waddington was a class act and Stoke City were looked upon as a quality side for the majority of his time in charge.'

Naturally, no Stoke City fan underestimates Tony Waddington's ability as a manager or his value to the English game. Over the years they were joined by some notable football figures in mutual admiration. Brian Clough described him as a 'man in a million'. And Waddington's achievements, Clough argued, were 'harder earned there [at Stoke] than at Liverpool, Everton or Manchester United. He put Stoke City on the map.'

Yet despite these warm words from a football genius and, admittedly, friend of Waddington, the man with the demeanour of a 1950s bank manager rather than a stereotypically hard-nosed coach enjoys little recognition in the wider footballing world. This is the story of how Tony Waddington brought us 'a working man's ballet'.

1

Firing up the Potters

COACHING and management seemed in modern footballing parlance a natural fit for Tony Waddington, a man with a deep love of football yet one enduring an unfulfilled playing career, blighted by injury and ending in inevitable frustration. From 1940s starlet at Manchester United he had gone to relative footballing anonymity with Crewe Alexandra before being forced to quit playing. In taking his first coaching and then managerial job at Crewe's neighbours Stoke City, he found himself in the embrace of fellow sporting travellers cursing their luck. It was a club in alarming decline.

Stoke in the late 1940s had harboured, as did Waddington as a young player, dreams of ultimate sporting glory. A club boasting England internationals challenged for the league title in the post-war years. But those dreams of winning silverware ended in a nightmare. Waddington, at a young age, loved a challenge. Stoke City, reduced from elite status to something of a basket case of a club by the time he walked through its doors in the 50s, presented him with the stiffest of footballing challenges.

One factor would work in his favour, passion for football in a proud working-class area. The people of the Potteries shared his love of the sport, the city of Stoke-on-Trent the smallest in England to host two full-ime professional Football League clubs.

On a Saturday afternoon, football provided the pottery workers and miners of north Staffordshire a release from the travails of everyday working life. Whether it was at Stoke's Victoria Ground or Vale Park, they went along to see teams fielding mostly local lads in their line-ups cast their spells over all-comers.

Their chief magician was Stanley Matthews, the 'wizard of dribble'. Yet incredibly, towards the end of that doomed 1940s campaign to bring league title glory to the Potteries he stunned Stoke City fans by walking out on the club. The Potters, minus Matthews, lost the title on the last day of the 1946/47 season with defeat to Sheffield United, leaving Liverpool as champions. Amazingly, Matthews, in what Waddington was later to term 'the worst deal in football history', had been allowed to leave Stoke for Blackpool just weeks earlier. From then on the club went into rapid and at times rancorous decline, from challengers for the crown of the champions of England to relegation fodder.

Waddington, as he built his career, became renowned and revered by most of his former players for supreme man-management skills, a master of psychology. The same can't quite be said of one of his predecessors Bob McGrory, the man who so nearly led Stoke to that elusive league title in 1947, losing out partly thanks to a bust-up with his best player. Losing the former Stoke captain Frankie Soo, the first non-white player to appear for England, a year or so earlier in a similar spat between manager and player was, to be polite, careless. Losing Matthews as his team was closing in on a league title bordered on insanity.

For McGrory to go on to lose Neil Franklin, one of England's finest ever defenders, a few years later was just plain shocking. Indeed, the nation was left stunned by the fall-out from Franklin's rows with his manager. So bad were Franklin's relations with not just McGrory and his club, but for good measure also the powers that be of the Football Association, he turned down the chance to compete in the 1950 World Cup finals.

Franklin and another Stoke player, George Mountford, turned up in Colombia in an ill-fated commercial venture. Naturally, Stoke's directors, their manager McGrory and the FA were furious, not that at the time English football cared much about FIFA's World Cup. It was the first time England had even bothered to compete. Franklin never played a game for Stoke City or England again.

In the short term it was a loss to both. Franklin's presence in the England team may well have prevented the embarrassing loss to the United States and humiliation at the World Cup of 1950. In the long term, Stoke were losers. The departure of Franklin and Mountford after falling out with their manager meant the club had lost all of its best players. These were all Potteries lads playing in the England team – in the case of Matthews a sporting icon. To sum up the decline, as Matthews celebrated cup final triumph with Blackpool in May 1953, his home town club suffered relegation with McGrory having been sacked some months earlier.

It was into this troubled environment Stoke's future manager Tony Waddington arrived as a young ambitious coach after being forced to give up his playing career at nearby Crewe. There seemed to be no prospect of an immediate revival of this provincial club. Yet he embraced and relished the challenge ahead. Lingering frustration at being unable to fulfil his playing ambitions may well have been a factor in him later becoming an inspirational manager for his players and supporters alike.

As a football-mad teenager his dreams were on the brink of fulfilment as he took up a contract as an amateur with Manchester United. Waddington may have considered United as his boyhood club but he also regularly went along to Maine Road to watch rivals Manchester City. Born in the city of Manchester on 9 November 1924, he no doubt looked forward to playing eventually in front of the packed terraces on which he once stood. At the age of 16, he made his Manchester United first team debut. But the year was 1941. The country was at war. He had been called up to join the Royal Navy as a radio telegraphist. Competitive professional football had been suspended, the sport a mere distraction from the perils the nation was facing.

As the war ended, the young naval serviceman thought his career in football was over even before it would be allowed to begin in earnest. Tony Waddington underwent a cartilage operation on a knee injury while serving on the minesweeper HMS *Hound* but he suffered complications, and was advised to give up any notion of going back home to play professional football.

A career at the highest level was out of the question. At first he took the advice until he decided to help out Crewe Alexandra, who were short of a player, for a friendly match against Hyde United. Crewe persuaded him to sign a professional contract. In settling for the chance offer of lower-league football at Crewe, he took with him a mantra from his training in the Royal Navy courtesy, bizarrely, of the Butlin's holiday camps. The navy had commandeered its Skegness camp as a training centre. Above the main gates Waddington noted the slogan, 'Our true intent is all for your delight.' He adopted it as his philosophy in football both as a player and a manager: always remember to go out and entertain the crowd, offer respect to the paying public.

It was as a manager, not a player, that he was to make an impact on those filing through the turnstiles to admire his 'working man's ballet'. One of his playing rivals of the day, and later a managerial rival, recognised his potential as a coach. Ruefully, Waddington recalled the verdict just prior to leading Stoke City to League Cup glory.

'Bill McGarry [a player with Port Vale and 1970s manager of Wolverhampton Wanderers] once said as a player I was a very good manager. Perhaps he got it right,' Waddington told *The Sun*.

His losing battle with persistent knee injuries at Crewe forced him to pack in the game as a player well before his 30th birthday.

A coaching and managerial career beckoned instead. As he acknowledged with regret, his knees would not stand up to the 'wear and tear' of playing professional football. He outlined the extent of the problem in a series of interviews to the *Staffordshire Evening Sentinel*'s Peter Hewitt. 'Both cartilages had been taken out of one knee, a number of operations had been needed on the other,' he explained. As a result, he had already embarked on an alternative coaching career, working with Crewe's reserves and Cheshire youth teams before the fateful call came from neighbouring Stoke City.

It meant a pay cut for young Waddington but given his circumstances, with an injury-plagued playing career at an end, he considered himself lucky to be offered the chance for an alternative coaching career at what he considered to be a 'big club'. Stoke City in 1952 was still a First Division club, though not for very much longer. Waddington's wage as a player at Crewe was £12 a week with a £2 win bonus. Stoke offered him £11 a week as their youth team coach and as he recalled years later had their 'pound of flesh' out of him.

His coaching duties were only part of the job. It also entailed assisting the ground staff and organising the playing kit. Indeed, far from being a coach hoping to learn his trade, he groaned at being treated as something of a dogsbody. Tasks included scrubbing out the dressing rooms, blowing up the lace-up leather-bound footballs, as well as helping the apprentices clean and cobble the first team and reserve players' boots. In an era long before multi-national sportswear companies sponsored teams, he even hand washed the players' socks, explaining they 'tended to run' if sent away to the laundry for washing.

The job offer for youth team coach and de facto part-time ground assistant was made by his former managerial boss at Crewe, Arthur Turner. A former player at Stoke in the pre-war years alongside the likes of Stanley Matthews, Turner had gone back there as assistant manager to former Wolverhampton Wanderers player Frank Taylor in a doomed attempt to turn around the Potteries club's ailing fortunes. Just a year after Waddington walked into the Victoria Ground, Stoke suffered relegation to the Second Division of English football.

Yet after taking over from Bob McGrory, who had finally paid the price for running a quarrelsome dressing room by suffering a string of disappointing results, this new managerial regime of Taylor, Turner and the 20-something Waddington were all full of optimism. They did fail to avoid what 1950s pundits considered to be inevitable relegation from the First Division. But, they felt they were the men to inject life back into Stoke in the long term.

Waddington had been tasked with nurturing local talent as part of the team rebuilding programme. It was one he relished. He explained, 'It seemed to me as if the club was really buzzing. It wanted to achieve success and so on. My responsibility was to deal with mainly the younger side of the playing staff. So the whole emphasis from my side of things was to bring on younger players, and we had quite a great amount of success in that respect.'

One of the young charges, Don Ratcliffe, joined Stoke at the same time as Waddington and followed him through the system from youth team to the first team. 'Funnily enough as I soared on, Tony moved on,' Ratcliffe remembered. 'I was taken to the A team [third team] when he first started. I got in the reserves and he was with the reserves. I got in the first team when he was looking after the first team. And then he was the manager.'

What was the secret to Waddington's success as a coach in Ratcliffe's mind? He answered, 'He was a bit of a con man but in a nice way. He conned you into believing in yourself'; a fine summation of the art of management. Another of Waddington's 1950s protégés, Colin Hutchinson, who himself eventually went into management with non-league Stafford Rangers, recalled training sessions in the concourse of the Boothen End during inclement weather. One-touch football was to the fore – 'Tip-Tap Tony' was the nickname Hutchinson fondly recalled.

As for the condition of the Victoria Ground when the new regime took over, it was in an appalling state; a sad reflection of the decline in the club's playing fortunes. Waddington remembered of those days, 'There was a huge stove in the centre of the dressing room and coke was constantly shovelled on, resulting in fumes all over the place. The stove supplied the hot water for the communal bath. Sometimes the water was not emptied for a week, so you can imagine the colour of it some days.'

Yet for all these apparent grumbles, Waddington was content at the football club. His mentor from Crewe, Arthur Turner, left Stoke to take up the manager's job at Midlands rivals Birmingham City and wanted Waddington to join him at St Andrew's as his assistant. This time, Waddington turned down a job offer from Turner. As Waddington put it, 'My heart was at Stoke.' It turned out to be a fateful decision for both parties.

Under Frank Taylor's stewardship, Stoke City made little progress, showing few signs of challenging for promotion back to the First Division. A fifth-placed finish was the best the club managed, coming in the 1954/55 season. The following season, much to the fans' ire and frustration, Stoke finished below neighbours and rivals Port Vale for the first time in decades, albeit both languishing in mid-table mediocrity in 12th and 13th. The consolation for Stoke fans was to see Port Vale relegated just a year later, finishing bottom. Any sense of *Schadenfreude* on the part of those Stokies was tempered by the club still finishing in mid-table mediocrity. Survival in the Second Division became the priority, the footballing struggle being sadly echoed by Taylor's constant battles with illness.

His first serious bout at the end of June in 1957 led to Waddington being appointed caretaker manager. Taylor collapsed after a swimming session and was taken to Stoke's City General

Hospital suffering from heart strain. Doctors made it clear he would need to remain in hospital for at least a month, then recuperate at home for at least another month before being allowed to resume his duties at Stoke.

Waddington took over what the *Stoke Sentinel* of the day described as a 'difficult job' with 'ability and affability'. He also began to shore up the Stoke side in the manner that served him so well in the 1960s and 1970s, bringing youth team players into the first team, blending them with experienced battle-hardened old pros. 'The dovetailing of youth into a very competent and experienced set of players who have served Stoke so well is probably the crucial operation upon which the club's chances of reaching their aim [of promotion] depends,' explained Waddington to the local press.

Above all in his caretaker stint, he showed early signs both of wheeler dealer qualities in handling the transfer market, not least his eagerness to recruit top-class goalkeepers. He did so in the latter case out of expediency with only one fit goalkeeper available to him for the start of the 1957/58 season. Sheffield Wednesday's manager indicated he might be prepared to loan out his experienced Scotsman Dave McIntosh on the proviso he was guaranteed first-team football. Waddington was happy to give such a guarantee and pounced. He considered it a 'lucky break' and thanked Wednesday's manager, Eric Taylor, for his 'wonderful gesture'.

Sadly, even with Waddington recruiting the help of Wednesday's trainer Jack Marshall, who had worked at Stoke, the deal fell through. It was a temporary setback as exactly a decade later Waddington managed to sign the world's best goalkeeper, Gordon Banks, on a permanent basis.

He had more luck in recruiting a top-class forward, one who would play a vital role in the early years of Waddington rebuilding his football club. It is difficult to countenance such a similar scenario in the Premier League era but Dennis Wilshaw, an England international with league champions Wolverhampton

Wanderers, was a part-time footballer. Wilshaw, originally from the Potteries, worked in his 'day job' as a school teacher. Among his teaching duties, he ran the Stoke-on-Trent schools' football team. He also lived in the area rather than Wolverhampton.

Once Wilshaw put in a surprise transfer request in early September 1957, Waddington tried to lure him to his home-town club, knowing full well he faced stern opposition from several First Division clubs. He also knew Wilshaw, given his circumstances as a teacher living and working in the Potteries, would be happy to join Stoke even if it meant dropping down to the Second Division. At first, Wolves demanded a prohibitive transfer fee. The deal initially fell through. But Waddington, with the backing of Frank Taylor once he returned to work from illness, persevered. Wilshaw moved to the Potteries three months after putting in a transfer request, Wolves selling him to Stoke for a fee understood at the time to be £12,000. Waddington had secured his first big signing, an England striker, albeit a player willing to move because he already lived and worked on his doorstep, ostensibly working not as a footballer but a teacher.

Under Waddington's guidance, Stoke enjoyed a fine start to the 1957/58 season, beating Middlesbrough 4-1 at home in their opening match. A certain Brian Clough scored Middlesbrough's solitary goal. The *Evening Sentinel*'s match report noted a change in tactics from Waddington's side after Clough's opener. Its correspondent did not mention Waddington by name. He wrote, 'The City evidently came out with new instructions for the second half when the forwards altered their methods and changed the outlook entirely. They no longer moved in line and one pass now was made where previously there had been several. In other words, the long open game was introduced with conclusive success.'

Further victories, at home to Bristol City and away to Leyton Orient, put Stoke at the top of the Second Division table. His players then faltered, Waddington blaming a heavy early programme of fixtures for a spate of injuries. He was encouraged though by the crowds beginning to flock back to the Victoria Ground, despite disappointing results after an encouraging start to the season. 'We have disproved the theory that crowds just come to see the home team win,' Waddington claimed. 'Five points have been dropped at home, yet the crowds still continue to come. The home results have been disappointing but it is some satisfaction to know that we have played well. It is true you have to make your own luck in this game, but there have been times when the breaks have been very much against us.'

Waddington was serving up entertaining football for the Stoke fans. He was also ruing his luck. He would do much the same a decade or so later with his team of the 1970s.

As the toll of crocked players built up, Waddington began introducing his promising teenagers from the youth team, most notably 17-year-old Tony Allen, a future England international, of whom more later. Overall, once Frank Taylor recovered from his illness and resumed his duties as manager, fans had been satisfied with Waddington's performance in his three months as caretaker. More importantly so had the board, promoting him to the role of assistant as a reward for his encouraging work.

But Stoke's mini-revival failed to last. Just a couple of years later, towards the end of the 1959/60 season, form slumped alarmingly. After beating Plymouth Argyle 1-0 on 27 February, Stoke lost ten games in a row. The club did not pick up a single point until the last game of the season on 30 April with a 2-1 victory away to Bristol City. The side narrowly avoided relegation.

Sadly it wasn't just the state of the football club in question but also, given his previous illness, the long-term health of manager Frank Taylor. Stoke's chairman Albert Henshall and his board decided not to renew his contract. On being given the news, Taylor responded, 'It is just one of those things.' Waddington was back in the role of caretaker manager. This time, he would remain in post.

It was for Waddington a predictably difficult return to managerial duties, facing another relegation battle on the one hand and factions among the board of directors on the other. Far from being the natural successor, Waddington was vulnerable to the axe himself especially as his relationship with Gordon Taylor, the man swapping the chairman's seat with Henshall from season to season, appeared a little fraught.

On joining Stoke in the early 1950s Waddington claimed to the *Stoke Sentinel* that he had been told, 'Make sure you keep on your toes because God is around.' Waddington dismissed it as something of a joke.

He soon worked out the man in charge of the boardroom did behave as if he was God. Gordon Taylor, an eccentric businessman with an interest in farming and a Potteries building firm, quite bizarrely appeared to consider himself footballing deity. Among his eccentricities was to insist on the club allowing his sheep to graze on the Victoria Ground pitch, much to Waddington and his groundsman's chagrin.

More infuriatingly, Taylor tried to interfere with team selections. Every Friday morning the chairman rang down on the phone to his acting manager demanding to know the team line-up for the following day. Waddington always politely gave him the side. Yet a few hours later Taylor would be back on the phone with alternative suggestions. Waddington took no notice. He explained, 'It was fortunate that I stuck by my decisions regarding team selection and finished high enough to justify my decisions. I hate to think what might have been our fate if I allowed the chairman to pick the side.'

Fortunately, Waddington had his supporters on the board, not least vice-chairman in the 1950s and eventually his trusted chairman Albert Henshall. His chairman's support over the years and their developing and enduring friendship proved crucial to the eventual success of Stoke in the 1970s.

Once Second Division survival was secured and the board made the decision in the euphemistic parlance of football 'to part company' with their ailing manager, Frank Taylor, Henshall became Waddington's sponsor. He wanted Waddington appointed manager. In contrast, Taylor and others insisted on the job being advertised. It was necessary under the terms of the football club's articles of association, the terms under which the club was governed. Waddington stubbornly took umbrage at formally applying for a job he thought was his after his spells in temporary charge. As far as he was concerned putting in an application in writing would be superfluous, the directors already aware of his credentials.

This complacent approach almost cost him the job. It took his mentor, Henshall, to smooth over egos and ensure good sense prevailed. Waddington may have enjoyed a managerial career at Stoke for nearly a couple of decades. His supporters considered him to be the most underrated soccer boss in the history of the game. But if it hadn't been for the diplomatic intervention of Albert Henshall in the summer of 1960, Waddington's career as manager of Stoke may never have even started.

On the night of a meeting of the board to decide on the appointment of the next manager, Henshall went into Waddington's office with a piece of paper. He gave him a pen. Waddington recalled Henshall then told him, 'Now write down, "I apply for the job of manager of Stoke City Football Club, finish." Do that or else.' Waddington dutifully complied with his friend's rather forceful request. Half an hour later on Thursday, 1 June 1960 he had been appointed manager. On the following morning the national newspapers dryly reported 'struggling Stoke City' had promoted their assistant Tony Waddington as manager after the departure of Frank Taylor due to illness.

On the phone to congratulate the young manager and offer his support was one of the managerial legends of the game Joe Mercer, then in charge at Aston Villa. Waddington recalled, 'He was the first call I received the following morning. He said, "Tony, I am just ringing to congratulate you and you'll do a marvellous job. Good luck and all the rest of it. And just one other thing, listen, don't trust anybody. And, when I have put this phone down, don't trust me either." That was Joe!'

Wise advice from the old sage. Given the parlous state of Stoke City Football Club in 1960 and the fickle nature of professional football, they were words of wisdom Tony Waddington did well to heed.

Sadly, he had inherited as its new manager a club he knew to be in a mess. It had no money. Instead, it owed survival to the banks, straining under a whopping overdraft of £100,000. That's getting on for £2.5m in today's money. Work had begun at the Victoria Ground on building a new main stand, the Boothen Stand, but it had been abandoned because of the lack of cash. Waddington dryly observed that it looked more like a 'pigeon loft' than a facility for paying spectators.

The task facing Waddington was monumental. He simply somehow needed to do a better job of rebuilding the football club than his predecessor, Frank Taylor, the man under whom he had served his managerial apprenticeship for the best part of a decade. In essence, he needed to build 'a wall' – Waddington's Wall!

2

Waddington's Wall

FOR a man who eventually gained a reputation in the game by loving his teams to play free-flowing balletic football, Tony Waddington's decision to send out his early teams in an ultra-defensive formation appears distinctly odd. It was, though, indicative of the perilous predicament he found himself in.

He was unapologetic. Stoke City's goal needed protecting at all costs. Only then could the flair players express themselves, dance and dazzle their way to victory. In truth the number of flair players on his club's books at the beginning of the 1960/61 season was to put it mildly limited. Logically, for this lover of the beautiful game, recruiting mercurial midfielders and natural goalscorers would have been a priority. Instead, his first signing was a goalkeeper.

Jimmy O'Neill, Everton's experienced Republic of Ireland international goalkeeper, signed for Stoke in the summer of 1960. Waddington declared his capture as 'significant'.

Given Waddington's eventual modus operandi in building teams during his managerial career, it is no surprise he made O'Neill his first signing. His recognition of the importance of goalkeepers stemmed from going along as a boy to Maine Road, watching

Manchester City with Frank Swift playing in goal. He rated Swift, an England international, as one of the greatest goalkeepers of all time. In Gordon Banks, Waddington would go on to sign another of the all-time goalkeeping greats.

Recognising the need for not just a good goalkeeper but a class goalkeeper revealed a pragmatic streak in a man considered something of a footballing romantic. 'Strikers have always cost the most, but there is not much point in scoring goals and leaking them at the other end,' he mused. Though he did acknowledge that if he hadn't seen Swift play he might have had a different attitude towards goalkeepers. Swift inspired him.

O'Neill considered it an honour to be Waddington's first signing. Yet in the opening weeks of the season he inadvertently found an odd way to repay the honour. Waddington craved national recognition and attention, yearning for his club's name to be plastered over all the daily newspapers. This soon came his way courtesy of the hapless O'Neill.

A relatively uneventful start to the season with an opening day 3-1 away defeat to Plymouth Argyle and a goalless bore draw with Sunderland in a midweek fixture at the Victoria Ground gave Waddington little to worry about. But notoriety for Stoke and its freshly appointed manager came with the following home game against Norwich City.

A bizarre match-fixing scandal unfolded courtesy of his new goalkeeper, an unwitting and innocent party. O'Neill contacted Waddington the night before the game and dropped a bombshell revelation. He informed his manager of an offer of a bribe to throw the forthcoming match.

Some hours earlier a telegram had been delivered to O'Neill's home with the correspondent asking the Dubliner to telephone him in the evening. The number given was that of a payphone, Swansea 55443. O'Neill obligingly met the request to call the number but with his wife Angela alongside him trying to listen in. A voice familiar to O'Neill answered and he made a simple request. Would Jimmy like to make some money by agreeing to make sure Stoke lost against Norwich?

Stoke were firm favourites to win. Norwich, who had just been promoted to the Second Division, were 11/4 outsiders. O'Neill refused to fix the outcome but the caller persisted, suggesting he might try to throw a future match. Instead of agreeing to do so, O'Neill ended the call and contacted his shocked manager.

Just a few short weeks into his managerial career, Waddington persuaded his directors to hold an emergency board meeting to discuss the match-fixing approach. The matter was duly handed over to the police and details of O'Neill's allegations were sent to the Football League. There was no public statement. For the moment, Waddington and his directors kept the scandalous revelation under wraps.

Despite being understandably unsettled by the bribery attempt, O'Neill played against Norwich, his manager simply telling him not to let the situation upset him. 'Just play as though nothing had happened,' Waddington advised.

The offer of a bribe to the Stoke goalkeeper did not stay secret for long. Once the *Daily Mail* broke the story some days after the Norwich game, Waddington quickly defended the integrity of his player. He commented, 'My directors take a very serious view of this approach to O'Neill, who is a good goalkeeper and a sportsman of the highest character.'

As a young and inexperienced manager he displayed a considerable degree of calmness under pressure, charmingly dealing with the unwelcome attention. Throughout his career he always tried to show total faith in his players regardless of the circumstances of a game. For the record, this particular encounter which a murky figure in 1960s football wanted to fix ended 1-1. Those betting on Norwich to win, with Stoke's stopper presumably throwing the ball into the net a couple of times, left disappointed.

Waddington addressed members of the national media, who turned up at the Victoria Ground in droves for the first time since the glory days of the likes of Stanley Matthews and Neil Franklin a decade or so earlier. Frustratingly for Waddington and his board of directors they probably wished these inquisitive news correspondents rather than sports journalists had stayed away. He told his interrogators, 'The police now have the mystery telegram. The Football League is holding an inquiry of its own and Mr Len Shipman, chairman of Leicester City, who is a member of the League's management committee, has been to Stoke to investigate on the spot.'

Waddington referred to a 'mystery' telegram, odd terminology given it was signed by a player familiar to both himself and O'Neill. They simply refused, at first, to reveal the name of the culprit.

Naturally the failure to name the alleged fixer only served to fuel further interest in the Potters and their goalkeeper. Just who was the man who had made the attempt to bribe O'Neill, a man being labelled Mr X?

Within a month, the national press had the name of the player allegedly responsible for sending the telegram to O'Neill. It was Alan Sanders of Swansea Town (now Swansea City). The *Mail* cautiously ran the headline, 'Is this what led to bribes quiz?' It outlined how Sanders claimed there had been a 'misunderstanding on O'Neill's part' during a telephone call between the pair the day before Stoke were due to play Norwich. He had merely asked the Irish goalkeeper whether he thought his team would win or not.

Sanders admitted to sending the telegram to O'Neill but insisted, 'That is all that took place which could have led to this terrible misunderstanding. My wife and I have been upset ever since we heard the allegations. It was a natural thing for me to ask an old colleague like O'Neill about his team's chances.'

Sanders, who had been tracked down by reporters at a race meeting with his Swansea team-mates, told them he was not interested in gambling. He did not understand fixed odds betting, despite frequenting race meetings. To sum up Sanders's response to the allegations, he didn't understand the fuss being made, seeing it as a matter of 'match fixing, what match fixing?'

Just days before he put his side of the story, Stoke had played Sanders and company at Swansea's Vetch Field. O'Neill and Sanders, former team-mates and friends at Everton, met up for a chat before the game. Sanders claimed they had just asked each other how they were getting on and denied he had asked O'Neill to cover up any further details of alleged match fixing.

Given a building media frenzy over the approach to O'Neill led to speculation of corruption in English football being widespread, bosses of the Football Association and Football League agreed to hold an inquiry. It turned out to be a meeting lasting just 45 minutes. Afterwards the FA and League bosses agreed to pass on whatever evidence they had of bribes being paid to professional footballers to the director of public prosecutions.

Twenty clubs were implicated, including, thanks to Sanders's alleged approach, Stoke and Swansea. There was insufficient evidence to accuse Sanders of any impropriety. Nothing came of the corruption inquiry, the football authorities closing ranks. Even the Professional Footballers' Association treated the bribery allegations as nothing more than a newspaper invention.

In particular, the PFA chairman Jimmy Hill questioned the *Daily Mail* in its campaign to expose corruption in football. The *Mail*'s correspondent, J.J. Manning, tersely responded, 'It is not too flippant or cynical a view to take that men who have difficulty finding a good England team could not hope confidently to probe the depths of the underworld of sport.'

O'Neill's revelation that he had been approached to fix a match was one of the first of a string of bribery scandals afflicting football during the early 1960s. This one was passed off as boiling down to a simple 'misunderstanding' on the part of the goalkeeper, a man who along with his manager was acting honourably.

Those wishing to pretend match fixing had not become a problem in early-60s English football acted less so. Corruption in football could not be ignored forever. Four years later ten footballers, including the then England centre-half Peter Swann, were jailed as a result of British football's biggest corruption scandal. The FA's bosses feigned shock. They had been warned of the dangers of match fixing thanks to the openness of O'Neill and Waddington.

For the pair of them it was best of course in the aftermath of this unsavoury event just to focus on football and the difficult task of rebuilding Stoke City. It began with what became swiftly dubbed by critics as 'Waddington's Wall'. O'Neill, in his role as goalkeeper, had the task of helping to supervise the human wall, a bank of defenders to frustrate, annoy and if necessary kick the opposition. He was not going to throw the ball in the back of the net, accidentally or otherwise.

O'Neill's summing up of Waddington's tactics in those early years was blunt. 'The first year here [at Stoke City] with Tony was quite a struggle because although we were talking about systems and 4-4-2s and all that sort of thing, I think we played 1-9-1! It was practically built on defensive breakaways because we didn't have a great lot up front at the time.'

The one player Stoke did have up front, Waddington considered a gem.

Johnny King had played with his new manager at Crewe Alexandra. He played up front at Stoke with the rest of the team lined up behind him and O'Neill stood in goal. At 5ft 10in, O'Neill, even by the standards of the day, was small for a goalkeeper but he was extremely agile, his agility regularly being called upon in a difficult season.

As for King, he needed to be a workaholic. 'He had the ability to hold the ball despite a slight physique and was a great asset in this respect, enabling me to play him as a lone striker,' Waddington explained. 'In those early days, playing defensively, it was essential to have someone who could hold the ball until support arrived.'

King served as a brilliant foil for deep-lying forwards, especially Dennis Wilshaw, who spent most of the game indulging in defensive duties. The rather negative tactics just about worked. King scored 12 league goals and Wilshaw 11 in Waddington's first full season in charge as the club escaped relegation. Their team finished just three points clear of the relegation zone in 18th place.

King and Wilshaw's goals accounted for almost half of Stoke's total. More significant was the goals against column with 59 conceded, only the top four sides leaking fewer goals. O'Neill and his defenders had put up Waddington's Wall and had done an effective job.

Among those defenders lined up in this 'wall' were young players, who proved in time to be stalwarts for Waddington and Stoke, notably Eric Skeels and local lads Tony Allen and Alan Bloor.

In the case of Skeels, the signing was a little fortunate. Waddington, while still assistant manager at Stoke, had gone along to Crewe to cast an eye over players at his old club. It was there he met a scout, the son of legendary Arsenal and Huddersfield Town manager Herbert Chapman. It was Chapman junior who alerted him to Skeels, who'd had a trial at Birmingham City but was turned down. On Chapman's advice, Waddington gave the 'teenager' a trial, only for Skeels to spring an unwelcome surprise.

'When we signed Eric he told us he was 18 but had lost his birth certificate,' Waddington explained. 'We played him in an FA Youth Cup game against Wolves and we lost, which was fortunate! It turned out Eric was 20 and two years over the age limit. He had not liked to tell us his real age in case we thought he was too old.'

Skeels was soon forgiven and assured by Waddington he had a future at Stoke. It turned out to be a prolonged future, playing more than 500 games for the club over the best part of two decades.

Waddington's signing of Allen in the mid-1950s, while still in the role of coach, proved to be equally fraught, even though he came from closer to home. Allen played for the Stoke-on-Trent schools team, which was being coached by Dennis Wilshaw, then still playing for Wolves. Thanks to Wilshaw's success with his young charges from the Potteries, Allen and one or two others had come to the attention of scouts coming from across the country to watch a group of kids under the stewardship of an England international.

To secure Allen's signing Waddington realised he had to act quickly, his fears of possibly missing out on the young player confirmed after offering his dad a lift to a schools game in Northwich. During the match, he heard a familiar voice pipe up, praising Allen as a brilliant player. It was a scout from a rival club and Allen's father naturally introduced himself, anxious for his son to take up a career in professional football. In his mind there was no guarantee Waddington would offer his son a contract.

At half-time, Waddington decided to take Allen senior to one side for a cup of tea and did his best to keep him away from any other scouts who'd been casting an admiring eye over his promising young son. He told Allen senior his son's future lay with Stoke. A few days later Allen signed for his local club and eventually settled into Stoke's first team.

Such was his talent that while still in his teens and playing for a Second Division club, he progressed into the England team. He won three caps but much to Allen and indeed Waddington's bafflement and frustration failed to pick up any more. A consistent pattern of Stoke City players being ignored for England call-ups constantly irked Waddington throughout his managerial career.

Having young home-grown players bursting into the team was a massive bonus for Waddington. If the club was to progress, though, more reinforcements were needed; experienced old pros. One of those veteran signings in the latter stages of the 1960/61 season was enforced, though it proved a significant signing in the history of the football club.

The Stoke manager urgently needed a replacement for his skipper Wilshaw. An FA Cup run had been a welcome diversion from the travails of fighting relegation thanks to Wilshaw's goals and leadership. Stoke had knocked out First Division West Ham United in a match marred by controversy over the state of the Victoria Ground pitch, a consistent complaint from visiting teams during Waddington's time in charge of his football club. More than often the ground staff, under instructions from Waddington, deliberately made sure it was in a mess, often with the assistance of the local fire brigade who hosed it down with gallons of water.

Ahead of this tie, ice on the pitch put the game in jeopardy. Braziers, flame-throwers, salt and sand were used in the effort to persuade the referee to go ahead with the game. He agreed. Ted Fenton, West Ham's manager, raged, 'It is scandalous to play on a pitch like this. All this sand is merely camouflaging the icy ridges underneath.' Perhaps not in the best of moods, West Ham lost 1-0, Wilshaw described by one observer as a 'limping hero' hooking the winning goal into the roof of the net.

After a marathon series of matches against Aldershot, the Potters made further progress. They finally saw off their Fourth Division opponents 3-0 in a second replay with Wilshaw scoring twice. Waddington had persuaded him to put off his retirement from playing a year earlier. His faith in the veteran striker was paying off.

Wilshaw served as more than just one of Waddington's most valued players, working alongside him as a part-time scout and coach at youth level. Wilshaw's alternative career as a teacher, coaching the Stoke-on-Trent schools team, ensured Waddington had eyes and ears in the recruitment of young local talent.

Just prior to the fifth round tie at Newcastle United, Wilshaw, as a result of his mixed activities, faced something of a dilemma.

If he recovered from an ankle injury, then Waddington wanted him in the line-up to play in the north-east at St James' Park. If not, then he was able to stay behind in Staffordshire and free to watch his Stoke schools team. This groups of lads, including some of Waddington's next crop of players, faced their counterparts from Barnsley in an English Schools Cup tie. It was impossible for Wilshaw to do both tasks.

As it turned out, Wilshaw was fit to play. One national newspaper, as a gimmick, offered to fly Wilshaw from Stoke to Newcastle by private plane on the Saturday lunchtime so he was able to watch the boys in the morning and play in the afternoon. He declined the 'kind offer' explaining, 'Time is against this trip and anyway my manager [Tony Waddington] knows that if I watched my boys in this match it would be like playing two games in one day.'

Waddington, recognised now by some national newspaper columnists as one of the 'bright young managers' of the game, agreed. He commented, 'Dennis takes his job with the boys very seriously and it is wonderful for the city of Stoke to have a man with his knowledge of the game.' He also revealed he had sent Wilshaw to 'size up' their Newcastle opponents in a league match at Leicester City.

In the event both men probably wished Wilshaw just settled on doing his scouting and coaching duties. Stoke lost. More significantly for Waddington his former England international inside-forward had broken his leg. Stoke were unluckily trailing 1-0 at half-time. But just two minutes after the interval Wilshaw was stretchered off the pitch, his right leg broken just below the knee. The tie ended 3-1 to Newcastle but from Stoke and Waddington's point of view the result was of the least significance. Wilshaw's playing career, let alone season, was effectively over.

Waddington described it as a 'shattering blow' to club and player. He urgently needed a new deep-lying striker able to play off his old Crewe Alexandra team-mate Johnny King. He also needed a new captain.

Finding a replacement for Wilshaw as a striker came first. It was off to Blackpool to sign Scottish international inside-forward Jackie Mudie, a friend of Stoke old boy Stanley Matthews and a member of the Lancashire club's 1953 FA Cup-winning team. At first Blackpool refused but Waddington persisted in his pursuit of the player. He remembered, 'I decided to ask Blackpool about Jackie Mudie. Ron Stuart [the Blackpool manager] was at first reluctant and we had little money anyway. The [Stoke] directors dipped into their own pockets to take out a new share issue and a last-ditch plea broke down Blackpool's resistance.'

It was a bold and surprising move but a sign of what was to come with Waddington's dealings in the transfer market. It was having an eye for what he considered a bargain, signing experienced, international players being neglected or even rejected by clubs obsessed with younger footballers.

He explained in his series of nostalgic interviews given to Peter Hewitt of the *Stoke Evening Sentinel*, 'The art of signing experienced players of calibre was based purely on pedigree. Players who had performed at the highest level could step down a shade and produce something. A player's legs tend to go in their mid-30s. Yet even at that stage the class players can make the ball do the work and do not need to do quite so much running.'

Mudie, however, at the age of 30 was still a willing runner. He needed to be, working in helping to shore up Waddington's defensive wall and then coming from deep, as did Wilshaw, to threaten the opposition goal. He signed for £10,000 and scored six vital goals in the closing stages of the 1960/61 season to ensure Second Division survival once again.

The first of those goals came just five minutes into his debut against Scunthorpe United. Mudie anxiously wanted to return to playing First Division football, hopefully with his new club. But as

Waddington put in interviews after his retirement from football, 'The name of the game at that stage was consolidation.'

Mudie may have been an emergency signing. But he was a more than useful addition to Waddington's squad, far too good for the Second Division even in what was considered at the time to be the twilight of his career.

Goalkeeper Jimmy O'Neill remarked, 'As the years went by you could see what Tony was aiming for. He was aiming to get Stoke back on the map, because they'd gone through quite a lean spell during the 1950s, by bringing in players with big reputations and their reputations didn't fail them when they got here. They did very well.'

He was aiming to do so by steadily signing quality players to supplement the local talent coming through the youth team system established by himself during the 50s. Waddington, as a manager, put himself under pressure to succeed. His mentor, chairman Albert Henshall, did much the same. He would put his head round the door of Waddington's office to comment in jest if a week had mysteriously gone by without Stoke signing or at least bidding for a player.

At least news of a bid would stimulate interest in the local newspapers, keep the dwindling band of fans happy. Crowds were declining, thanks in part to the team struggling to win matches but also because of the awful standard of football on offer at the Victoria Ground. Waddington eventually did become known for insisting on the playing of attractive football with his talk of directing a working man's ballet. Sadly out of expediency, his early 1960s side looked more like a morris troupe, a gang of clog hoppers.

Among players needed to freshen up the side, ultimately challenge for promotion and stimulate interest in the football club, Waddington craved a marquee signing, a star name. He put it simply, 'One of my maxims was that if you don't grab the opportunity, then you will never sign star names even if you were not always successful.'

At first, quite remarkably in view of future events, he thought of signing England winger Tom Finney from Preston North End. To put Stoke City on the map Waddington recognised, 'We needed a personality to excite local interest and create a spark in the club.' There was one obvious choice at the back of his mind. Yet Waddington, at first, opted for Finney instead. Indeed, the Preston plumber, as he was fondly known by English football fans, expressed an interest in joining Stoke. The proposed deal fell through. 'Finney couldn't sign because he's already drawn his annuity from the league's provident fund,' Waddington rather prosaically explained to the *Sentinel*'s Hewitt. It forced him to look elsewhere.

It was while on a trip to Turkey with Albert Henshall that inspiration supposedly came to the two men – actually surreal confirmation of what they were thinking of in the first place. They came across a fortune teller.

Waddington recalled, 'We were all there in Istanbul, and sitting down having a cup of coffee and we saw a lady, a very old lady. She was a fortune teller. She sat down. She said it was very, very interesting that there was very much evidence of success, a person associated with success. He would play an important part and that person was "an old man from the sea".'

According to the fortune teller this 'old man from the sea' would help them to achieve their ambitions. They knew the fortune teller was alluding to a footballer living on the Lancashire coast. The 'old man from the sea' was Stanley Matthews.

3

An Old Man from the Sea

GOING off to Blackpool in the autumn to take in the illuminations had long served as a popular mini-break for working-class lads normally content to be dazzled by their heroes' exploits on a football pitch. Tony Waddington and his mate Albert Henshall decided on their own 'lads' day out' to the Lancashire coast, going along to visit the lights and more importantly pop into the home of the greatest star born into the land of pots and pits.

Persuading Stanley Matthews to return from Blackpool to Stoke was a monumental transfer coup for Waddington, explosively reigniting interest in his football club. Yet in many respects it may well have been seen as a desperate gamble. On the one hand there was a national idol embarking on a triumphant homecoming to the delight of Stoke fans starved of football success. On the other was a player in his late 40s, a bloke quite possibly living off past glories.

As an eternal optimist, Waddington took the former rather than the latter view. Along with his chairman Henshall he would be more than aware of any reservations expressed by die-hard older

Stoke fans angered by Matthews's departure to Blackpool some 14 years earlier. Those views were to be ignored, a minority opinion of little value. Matthews was box office. His signing proved to be the catalyst for success, the man Waddington wanted to help him revive interest in Stoke City.

Never burn your bridges is a mantra for any employee demanding a P45 from the bosses to wander over to pastures new. If given this advice in the spring of 1947, Matthews ignored it as he agitated to leave Stoke while his club was in the latter stages of challenging for the league title.

From the Stoke fans' point of view, allowing their most renowned player to leave amounted to an act of insanity. Many blamed both parties, manager Bob McGrory and player Matthews, for the debacle. Perhaps the board had enough of Matthews and his financial demands, eventually agreeing to his request to join Blackpool.

McGrory clearly appeared to have lost patience with Matthews, and Matthews was equally unhappy with McGrory. The pair had been metaphorically at each other's throats for the best part of a decade, before and after the war.

He first put in a transfer request in 1938, sparking uproar in the Potteries. The local newspaper, the *Evening Sentinel*, thundered, 'Without Stanley Matthews, Stoke City would not be Stoke City. Stanley Matthews must not be allowed to go.'

Such was the level of anger a protest meeting was convened in the Kings Hall, Stoke, with an estimated 3,000 people packed inside and another 2,000 locked out on the streets outside. A motion was put to the assembled gathering. It read, 'We the supporters of Stoke City Football Club present at the public meeting being concerned for the welfare of the club and the district earnestly urge the directors to strive their utmost to secure the retention of Stanley Matthews. We believe it is possible, if good will is shown by all parties, to satisfy him that it is in his best interests to remain with Stoke City, and convince him that he will be as happy and comfortable with Stoke as any other club.'

Most fans blamed the manager for Matthew wanting to leave. Matthews later said he was 'touched' by the strength of feeling from fans, the people who paid his wages, something he readily acknowledged. He agreed to stay.

Less than a decade later, it was a similar story only with a twist. This time there was no concerted effort to keep Matthews at City. Both the manager and the board foolishly believed the 30-something player was well past his sell-by date. Fans and his team-mates disagreed. Just as a decade earlier, the rumour mill started with tales of unrest in the dressing room, jealous spats in the camp, the jealousy directed at Matthews, the superstar of the team.

It mattered little there were other regular England internationals in the Stoke line-up, namely the centre-half Neil Franklin and centre-forward Freddie Steele. Matthews attracted most attention. In a bizarre move Franklin wrote to Matthews assuring him there was no animosity from the rest of the squad towards him.

Franklin later observed, 'It was rubbish to say Stan was not popular. He was a man loved and admired by us all.' To add to the speculation Matthews was put in the reserves despite recovering from injury, much to his evident dismay. He only regained his first-team place after an injury to another player.

Stoke were trying to win the league title. Yet in an absurd act of self-harm they were about to let their star player go. A deal between Stoke and Blackpool was struck in Glasgow where the great and the good of British football had gathered for a charity game at Hampden Park between a Great Britain XI and Rest of Europe XI.

Bizarrely, Matthews was playing international and representative football but not club football, left out of a Stoke team hoping to win their first top-division championship title. Instead, he was off to Blackpool, much to the dismay of the fans. Many blamed the then Stoke manager and his board of directors. They accepted

Matthews's view of him being sold because McGrory disliked his 'high profile in the game'. Other disgruntled fans, though, saw it as an act of betrayal by Matthews, who they dismissed as a fan of local rivals Port Vale all along. Eventually Stoke would lose out on the league title to Liverpool on the last day of the 1946/47 season, heartbreak for fans and players alike.

Did the transfer of Matthews cost Stoke the championship? Quite a few of his disappointed former team-mates thought so. They also blamed the club, and in doing so the manager, for missing out. Goalkeeper Dennis Herod described the funereal mood among his colleagues, 'The atmosphere was dreadful. I can't tell you how depressing it was. Actually, it took me six months to get over it.' Condemning the then Stoke manager, McGrory, Herod added, 'How could he sell Matthews? I am not taking anything away from McGrory who did a great deal for Stoke City, but he wanted the limelight himself and was jealous of players like Stan and Neil Franklin. To sell the best forward in the world to Blackpool was sheer stupidity.'

Franklin, in an interview with the *Sentinel* some years after the event, agreed and said, 'Stan was the best player I ever played with. If he had not been sold to Blackpool in 1947, I am sure Stoke would have won the First Division championship.'

Waddington later described his predecessor's decision to sell Matthews as 'the biggest blunder of all time'. Waddington, unlike McGrory, was never guilty of wanting to hog the limelight for himself, He coveted the best players for his club. He was never jealous of them, including Matthews. He appreciated their value.

Matthews, as he contemplated a return to his home-town club in October 1961, would no doubt reflect on his acrimonious departure from Stoke. There was no guarantee of him being hailed as a returning messiah.

In his autobiography, *The Way It Was*, he wrote mournfully, 'Whether or not my presence in the team would have aided Stoke in their quest for the championship is a matter of conjecture. Suffice to say that Stoke not winning it that season was, for me, a sad end to what had been 17 wonderful years with my hometown club.'

As Matthews negotiated his return with Waddington, Stoke were by then in a very different state to the club he left. Instead of challenging the top teams in the land for the league title, the club was in a parlous state. Yet Matthews, for all the jibes from disgruntled older Stokies of being a Port Vale fan whose desertion scuppered the Potters' title challenge, was well aware of the potential of his former club. It was a matter of personal and professional pride. There was unfinished business to be done.

Both Waddington and Matthews recognised Jackie Mudie's key role in the return of the man known as the 'wizard of dribble' to the Potteries. For Waddington, Mudie added, as a player on and off the field, what he considered to be 'the most important contribution' to the club's early survival. He thought 'the most important of all' was helping him to sign Matthews.

Mudie suggested to Waddington that Stoke ought to try to re-sign him. In his vision of securing a marquee player with the ability to re-ignite interest in the football club Matthews shone out as the ideal candidate, regardless of any bitterness over his departure all those years ago. After all, in Waddington's opinion it was not Matthews's fault. It was McGrory who had driven the club's most famous player away.

Quite remarkably, as the current manager, Waddington contemplated signing a player he had watched from the terraces as a kid. 'I'd sat on my dad's shoulders among the 80,000 at Maine Road to watch Stan for the pre-war cup tie [Stoke City] against Manchester City and was hooked for life,' Waddington recalled.

'I always believed in having a player the crowds wanted to watch, and we desperately needed to bring back the public because we were down to eight thousand or so.' According to Waddington there was constant talk at the club of 'bringing back Stan'. Now there was the opportunity to bring him, and also the crowds, back.

As for Matthews, he recalled Mudie's crucial involvement in helping to bring about the deal. 'Ron Stuart [the Blackpool FC manager] had made it known that he would happily release me if I wanted to continue playing, which I told him I did,' Matthews wrote. 'I didn't have a clue what I was going to do next and it was my old Blackpool team-mate Jackie Mudie who came along to rescue my career.'

Matthews described his old club as 'wandering up and down the nether regions of the Second Division like a dog which had lost the scent'. He wanted to save his career. He wanted to do his old club a favour. According to Matthews, Mudie had told Waddington his old mate Stan 'had a few years left' in him and would 'do Stoke a job at outside-right'.

Crucially for Waddington, Dennis Wilshaw felt the same. His trusted advisor had seen Matthews play in Vancouver and assured him Matthews seemed very fit for his age. He was in his 40s but would pass off as a 30-year-old, according to Wilshaw. Waddington decided to make a move for the player, one calculated to add class and charisma to his football club.

On 7 October 1961 Waddington's Stoke were in London to play Leyton Orient. Matthews's Blackpool had a more glamorous fixture at Arsenal. Both Stoke and Blackpool stayed at the same West End hotel, the Russell Hotel. It gave Waddington an ideal opportunity to make his initial approach. He explained, 'I could see he [Matthews] was unsettled during a brief conversation and I took it from there.'

There was just one snag in that he needed the support of his eccentric chairman, Gordon Taylor, who had travelled on the team bus to London, in theory to see them play but in reality to watch his horse, Concealdem, run at Lingfield Park. Taylor gave him permission to make Blackpool an offer for Matthews but did not think much of his chances of securing Stan's signature. Waddington was better off just betting on his chairman's horse. He did just that and it cantered home to victory, an omen for Waddington. He then went off in pursuit of Matthews.

Blackpool's 3-0 defeat to Arsenal turned out to be Matthews's last appearance for the Seasiders. Critics questioned his continuing presence in the side, doubting that he was still up to playing First Division football. Many felt he ought to pack the game in. Once it emerged he may be leaving Blackpool and returning home to Stoke, one sneering critic wrote, 'To hear that the old master of soccer Stanley Matthews will soon be playing in the Second Division [for Stoke] is like hearing that Sir Laurence Olivier [the great Shakespearean actor of the day] is joining a provincial Rep.'

It had also been noted some fans even booed the veteran winger in the game at Highbury. Stanley Matthews, one of England's greatest ever players, was finished, it seemed. Waddington begged to differ.

Given the negative press over the proposed move, Waddington felt he needed to offer reassurance to Matthews, fearing the old master might just decide to pack the game in altogether. He gave him words of comfort, telling him to ignore the column inches of bile being written by the naysayers.

The criticism irked Matthews. He commented, 'Tony Waddington rang me to reassure me age was not an issue. He wanted me back at Stoke because he thought I would do well for them and he had the full backing of the board, especially vice-chairman Albert Henshall. When a manager angles out a specific director as being in support of a player a club are wanting to buy, it's not an indication that the other directors aren't in favour, it's a sure-fire sign that the director in question is putting up the money. So with the intimation that all were in favour of my return to Stoke, I was only too happy to sign and the quicker the better.'

Even then the deal did not go through smoothly. Blackpool demanded a transfer fee of £5,000, though Matthews wanted the club to waive the fee and offer a free transfer. The club refused point blank, one director even telling Matthews, a player Blackpool had signed as a seasoned international at the age of 32 from Stoke, the seaside club had 'made him'.

A row ensued between Matthews and the Blackpool board so a compromise was sought, Waddington and Henshall even going on their trip to Blackpool ostensibly 'on holiday' to take in the illuminations but actually on a mission to sign their superstar player. Eventually Blackpool and Stoke agreed a fee of £3,500. Even then Matthews was annoyed by the Blackpool directors' behaviour, especially their decision not to inform Waddington and Stoke of the player's niggling knee injury. Matthews commented, 'To ask for a fee for a player who had given 14 years' loyal service to the club and who was now 46 years old with a dodgy knee seemed a bit rich to me.'

Once he was back in Stoke to negotiate his wage demands, Matthews was taken aback by Stoke's offer, not because it was too measly but because it was, to his surprise, too generous by the standards of the day. Waddington had set out terms of £50 a week for a two-year contract with an extra £25 as an appearance fee. It doubled his weekly wage at Blackpool. If Matthews played, come Saturday afternoon, it was treble his Blackpool wage. Perhaps mindful of yet failing to inform Stoke of his dodgy knee, something the club would soon discover, Matthews settled for a one-year contract of £50 a week and waived the offer of appearance money. He was happy to sign, bizarrely live on national television.

Waddington had an eye for publicity. Matthews might well have been past his prime, stubbornly resisting the course of nature and the laws of human physiology. He might well have been written off by his critics but then again much the same was deemed to be the case when he left Stoke for Blackpool 14 years earlier.

To Waddington this was the staging of a superb transfer coup, a chance to generate maximum publicity for Stoke. Such was the interest in the 'Wizard of Dribble' going back to the Potteries to play for his old club, the BBC's *Sportsview*, a midweek sports magazine programme, offered to televise live the signing of the contract. Waddington was delighted to oblige. Matthews was a little reluctant but was eventually persuaded to go along with the broadcast for the good of a club he first signed for more than 30 years earlier.

As they arrived at the television studios, Waddington was in for a shock. One of the Blackpool directors turned up and told him the deal was off. A master of subterfuge, Waddington informed him it was too late. Matthews had already gone through the formal motions of signing for Stoke, according to the club's manager. The TV show just served as a publicity stunt.

That was not quite true. Yes, there had been a verbal agreement. But Matthews had yet to put pen to paper and the documents were still to be lodged with the Football League. Matthews duly signed them in front of the television cameras and after they had been inked, Waddington told Matthews, 'Welcome home, Stan. For years this club has been going nowhere. Now we're on our way.' As Matthews later commented, 'Nobody realised at the time how prophetic his words were to prove.'

Gerald Williams of the *Daily Mail* summed up the mood among sports correspondents and fans nationally. He wrote that Stoke had pulled off 'the biggest short-term transfer bargain in history'. He noted, 'They will pay £3,500 for 46-year-old Stanley Matthews, the most famous name in soccer, to finish his great career where it began – in the Potteries.'

For the *Daily Telegraph*, Donald Saunders observed, 'Stoke have long wanted back the genius who served them from 1929 to 1947. When Matthews first joined them they were in the Second Division. Within four seasons he had helped them into Division One. In 1953 they returned to the Second Division and now fourth from bottom need Matthews to inspire them again. They also requite his magic name to halt a dangerous slide in attendances which on Saturday dropped to a miserable 8,400.'

Given this transfer coup, it seemed logical to field Matthews in the very next game. Waddington thought otherwise. The 'miserable' attendance figure at the Victoria Ground being quoted by the press played on his mind. Stoke were due to play away at Plymouth Argyle, just days after Matthews became his prize signing. Yet for the next available fixture he was left out of Waddington's side.

In the hope of ensuring a bumper crowd at the Victoria Ground, he decided that Stoke's prodigal son would make his return debut at home. Matthews had no complaints. He knew what his wily manager was up to. 'It was a great marketing ploy on his part,' explained Matthews. He went on, 'By delaying my debut until Stoke's next home match, Tony hoped to attract many stay-away supporters who he believed would turn up not only to see me play but for the additional reason they could say "I was there" when Stanley Matthews made his return debut for Stoke.'

Curiously, in interviews after retirement, Waddington refused to take credit for delaying Matthews's debut, claiming it was the player's idea. Whoever's idea it was, it worked spectacularly.

The magnet of Matthews gripped the Potteries public. They flocked to the Victoria Ground and tens of thousands turned up to watch Stoke play Huddersfield, though more importantly to take a glimpse of Matthews back in the club's famous red and white stripes.

Just to stir up the excitement on the morning of the game, Matthews elected to walk from his hotel to the ground followed by thousands of his enthusiastic fans.

As *The Times* correspondent observed, 'This was a communal celebration, a relief from greyness. It was the day this Mr Matthews, now an international sporting celebrity, returned to his birthplace of the Potteries. So the people of the six towns retraced their sentimental steps in full force. Stoke had not had a day like this for a long time. For a decade and more an older generation had told the young about the departed idol. Now all were joined in one spontaneous welcome home.'

The article described Waddington's early strategy for the football club in a nutshell – revive an ailing institution by lighting an incendiary torch with Matthews as the accelerant.

The Times's writer anonymously described as its 'association football correspondent' may well have been unaware of the antipathy felt by a tiny minority of Stoke fans towards Matthews given his controversial departure almost a decade and a half earlier. As a kid in the Potteries, I remember the old sages still complaining of what might have been if he had stayed. There was a rapprochement on his return, an absolute outpouring of joy.

Waddington's cuteness as a football manager, turned part-time PR guru, ensured a generous welcome without fear or favour. After all, why not indulge in the ridiculous fairy tale of a footballer being hailed as a saviour, yet 14 years earlier considered surplus to requirements on the spurious notion he was too old? Yes, a flawed genius to those still smarting at his earlier departure, yet a footballing idol to all.

His return ensured Stoke fans falling out of love with football rediscovered their passion for the game. From a previous gate of around 8,000, almost 36,000 crammed into the Victoria Ground to watch their returning hero. Already by signing Matthews Waddington had seemingly achieved overnight success by grabbing the attention of the nation for a struggling Second Division football club with public relations cunning. He had his man. He had the attention of the mass media. As Matthews remarked in his autobiography, 'Rarely was I out of the headlines as the debate raged about whether I could make an impact in top-flight football. Tony Waddington loved it.'

There was just the not so small matter left now of winning football matches, starting with victory over Huddersfield.

Once everyone had gathered in the dressing room for the game, early signs from Matthews failed to augur well. With kick-off looming and the Victoria Ground packed to the rafters for the first time in more than a decade, Matthews's ambitious boss suffered an unwelcome scare. Stoke's star signing, the man the fans had come to see in their tens of thousands, was being violently sick in the toilets. Understandably, Waddington suffered a bout of empathetic illness. He was worried sick.

Jackie Mudie's next task as the man who had helped to facilitate Matthews's transfer was to put the mind of his boss at rest. It was all simple, if not bizarre and a little tortured in forming part of the great man's preparations for games. Mudie explained to his panicking manager how, as part of his new signing's routine, he deliberately threw up any food he may not have digested properly. There was no need to panic. Stan would be out on the pitch and ready to play.

As Matthews trotted out on to the pitch, he was weaving his magic, both on and off the field of play. The crowds were there. Now the man jealous of the fortunes made by Hollywood and matinee film idols needed to perform his boss's famed 'working man's ballet'. Waddington recalled, 'The arrival of Stan was just like a fairy tale. There was a transformation from the day he walked into our dressing room, for he rekindled the atmosphere. One or two players may have lacked a little confidence and it needed the signing of Stan to improve them.

'I could sense the difference even before the team sheet went out and his very presence meant that the attitude in the camp was that we were not going to lose. The younger players were mesmerised by his presence.'

They were also inspired for Matthews's first game back in Stoke's red and white colours to go out and win.

Matthews had a relatively quiet game. The players around him though seemingly felt inspired by the fans' idol lining up alongside them. They enjoyed a 3-0 victory with two goals coming from Tommy Thompson and the other being scored by Jimmy Adam.

In just pure sporting terms it was merely a welcome victory, one preventing the side sliding further into relegation trouble. Yet in reality this was more than just a game. It was a grand occasion. Waddington, by unveiling his new signing Matthews, had engineered a cultural and communal celebration. He had put on a thrilling show.

Cast in the role of pantomime villain was a man born in the year Matthews made his international debut. Ray Wilson had just broken into the England team and would go on to achieve his own footballing immortality by helping to lift the World Cup. On this occasion, he gamely tried to neuter a force of nature, a veteran refusing to give into the march of time. A couple of times Matthews's twinkling feet left Wilson on his backside. Yet by and large the Huddersfield left-back coped admirably with the threat from Stoke's right-winger.

But Matthews's mere presence on the pitch lifted the spirit of his team-mates, giving them confidence to go out and win. Their opponents felt Matthews also influenced a starstruck referee, who gave the Stoke winger over-sympathetic treatment. Wilson lamented, 'We were on a hiding to nothing from the start.' In a sporting gesture, Stoke's trainer Len Graham walked on to the pitch to congratulate not Matthews but Wilson, on what he called 'a job well done'.

Waddington purred, 'He [Matthews] had a steadying influence on our attack. Every time he got the ball he brought order out of chaos.' As for his team-mates, Matthews had also helped to line their pockets. In an era of a maximum wage for footballers, Waddington had cunningly written into their contracts an attendance bonus – the larger the crowd the more money they were paid.

To watch Matthews make his return debut, a crowd of 35,974 packed the terraces, in contrast to an attendance of 8,409 for the previous home game. If such a level of support was maintained for the rest of the season, it meant an additional £200 each for the Stoke players. For the board, in particular Albert Henshall, who had bankrolled the Matthews transfer, there was the bonus of recovering more than the £3,500 paid out in one game alone.

By the end of the season gate receipts had risen by more than 60 per cent on the previous season to £80,680, turning a yearly loss of more than £7,000 into a profit of more than £16,000. Henshall recognised that the return of Matthews was a stroke of genius on the part of Waddington. It meant by now the board, despite being notoriously tight with the purse strings, might be able to reward him with a small war chest for fresh players.

It is no wonder Henshall commented once the season was over at the club's annual meeting, 'Stan's return was undoubtedly the highlight of the season. Apart from pulling the crowds in, he had an almost magical effect on his team-mates and supporters alike.'

One fan welcoming the return of Matthews was Henshall's successor as club chairman, Peter Coates. He is fulsome in praise for Waddington in pulling off a masterstroke. 'Bringing back Stanley Matthews was quite inspirational,' he told me. 'It showed how smart and shrewd he was because he brought quite a fine number of players as well. [Dennis] Viollet was one of the best players of his generation. He [Waddington] was extremely canny and clever and he had the charm and the skill to do it.'

Given the 'Wizard of Dribble's' rapturous reception on returning to Stoke City, Matthews reflected, 'I was filled with a mixture of humility and delight. The delight, for the most part, was for Tony Waddington and the club's directors who, in having faith in my ability and giving me a decent wage, had been rewarded in full.'

Waddington was less effusive. He recognised the day had been a success, something of a triumph with the bonus of a comfortable victory to kick-start a stuttering season. Yet Waddington craved long-term success. One player, however much revered by fans starved of success, hardly made a team. As Peter Coates alluded to, all along Waddington knew he needed more class players to play alongside Matthews. He needed to build. He needed top-flight football. Only then would the crowds consistently flock to the Victoria Ground, Matthews or no Matthews.

4
Winning Promotion

HOW do you keep parsimonious directors at a cash-strapped professional football club happy and still build a strong enough squad to enjoy success and satisfy expectant fans? This was the dilemma facing Tony Waddington in the early 1960s. He had a growing friendship with Albert Henshall, the pair working in harmony to bring home Stanley Matthews as the pied piper leading thousands of fans back into the Victoria Ground. His relationship with many of the other directors, especially Gordon Taylor, the man swapping the chairman's seat with Henshall from year to year, appeared less than harmonious.

Even for all his keenness to open the cheque book to spend money on players deemed necessary by his manager, Henshall, as a fastidious accountant, still insisted on financial prudence, both in terms of outlay in transfer fees and crucially players' wages. As the Professional Footballers' Association, led by Jimmy Hill, agitated for the end of the maximum wage, Henshall and Stoke were among their sternest critics.

Waddington, a young manager with some players of his own age and in one case considerably older than him, backed his board when it came to wage demands. Stoke's directors were furious at suggestions the Football League might cave in to the players' demands once the PFA threatened strike action. Those suggestions largely came from bigger clubs able to pay larger wages.

Stoke's manager and directors felt, as a struggling league club, they were unable to do so. In criticising the PFA and its allies, Henshall ranted, 'I should like to know how they think we are going to augment our income.' He dismissed the PFA's demands as 'unreasonable'. Yet by the time he was welcoming Stanley Matthews back, his club had been forced, along with everyone else, to scrap the maximum wage. Waddington, as a result, had simple instructions from the Stoke board: keep the wage bill down and go bargain-hunting in the transfer market. He was happy to oblige.

Frankly, given the tight budget, Waddington had to plot and scheme ways to raise the money needed to bring in players of experience and quality. As a manager he needed to innovate to raise funds to suit his spending plans on players. Income from gate money, even boosted immeasurably by the return of Matthews, would not be good enough. For clubs in the 1960s fans paying at the turnstiles were the prime source of funding along with money from the sale of players in transfer deals, unlike in the modern era with tens of millions of pounds in TV money swelling the coffers.

Waddington came up with a plan to raise extra revenue thanks to an aborted scouting mission. He had gone to Stockport County to watch a player who failed to live up to his expectations. Just as he was about to leave, County's commercial manager, an old friend, tapped him on the shoulder to offer valuable advice. It seems obvious now. Back then it was revolutionary. How to run a lottery.

Jack Connor had played against Waddington in the lower divisions as a centre-forward mainly for Rochdale and Stockport County. Connor told him about the Stockport scheme, lottery cards offering daily prize draws bought by the fans as they arrived at the football ground. To Waddington it seemed a superb idea, so instead of leaving Stockport with the signing of a new player, he headed back to Stoke-on-Trent with instructions on how to run the lottery and the address of the printer.

Waddington recognised that his football club 'badly needed' some additional revenue. The directors agreed to adopt his lottery scheme and it proved a success. A maximum of 15,000 members were signed up at one shilling per ticket over the course of a fortnight. Such was the popularity a parallel scheme was launched, attracting thousands more members. It meant more than £3,500 a week was coming into the club in additional revenue. Waddington proudly recalled, 'That was an incredible amount of money to say the least. That was one of the ways that I was able to raise money to buy more expensive players.'

The money allowed him to start team rebuilding in earnest. Given the propensity of clubs in the 1960s to offload veteran international class-players still in their prime, it allowed him to go bargain-hunting.

For all the hullaballoo and fanfare for the signing of Matthews, Waddington's activities in the transfer market largely went under the radar of the football world and its followers in the national media. Going quietly about his business proved a useful policy for Waddington. He did so while dealing with a tight-fisted board reluctant to splash any cash coming into the football club. Opportunities still arose though for Waddington to sign quality players, partly because of the tendency of his rivals to favour youthful potential over experience in their own transfer dealings.

When it came to signing experienced, battle-hardened professionals, Waddington was quite happy to go bargain-hunting once an opportunity arose. At the same time, talented home-grown players were progressing through his youth ranks. Dennis Wilshaw proved a useful ally as he worked in tandem with his successful Stoke schools team.

Ostensibly he was still looking for experienced players to supplement his young defenders who had been doing a reasonable job in manning 'Waddington's Wall'. Reinforcements were still needed. It was no longer 1-9-1 as in goalkeeper Jimmy O'Neill's comical description. There was a lot more finesse thanks to the presence of Mudie and Matthews further up the field. It meant an improvement in results and the style of play.

Defence remained a priority. Yet with an eye for a bargain, once the prospect loomed of signing an international centre-forward on the cheap, Waddington acted. As a former Manchester United trainee, Waddington maintained a warm relationship with Matt Busby, the manager who released him because of his injury problems soon after becoming the Old Trafford boss. He also kept a keen eye on his boyhood club's playing fortunes.

Around Christmas in 1961, Dennis Viollet lost his first-team place. At his best he was one of the country's most prolific strikers, notably a year so after surviving the Munich air disaster by setting a Manchester United record in the 1959/60 season with 32 goals in 36 games. But by the end of 1961, he was out of the side.

Sniffing an opportunity to snatch a bargain in the transfer market, Waddington made his approach to Busby. Yet despite leaving Viollet out of the United side the wily old manager was reluctant to sell. As Waddington noted he clearly still had a 'special relationship' with the player. Waddington refused to take no for an answer. He badgered Busby into giving him Viollet's home address and the Stoke manager went off to pay him a visit. The pair talked long into the night without Viollet agreeing to sign for Stoke. He did agree though to watch them play in an FA Cup replay against Leicester City at the Victoria Ground. In the previous drawn game, Matthews had excelled.

Among those waxing lyrical about the performance of Matthews and Stoke City in the 1-1 draw with Leicester at Filbert Street was the *Daily Mail*'s Ian Wooldridge. Sensing that Waddington had built a team with promotion-winning potential, he wrote, 'Friend and foe, united in admiration of an idol, stood to cheer Stanley Matthews from yet another scene of triumph. The old man, shivering slightly, waved modestly. Saving Stoke it seemed was just another night's work.'

The key moment turned out to be a free kick taken by Matthews, which was weighted perfectly for his old mate Jackie Mudie to head in an equaliser. For the replay, Waddington had another experienced reinforcement waiting in the stands to see Stoke carve out an impressive 5-2 victory with Matthews among the scorers. After the match an impressed Viollet turned around to Waddington who claimed he told him, 'I'm not sure why you want me. I will have a job to get into this team.' Viollet signed for Stoke. Forget the acquisition of Matthews and later Gordon Banks, the world's best goalkeeper, Waddington insisted years afterwards that his 'most significant capture' was Dennis Viollet. At £23,500 he considered the signing one of the best he ever made.

Not everybody at Stoke was so happy with the deal. Support for Waddington's dealings in the transfer market remained forthcoming from his friend Albert Henshall. Other directors felt that the purchase of Viollet was too much of a financial gamble, that the club was over-reaching itself.

Any boardroom dispute over transfer dealings coincided with haggling over the botched project to build the new main stand at the Victoria Ground. The board needed the cash to complete the construction, rather than to buy yet another former international player. It meant a couple of directors resigned in a huff to be replaced by another couple of friends of Waddington's nemesis as chairman, Gordon Taylor.

His influence, though, was on the wane. Henshall was about to take over on a permanent basis, fresh from the success of seeing through the Matthews deal. For Waddington he was an essential ally in recruiting the players needed to bring success to the football club, a man appreciative of Waddington's commercial savvy both with his money-raising schemes and shrewd dealings in the transfer market. The pair established a strong, enduring relationship built on trust and mutual respect.

Further recruits, experienced players of international class but curiously deemed surplus to requirement by their clubs, arrived at the Victoria Ground in the summer of 1962. Among them was Eddie Stuart from Wolverhampton Wanderers for the modest fee of £10,000. At Wolves, Stuart, a South African international, had mostly played at full-back as the club won three league titles. Waddington, describing him as 'a model of steadiness in defence', moved him to centre-half. He also appointed him captain.

In his role, Stuart made a significant contribution in helping to influence his new manager's transfer dealings. He suggested that Wolves's former legendary 'hard man' Eddie Clamp might be available, an odd tip-off given that Clamp had only recently signed for Arsenal. Quite correctly, Stuart calculated his old mate might not last long in the marble halls of Highbury.

Clamp had moved to Arsenal from Wolves for £40,000 and found himself reunited with his former skipper Billy Wright, the new manager at the north London club. No doubt Wright felt confident he might be able to control Clamp's more aggressive tendencies. He was wrong.

Stuart suggested to his manager that he ought to go along in midweek to Highbury to watch Arsenal play Aston Villa. Specifically, he ought to keep an eye on Clamp. Waddington, sensing Stuart knew something was afoot, took the advice and went along to watch Clamp take to the field against one of his former club's fierce local rivals.

Waddington described what unfolded before his eyes, telling the *Stoke Sentinel*, 'Perhaps Eddie had a feud boiling over from the past, but he went into a crunching tackle right in front of the directors' box. The directors and their wives were horrified and to make matters worse, it seemed that Eddie had hit the wrong player. He had meant to tackle someone else!'

Villa's left-back Charlie Aitken was the unfortunate victim of Clamp's assault. Stuart warned Waddington that his mate would lose his cool. He just thought ahead of the game that Clamp was intent on targeting someone else. As a result of Clamp's dubious antics, Wright hurriedly ushered his old Wolves team-mate out of Arsenal. Waddington offered Wright a £15,000 fee, £25,000 less than the figure paid to Wolves only a few months earlier. The Arsenal manager and his horrified board of directors readily agreed to the knock-down price just to get rid of Clamp and he became a Stoke player, but significantly not any old player. Waddington had one specific role in mind; that of Stanley Matthews's 'minder'.

It was a perfect bit of business for Waddington, even if it came as a result of an act of thuggery bordering on farce. Recruiting an aggressive hard-tackling player such as Clamp seemed at odds with Waddington's philosophy of directing a 'working man's ballet'.

But Matthews, for one, appreciated the signing. Both the manager and his star player saw Clamp as a loveable rogue. Opponents viewed him differently. He was a man to be feared. According to Matthews, Clamp told him all he had ever wanted to do was to kick him into row G, physically and not metaphorically. Now as a team-mate he was going to look after him.

Clamp had earned a reputation as a hard man but he was a decent footballer with a couple of league championship medals and an FA Cup winner's medal in his back pocket. He had also earned a handful of England caps. 'I may be an artisan but you'll find I will always pass to a red and white shirt,' he assured the fans.

Waddington, with Clamp and Stuart adding experience and bite to the defence, had moulded a team capable of challenging a promotion challenge. As he sat around in the dressing room taking note of the average age of the Stoke squad Clamp wittily observed,

'Our original National Insurance stamps are more valuable than penny blacks.'

Waddington's mixture of veteran players and local young talent though was about to pay dividends. It did so after a terrible start to the 1962/63 season.

They failed to win any of their six opening games, losing to Leeds United and Swansea with draws in the other four. A couple of matches in the space of a week against Charlton Athletic then served to kick-start the stuttering campaign. Everything clicked for what Matthews described as 'a curious combination of a team' once Charlton's players turned up at the Victoria Ground. They were thumped 6-3, Dennis Viollet scoring four goals.

Buoyed with confidence, Waddington's men played Southampton at home a few days later and again enjoyed a comfortable victory, this time 3-1 with Jackie Mudie scoring a brace of goals. Then it was off to The Valley for the return midweek fixture against Charlton, crowd numbers boosted by those wishing to see Matthews in action.

One over-enthusiastic correspondent mused that fans 'long starved of soccer wizardry welcomed and saluted genius' in the guise of Matthews. He ran the show against an inexperienced Charlton side. Stoke signalled they were intent on mounting a promotion campaign with a comfortable 3-0 victory, their first away win of the season.

Those clashes with Charlton marked the beginning of an 18-match unbeaten run until Leeds United turned up at the Victoria Ground just before Christmas. A 3-1 defeat was followed by a 2-1 Boxing Day victory over Rotherham United before the harsh winter of 1963 struck and professional football came to a halt. The bitter winter meant an enforced rest, though not for Waddington. He kept his eye on the transfer market.

To match the awful icy weather, there was a freeze in relations between Burnley and Northern Irish international Jimmy McIlroy, a key player in their First Division title-winning team of 1960. Three years later he was inexplicably out in the cold. Much to the astonishment of the player and the anger of Burnley's fans he had been put on the transfer list. National newspapers of the day described his transfer-listing as something of a mystery. For many Burnley fans it remains a decision of intrigue to this day.

McIlroy himself expressed his bafflement years later, telling the BBC, 'I remember the morning the manager Harry Potts told me he was putting me on the transfer list and I asked why? He said you haven't been turning it on in these last couple of weeks, so I said why the blazes didn't you drop me? He looked astonished and said don't be silly, you don't drop players of your calibre.'

Waddington, even with Matthews, Mudie and Viollet in his side, craved a player of McIlroy's class, identifying him as 'the missing link' in building a promotion-winning team. He seized the opportunity to strengthen the Stoke squad with the signing of yet another international veteran who was, in a familiar theme, deemed surplus to requirements by his club. The deal, much to the dismay of Burnley's fans, went ahead but not without difficulty.

One imposing figure stood out as a notoriously difficult and uncompromising negotiator in 1960s football: Burnley chairman Bob Lord. He demanded £30,000 for McIlroy's services but Stoke were not going to pay more than £27,500. Neither club would budge. Rather cheekily Waddington made an offer to Lord. He told him if Stoke beat Walsall in their following match then given McIlroy might be surplus even to Stoke's requirements as a Second Division club, the offer would drop to £25,000. Stoke duly won 3-0 with Mudie scoring a hat-trick.

Waddington was back on the phone to Lord, who quoted £27,500, but Waddington stuck to his figure of £25,000. Remarkably and somewhat out of character, the Burnley chairman caved in. Given the original decision to sell McIlroy had been deeply unpopular among Burnley's fans, Lord perhaps felt it was better for the player to be out of sight and out of mind. He accepted Waddington's offer. 'I was not made welcome in the Turf Moor boardroom afterwards,' Waddington later reflected with wry amusement.

His sense of humour was sorely tested on McIlroy making his debut for Stoke away to Norwich City. Stoke were thumped 6-0, a chastening experience for McIlroy. He later reflected, 'I wondered what I let myself in for. We were hammered 6-0 that day. I'd left a successful club, Burnley, and here I was in the Second Division and on the losing side. The only consolation was at the end of it I heard Tony on the radio saying that he was pleased with the way I played.

'It was a terrible day really because all the sports press were there, hoping for big things with Stoke's players on the right wing being Matthews and McIlroy. I don't know what they expected. Fortunately things got better.'

Indeed, despite suffering a heavy defeat, it proved to be a hitch rather than a major setback in Stoke's campaign for promotion. As for McIlroy's performance in that 6-0 defeat, Waddington observed, 'My faith and judgement in Jimmy were realised, for we then embarked on a good run, and that gave us the impetus to clinch promotion and the Second Division title.'

To go on this promotion- and title-winning campaign, Waddington resorted to desperate, some might consider underhand, measures. To assist his injury-prone veteran star players, especially Matthews, he deliberately turned the Victoria Ground pitch into a bog. Feeling quite proud of his fiendish tactic, Waddington explained in an interview with the *Stoke Evening Sentinel*, 'It was the winter of the big freeze with pitches bone hard and Stan preferred the surface to be soft. That started the water treatment. We obtained some special anti-freeze liquid and the fire brigade came in and flooded the pitch.'

Even then, Matthews wasn't always satisfied. 'He would test the pitch was the water came up around his ankles and say "It could do with a little more water, Tony",' recalled Waddington.

The tactic infuriated opponents and many, as had been the case for West Ham with their earlier FA Cup tie played on a virtual ice rink, believed the Victoria Ground pitch was not fit for playing on. For the most part mud, rather than ice, was the problem. Waddington admitted there was barely a blade of grass. It was a disgusting mud-heap, a glorified bog.

On one occasion, the Swansea manager Trevor Morris took matters into his own hands after suffering a 2-0 defeat. Morris grabbed a bucket of water and marched up to Waddington, who thought his opponent was going to chuck it all over him. Morris simply yelled to him, 'Here is another bucket of water to tip on your flaming pitch.' It mattered little to Waddington. His players were happy and they were on course to win the Second Division title.

This little act of subterfuge, as he proudly pointed out without any sense of contrition, continued throughout his time in charge. Indeed, it amused Waddington, unapologetic at commandeering public servants from the fire brigade to help him out. After all, they were Stoke fans so did not care.

It wasn't just Matthews either as in later years all of Waddington's playmakers benefited from the 'water treatment', especially those carrying injuries. By giving them a 'soft top' on which to play, Waddington reasoned they could work their magic. In Waddington's working man's ballet they were able to skip and dance through, rather than wallow in, mud.

Swansea's Morris was not the first, given earlier complaints from various clubs over the state of the Victoria Ground pitch, nor the last to feel disgruntled about what they considered to be the doctoring of the playing surface. With the River Trent running alongside the ground, blaming the high water table provided a less than convincing defence offered by the club for the awful state of the pitch.

Inevitably, success over the Easter period proved crucial in determining the outcome of the season, given the tight fixture schedule at that time of year. Stoke travelled to Sunderland to play their promotion rivals at Roker Park on Good Friday. A crowd of 62,138 turned up to watch the sides grind out a goalless draw.

It was then back to the Victoria Ground to face Cardiff City the following day. Dennis Viollet scored the only goal of the game, setting up nicely the return clash with Sunderland on Easter Monday in front of a crowd of 42,366. Once again Viollet scored to give his team the lead. After Sunderland equalised a draw seemed the likeliest result but Stoke were awarded a late penalty, one their aggrieved opponents felt to be extremely dubious. Even Stoke players afterwards admitted the award was 'soft'. It was converted and Waddington's dream of guiding Stoke back to the top flight of English football was turning into reality. There remained one more crucial game against a promotion rival, away to Chelsea.

More than 66,000 fans packed into Stamford Bridge, with a further 10,000 or more disappointed Chelsea supporters locked outside the ground. Matthews remembered the tense atmosphere among the players in the dressing room before the game. He wrote, 'It would be gung-ho stuff and despite all the invaluable experience in the Stoke team, I think at the back of our minds we would worry that this young Chelsea side would run the legs off us if we weren't careful.'

Just to break the tension, Eddie Clamp rose to his feet with not so much as a pep talk but one of his stand-up comic routines. Within minutes he had his team-mates in fits of laughter. In contrast the neighbouring Chelsea dressing room was silent.

Once they ran out in front of Stamford Bridge's biggest crowd for decades, experience triumphed over youth. It was not the first time Stoke's veteran players had sampled such an electric atmosphere, boasting a clutch of league championship medals, FA Cup winners' medals and dozens of international caps. For Chelsea's youthful players, it was a new experience, the biggest game of their lives so far. Even so their fans jammed on to the terraces anticipated a home victory. A section mercilessly chose to mock Waddington's bunch of ageing players, in particular Stanley Matthews, a man just voted Footballer of the Year a remarkable 15 years after he first picked up the award.

For the first half-hour Chelsea dominated with Matthews coming in for some harsh treatment on and off the pitch in the form of jeers of derision from the crowd and a string of crunching tackles from young full-back Ron 'Chopper' Harris. This, naturally enough, brought Harris to the attention of Clamp, the pair of them ending up in a wrestling match. According to Matthews, Clamp threatened to put Harris in hospital. Once the referee separated the warring pair, politely asking them to concentrate on playing football, Clamp came up with one of his classic one-liners. He commented, 'That's the trouble with you referees. You don't care which side wins.' Remarkably, neither Harris nor Clamp were booked for their antics, either physical or verbal.

Once Clamp finally delivered on his promise of more or less taking Harris out of the game, Stoke were able to settle down and began to dominate proceedings. In Clamp's final act of thuggery in his feud with Harris, he rose off his feet and clattered into the Chelsea player, sending him into the air and crashing into the advertising hoardings. Menacingly he told the prostrate Harris, 'Next time they'll just slide a stretcher under thee.'

Clamp's manager prided himself on his teams being exponents of the best the beautiful game had to offer. Yet as a glaring contradiction in Waddington's managerial character he also indulged hard man characters such as Clamp. In describing the tackle, Matthews commented, 'Never in 30 years of football had I seen a tackle like it.' To Clamp, it was something of a back-handed compliment from the 'Wizard of Dribble'.

Clamp had done the job assigned to him of minding Matthews. It worked. In the 37th minute, Matthews, described by one commentator as 'spry as a monkey', exchanged a triangle of passes with Jackie Mudie to set free Jimmy McIlroy. He avoided simultaneous lunging tackles from Eddie McCreadie and Harris to shoot past goalkeeper Peter Bonetti, the ball ricocheting off the post and into the net. It turned out to be the winner.

Stoke grew in confidence, McIlroy buoyed by scoring his goal orchestrating matters from midfield. Waddington was able to sit back and watch his 'working man's ballet' unfold, though not before Clamp had got up to his bone-crunching antics. There was one last scare with Chelsea hitting the post but a 1-0 scoreline belied a comfortable win for Stoke. Promotion was beckoning and one more win was needed.

But just a couple of days later Stoke suffered a shock defeat away to Bury. Matthews was absent, sat at home nursing his injuries after being kicked all around Stamford Bridge by Harris. It meant that Stoke, in their final home game of the season, needed to beat relegation-threatened Luton Town to secure promotion.

More than 34,000 fans turned up for the game in eager and nervous anticipation. Stoke were going for glory while Luton were fighting for survival. If they lost, it meant Third Division football for them. To coin the footballing cliché, they were 'fighting for their lives' and proved understandably awkward opponents for the Second Division championship pretenders.

Mudie settled nerves to give his side a 1-0 lead at half-time but with quarter of an hour to go it was looking shaky and Luton were still stubbornly in the game. Then came a moment of magic recalled by McIlroy, 'I picked the ball up and was fiddling about with it. Out of the corner of my eye I noticed Matthews, streaking towards goal. I couldn't believe it seeing Stan streaking for goal. So I whipped the ball over the full-back's head. I put Stan in the clear and he just waltzed past the keeper and tapped it into the net and that sealed promotion at a stroke,' he recalled.

Matthews savoured the memory in his 2000 autobiography, *The Way It Was*. He wrote of the moments after receiving the pass from

Mudie, 'I headed straight for goal, the tell-tale click-clack of boots running through mud telling me two or three defenders were in hot pursuit. I took to my toes as the Luton goalkeeper Roy Baynham came out to narrow the angle. It was a simple job of feinting one way so he committed himself and going the other. Taking the ball wide of Roy, I took a moment to glance up and see the open goal before side-footing the ball into the net.'

Cue pandemonium as the Stoke fans went wild, 'ecstatic, prolonged cheering' to the ears of one local correspondent. Once the final whistle went, thousands invaded the muddy pitch, the players needing a police escort to the dressing room. It was a fairy-tale finish, the legendary Matthews scoring the goal to seal the Second Division title and a return to the top flight of English football.

For Waddington, it was a day to treasure in his mission to revitalise a failing football club. Yet he left the plaudits to Matthews, the local hero, and the rest of the players as they took a bow from the directors' box to the adoring crowd below.

McIlroy, for one, understood and appreciated his manager's show of modesty. 'There was one man missing, Tony Waddington,' remembered McIlroy. He went on, 'The crowd chanted and called for him to appear. But there was no sign of him. You know just for that action Tony went up in my estimation because it's very easy for a manager or a player to wallow in the adulation of the fans when things are going well. In football, six months later you can become a villain as many managers have found out.'

McIlroy felt it wise of Waddington to stay out of the way and let the players take all the credit. Football fans can be fickle. If his project of ensuring a footballing renaissance for Stoke unravelled then chants of 'Waddington out' might be ringing from the terraces. Sustained success could not be guaranteed.

After all, his policy of bringing in veteran players, some with big egos, meant they had a short shelf-life. At most they were only able to stay at the football club for three or four years. It did not help that one or two players, including Mudie, discovered they were not being paid as much as the others and became unsettled.

Mudie dismissively suggested Waddington was a 'lucky' manager. The luck, according to Mudie, came in persuading Matthews to return to Stoke. In the former *Telegraph* and *Times* sports journalist David Miller's authorised biography of Matthews, Mudie commented, 'We weren't looked after by Stoke the way we should have been. When we had a celebration dinner after promotion, we had to pay ourselves. We were promised an overseas tour, taking our wives, but it never happened. Waddington wasn't straight with me. He said we were all getting the same, then I found I was on £40, [a week] and Viollet and McIlroy on 50.'

The answer to dealing with disgruntled players, despite their undoubted success, was to show them the door.

It meant a quick turnover of players as Waddington embarked on the next challenge of consolidating Stoke's position in the top flight of English football. Goalkeeper Jimmy O'Neill observed, 'Tony was very keen to get Stoke back on the footballing map by bringing in the likes of Matthews and Viollet and people like that. They came to Stoke with big reputations and their reputations didn't fail them when they got here. They did very well.'

As much as Waddington admired both of the men mentioned by O'Neill, especially Viollet, they, along with Mudie, Clamp and Stuart, soon needed to be replaced. Once again blending youth with experience proved key as Waddington aimed, as O'Neill commented, to put 'the football club on the map'.

His club's fans demanded entertainment. They craved success. History beckoned for Waddington; his historic challenge to bring major sporting honours to the Potteries.

5
Centennial Celebrations

FOOTBALL club saved from oblivion, able to celebrate promotion to the top echelons of English football in its centennial year; Tony Waddington deserved the gratitude of the Stoke City fans. Yet as he sat in his office in the summer of 1963, sheep still grazing on the pitch outside, Waddington realised he faced a herculean effort in continuing to transform a failing provincial club into one able to challenge for major honours.

The bizarre sight of the chairman herding his sheep in and out of the Victoria Ground served as a reminder. Promotion merely whetted his appetite for the task in hand. The club's centennial celebrations, with the masterstroke of persuading the then kings of European football, Real Madrid, to play a friendly match at the Victoria Ground, further fuelled ambition. It attracted national and international attention.

Waddington wanted the eyes of the football world permanently fixed on the Victoria Ground, Stoke-on-Trent. For the metropolitan elite of the game this was a deluded notion. The quietly determined boss thought otherwise.

Waddington took almost as much pride in staging the match against Real Madrid, then unquestionably the best club side in the world, as he did winning promotion. In persuading the Spanish team's aristocrats to turn up in the Potteries to play a Second Division outfit, there was one draw card – Stanley Matthews. He was revered by such greats of the game as Ferenc Puskas and Alfredo Di Stefano. A £10,000 match fee also served as an incentive.

For a two-day celebration the former European champions were put up in the North Stafford Hotel outside Stoke Railway Station, not the most salubrious of venues but the event proved a success. Additionally, Stoke invited the chairmen and their wives of every Football League club along with senior officials from the FA to the hotel, all of them to be wined and dined at a banquet before the unlikely clash of Stoke against Real.

It brought a frisson of anticipation throughout the Potteries as nobody had ever seen any of these international superstars play. Television coverage of football was still in its infancy with the wall-to-wall coverage of the sport still decades away. It was a rare opportunity to view the greats of the international game.

In staging the match, Waddington was well aware the club was taking a risk with it being scheduled in the middle of the closing stages of a tight promotion campaign. For Waddington though, a man with a keen eye on PR opportunities, the game was key to building Stoke's reputation as a football club, both at home and abroad.

He asserted, 'Stoke City versus Real Madrid rippled away to all parts of the footballing world. I think a lot of our standing was built upon that particular game. It certainly attracted not just national, but international attention.'

Almost 45,000 spectators packed into the Victoria Ground, a bigger attendance then for any of Stoke's home matches during the promotion-winning campaign. The national press, able to avail themselves of a fleeting chance to see Real's original 'Galacticos', also turned up in force. Stoke's young defender Tony Allen recalled, 'I remember standing there, ready to go on the pitch and thinking,

"We could get a right pasting here." I didn't know what to expect. I knew they were legendary players, but I had never seen any of them play.'

He remembered his manager's pep talk, 'Before the game Tony Waddington told us to go out and enjoy it. He said, "You don't have many opportunities to play against players like this – this is something special."'

At the time, Di Stefano was considered by some as the greatest centre-forward in the history of the game. Puskas enjoyed the same legendary status as Matthews, though both men were very much in the autumn of their careers.

Despite Stoke's Second Division status for this game, one curiously being staged right in the middle of the run-in of a promotion season, correspondents hoped that the Potters, with their contingent of experienced veteran internationals, would prove worthy opponents.

David Miller of the *Telegraph* wrote, 'Four of Britain's most worthy artists – Matthews, Viollet, Mudie and McIlroy – may emulate their visitors and show that there are better things in British soccer than the shoulder charge and the eternal "get stuck in" mentality.' Miller would not be disappointed.

Waddington's team managed to hold Real, at that point five-time European Cup winners and runners-up to Benfica the season before, to a creditable 2-2 draw, a result hailed as a 'triumph'.

Di Stefano worked his magic to set up the opening goal. He sliced open the Stoke defence to send his right-winger Arnancio clear. His cross found Ruiz, who slammed the ball past O'Neill and into the net.

Stoke went into the dressing room at half-time just a goal down and Waddington didn't need to do much of a pep talk. His players were re-energised, reminded to enjoy themselves and relish their task. Just three minutes after the break, Mudie passed to Viollet, who came off the wing to lash the ball past Real Madrid goalkeeper

Vicente Miera. Within another four minutes delirium broke out as Stoke took the lead. This time McIlroy sent the ball screaming past the keeper via a deflection.

The massed ranks of fans hoped for a famous victory. It failed to materialise as Stoke, complete with their quota of Waddington's veterans, began to tire. For them to take the lead was in the words of one correspondent an act of 'brazen affront'. A lazy foul on Puskas in the penalty area gave the Spaniards the chance to equalise so the Hungarian dusted himself down and took the penalty to make it 2-2. Real finished the game strongly, Puskas and Ruiz both smacking the ball against the post. But Stoke held on for what satisfied fans considered to be a creditable draw.

Real Madrid, by bringing their own brand of footballing glamour to the Potteries, did Stoke and Waddington a favour, albeit for a match fee of £10,000, roughly £200,000 in today's money. It might be peanuts by the standards of the modern-day Premier League, but back then it was a small fortune for an English Second Division side to pay out.

Afterwards a grateful Waddington proudly remarked, 'Real Madrid told us that in all their travels, and they have visited most parts of the world, they have never been treated quite so magnificently by anyone.'

Months after the game, the Real Madrid president was on the phone to Waddington to tell him the Real players were 'eagerly following' Stoke's results. Perhaps they were not too offended by the cheek of the upstarts from the English Midlands threatening to embarrass them with a shock victory.

As far as Waddington was concerned Stoke City had been put on the footballing map thanks to the visit of the Spanish superstars but the event was not just a triumph for the football club. It was a personal triumph for Waddington.

For their participation, the Real Madrid players returned to the Spanish capital laden with gifts to remind them of their visit to the Potteries, including Spode china coffee sets and Royal Doulton character jugs. There was also a specially commissioned Doulton ceramic bull and matador figure to go in the trophy room at the Bernabeu, a well-meant gift but odd artefact alongside a host of European Cups. These served as tokens of gratitude for helping Waddington and Stoke further raise their profile. Real Madrid's visit whetted the appetite for top-class football of the Potteries sporting public.

Fortunately the centennial celebrations did not serve as too much of a distraction as Waddington's team went on to secure promotion. But he realised that further changes needed to be made and many of the players who served him so well were to be discarded.

He also, in the meantime, needed to get rid of the pesky sheep grazing on the Victoria Ground pitch. Waddington eventually succeeded in persuading his chairman, Gordon Taylor, to take his sheep elsewhere. As he recalled, 'Oh my God did we have trouble? What they used to do was lie on the side and rub their sides and burn the grass off so we got great big bare patches all over the ground. It was quite some time before I managed to persuade the chairman of the club that, horses for courses, but no sheep for football grounds.'

The sheep left quite happily. In contrast, moves to discard players and bring in fresh talent surprisingly brought the first hints of criticism of Waddington's management of his football club. His reward for gaining promotion was the offer of a five-year contract.

He also had to endure the brickbats from sceptical national newspaper writers, a familiar theme for any manager of a club newly promoted to the top flight of English football.

One Fleet Street columnist observed, 'Life must seem a little hard to some of the men who helped Stoke City win promotion. Already the club are sniffing around the transfer market, before last season's heroes have had the chance to prove themselves in the First Division.'

In particular he objected to what he called 'run of the mill players' being approached. Bizarrely the critic felt new quality players were not needed because Stoke's first set of home games against Tottenham Hotspur, Aston Villa and Leicester City would guarantee full houses at the Victoria Ground. Waddington begged to differ.

As much as he wanted to pack the terraces with fans watching the star players of the day, it was more than just a cosmetic exercise. A working man's ballet, yes. A poor man's branch of show business or a freak show for the curious, no. He wanted to win football matches and secure his club's long-term future in the top echelons of the English game. He pressed ahead with his transfer plans.

Among those being approached by Waddington was charismatic Rangers and Scotland playmaker Jim Baxter. A fee of £70,000 was agreed by the clubs with Baxter indicating a willingness to move from Glasgow to English football. Frustratingly for Waddington, he was unable to close the deal with the formal agreement of Baxter, who later went to Sunderland instead.

Waddington's attention then strayed elsewhere, much closer to home than Glasgow. Specifically, it was to his adopted home town of Crewe, and a Manchester City player living there; one considered by snobbish Fleet Street critics to be one of those 'run of the mill' average footballers. He moved to sign his future captain, Peter Dobing. As a young player, Dobing first made his name at Blackburn Rovers, being a part of their losing 1960 FA Cup Final team to Wolves. But Dobing grew up near to Stoke-on-Trent in the Cheshire town of Nantwich, a young prospect originally missed out on by Waddington's youth scouting system.

Rivals Port Vale had given him a trial as a teenager. Stoke had ignored the young lad, a player who would end up lifting the club's own major trophy as captain. Dobing had moved from Blackburn to Manchester City but became unsettled there.

Waddington got word of his unhappiness. The tip could not be more reliable. It came from Dobing's dad, an hotelier in Crewe. It meant for Waddington a call to his old mentor Joe Mercer, by then the Manchester City manager, to arrange a pre-season friendly and the possible transfer of an unsettled player. Mercer duly obliged but for what was considered back then a high price.

As Stoke were being forced to pay a club record fee of £38,000 for Dobing, any lingering hopes of completing the more ambitious transfer of Jim Baxter from Rangers came to an end. Chairman Albert Henshall and his board of directors steadfastly refused to ease their tight grip on the purse strings.

They did so despite a financial windfall with intense interest in Stoke City sweeping through the Potteries. More than 6,000 season tickets had been sold before the club's first season back in the top flight had kicked off. It was estimated that more than £50,000 was in the kitty from ticket sales without a game being played, back then deemed a considerable war chest. The money was there but Waddington needed to plot his transfer strategy carefully. He still needed an eye for a bargain.

In opting to go for Dobing, he explained, 'In the transition to the First Division I felt it was essentially about pace and ability. Dobing had this swift burst of speed and the deal was completed after the friendly match with Manchester City. If Dobing had one problem it was a lack of confidence and I feel I helped to give him greater assurance by appointing him captain.'

It turned out to be an inspired move but not without its problems. Dobing may, in Waddington's opinion, have lacked confidence. Yet he had a tendency to be headstrong and would later test his manager's patience to the limit. As Waddington prepared for Stoke's return to the First Division, though, Dobing for him was an ideal signing.

Aside from a new goalkeeper to replace Jimmy O'Neill, the Northern Irish international Bobby Irvine from Linfield, Dobing turned out to be the only significant capture of the summer of 1963 for Waddington. But he had waiting in the wings a signing who would go on to play alongside Dobing in Stoke's League Cup-winning team and enjoy legendary status among the club's fans.

John Ritchie was one of Waddington's greatest signings. He was also the subject of one of his biggest mistakes.

More than often Waddington would scout a player before signing him, but not on this occasion. He poached Ritchie on being alerted of his potential by a rival manager trying to sign him. It was an act of subterfuge to test relations with others in the game. As Mercer insisted, never trust anybody in professional football, including Waddington.

The tip-off came from Arthur Turner, the manager at Headington, now Oxford United. His directors had refused to stump up Kettering Town's full asking price for Ritchie, their young centre-forward. Turner vented his frustration to his friend, Waddington. Given Turner's enthusiasm for Ritchie and his thwarted plans to sign him, Waddington sensed an opportunity.

He explained, 'I made a few phone calls and built up a mental picture of this goalscoring centre-forward. I knew Arthur was a good judge of a player and for £2,500 it was worth taking a chance. I persuaded the board to give me the £2,500 and so I went to Kettering and signed John Ritchie without ever seeing him play.'

It was not until the closing stages of Stoke's promotion season that Ritchie made his debut. For the start of the campaign in the First Division, he remained out of the side but was a more than useful back-up for Mudie and Viollet.

Ritchie's league debut came against Cardiff City in April 1963 with Stanley Matthews, in the role of welcoming local hero, taking him under his wing. Ritchie remembered being 'terrified' as he prepared to go out to play. He recalled, 'Sir Stanley took me down on to the pitch about an hour before the game. He said, "Come on, let's warm up together." He said, "These people are just waiting for a hero to come along. They need a hero. They need a centre-forward that can score goals and you can be that man. If you can do that for them, they'll never forget you.'"

It took a while for Ritchie to establish a regular spot in the side. Once he did he became a hero, as Matthews predicted. Therefore it was all the more mystifying, to outline later, why Waddington would sell him before realising his mistake and trying to sign him back as he was going out of the door.

In the summer of 1963, the only thing on Waddington's mind was how to establish his side among the elite of English football. His mixture of youth and experience had shown in the centennial game against Real Madrid they were capable of competing with the best. Now came a sterner test, competing on a regular basis in the top division of English football.

Such was the feverish interest in the Potteries that the police insisted that Stoke's first three home games, starting against Tottenham Hotspur, were all-ticket affairs. Nobody was able to pay on the day at the turnstile. For Premier League matches these days, the equivalent of the old First Division, this is standard practice. Back then it was rare.

So the first to turn up at the Victoria Ground were Spurs, winners of the English league and FA Cup double only a couple of years earlier. They had also become the first English team to win a European trophy a few months earlier with UEFA's Cup Winners' Cup.

Given Spurs' reputation, many of the 40,000 Stoke fans must have feared the worst as they went to the stadium. Their fears seemed justified within the first minute of the game. Waddington must have also wondered whether he had made the right move in signing Bobby Irvine as his goalkeeper. The Irishman fumbled a shot from Jimmy Greaves and Spurs centre-forward Bobby Smith pounced to open the scoring.

From then on though Stoke dominated with Matthews, returning to the First Division at the age of 48, carving out the chance for the equaliser. He exchanged passes with Don Ratcliffe before sending over a pinpoint cross to Jimmy McIlroy. He trapped the ball before firing past the Spurs goalkeeper Bill Brown.

McIlroy was once again enjoying a virtuoso performance in the harsh spotlight of top-flight football. Just before half-time he was the beneficiary of new signing Dobing's act of larceny, robbing Spurs' famed uncompromising half-back Dave Mackay of the ball. McIlroy seized on Dobing's cross and scored what turned out to be the winner. Despite the much vaunted reputation of Spurs and conceding a goal in the first minute, Stoke ended up comfortable winners.

It was the ideal start to the season. Don Ratcliffe, who left the club shortly after playing in the game, recalled, 'Taking on Spurs at home for our first game back in the First Division made it a wonderful occasion.' While praising McIlroy as 'one hell of a good player', he also singled out Eddie Stuart and Eddie Clamp for praise, noting 'they would scare anybody'. On this occasion it was Tottenham's international forward line who were scared.

Young full-backs Tony Allen and Eric Skeels also played their part. Allen remembered, 'It is always important for any promoted team to get off to a good start and we certainly did that. I was up against Cliff Jones. He had a big reputation and the thought of marking him scared me at first. But, like the rest of the Stoke team, I soon settled into my game.'

Stoke then settled into their next match by beating Aston Villa 3-1 with Dobing scoring a couple of goals. But from then on it was a struggle.

They went ten games without a win although Waddington refused to panic. He gave Ritchie his chance to establish himself in the side, a chance he took. Defensive reinforcements also arrived, including deep-lying midfielder Calvin Palmer from Nottingham Forest for £30,000 with Waddington feeling he was able to keep the player's volatile nature under control. He had managed to do just that with Stuart and Clamp– at least he thought he had.

A 3-2 victory over West Bromwich Albion had stopped the rot, Palmer scoring the winning goal. But then Stoke came up against McIlroy's old side Burnley, prompting an inevitable surge of interest. McIlroy never wanted to leave the Lancashire club. He never got a satisfactory explanation as to why he was forced out. Yet he had settled at Stoke and was happy to play under Waddington. Like so many of his colleagues, he admired 'Waddo', as the players fondly nicknamed him. As far as McIlroy and Waddington were concerned, the game against Burnley didn't need to be a grudge match. Eddie Clamp had other ideas.

With just ten minutes left at the Victoria Ground, Stoke were winning comfortably 4-2. But for some inexplicable reason Clamp singled out Burnley's England winger John Connolly for one of his trademark karate-style tackles.

Waddington takes up the story, 'Connolly went down poleaxed and the referee sent Clamp off the field. Burnley scored twice to level 4-4 and I stormed into the dressing room to inform Eddie that he had played his last game for Stoke. Hard man Eddie broke down at that moment, but he never turned out again in Stoke's first team.'

Notwithstanding the signing of Palmer and the emergence of youth team player Alan Bloor in the senior ranks, it was a risk. For all his temperamental flaws, Clamp remained a decent defender, a popular player in the dressing room and on the terraces. Reluctantly Waddington let him go. Stoke eventually escaped relegation without their hard man in their ranks. However, his absence might well have cost them in the League Cup Final against Leicester, which was played just weeks after the Burnley game.

Getting rid of Clamp turned out to be more difficult than his boss envisaged. Peterborough United offered to sign him for a nominal fee but the player had gone missing on the day of the deal. There was a race meeting at Wolverhampton so Waddington gambled that Clamp would be there. He was on to a sure-fire winner. Once a message from Waddington went blazing out across the tannoy system on the racecourse for Eddie Clamp to contact Stoke City, the player felt he had no choice but to respond.

Sending Clamp to a football club nicknaming itself 'The Posh' was possibly not the brightest idea. As club policy, Peterborough insisted players wore a collar and tie on match days, almost an impossible demand for Clamp as he never wore a tie. He played a handful of games for Peterborough but failed to turn up for extra training after one heavy defeat. Clamp told his manager he always attended church on Sundays but his brief spell as a Peterborough player came to an end.

By showing Clamp the door at Stoke, Waddington had effectively ended his career. Clamp was a footballer renowned for his hard-man reputation but he was also a fine player, a First Division title and FA Cup winner as well as an England international. It was brutal, if necessary treatment from Waddington.

There were no hard feelings. Clamp, despite being a lifelong Wolves supporter with his mother working for decades in the club's laundry department, occasionally returned to the Victoria Ground to watch Stoke games. He delighted fans of the era perhaps for different reasons than the likes of Matthews or McIlroy. Yet he still played a valuable role in the early years of Waddington rebuilding Stoke into a competitive First Division team.

As the first season back in the top tier of English football closed, the threat of relegation almost disappeared with a remarkable 9-1 victory over Ipswich Town, still the biggest top-flight win for the club.

Ipswich had stunned the nation by winning the league title a couple of seasons earlier under the guidance of future England World Cup-winning manager Alf Ramsey. Now they were in free-fall and Waddington's men were happy to give them an extra push, especially on their notorious muddy pitch.

The Ipswich defenders were barely able to stay on their feet as Stoke's fleet-footed players tore past them. Dennis Viollet scored a hat-trick and John Ritchie scored twice, ending an 11-game run without a goal. McIlroy also scored a couple and Keith Bebbington and Peter Dobing were on the scoresheet. But for Dobing having a goal ruled offside it would have been ten.

Ipswich went on to be relegated but Stoke survived thanks to further impressive wins over title challengers Everton and Manchester United in the last few weeks of the season. The 3-1 defeat of Manchester United ensured the league title went to Merseyside with Liverpool. It also ended any lingering fears of Stoke being relegated. At a century old, Waddington's club was re-established among the top sides in the land. Yet despite offering pay rises at the start of the season, the club hardly appeared in the mood to offer further rewards to its players.

'Footballer buys house' hardly rates as a news story. In the case of Stoke's Gerry Bridgewood it was for the *Stoke Sentinel*. The fact he stumped up the cash from his wages rather than his employers served to the *Sentinel* as a sign of the football club's directors' frugal nature. They had divested themselves of their property portfolio of players' houses, no longer offering free temporary accommodation for players and their families.

Waddington defended the policy. He explained, 'It used to be the policy of Stoke to buy houses for players. Now the club are encouraging players to acquire their own homes. It is an economic proposition for them and it encourages thrift.'

It failed to encourage them to win a major honour. The League Cup Final of 1964 gave Waddington his first chance to lift a major trophy but it was blown. One of the men to blame was one of Waddington's greatest players, Gordon Banks.

6

Banks of England

UNLIKE many of his managerial rivals of the day, Tony Waddington, with Frank Swift chief among his boyhood heroes, valued goalkeepers. Little in his wildest dreams did he think the world's best might become available.

It seemed inconceivable he might agree to join what critics viewed as a sleepy provincial club rather than the established trophy-hunting elite of the game from London, Manchester or Merseyside. Stoke City fans, even the most optimistic, were stunned by the signing of England's World Cup-winning goalkeeper Gordon Banks from Leicester City in the summer of 1967. For the Stoke faithful, he was a gift from the footballing gods. Yet in the club's first season back in the First Division those same fans had reason to curse Banks and his Leicester team-mates.

The League Cup was in its infancy and while counting as a major trophy it lacked even the admittedly limited prestige it enjoys in the Premier League era. In the early 1960s there was no place in European competition on offer for the winners. There was no showpiece Wembley final either. Instead Stoke met Leicester in the 1964 final over two legs, home and away. Prior to the first leg there had been heavy rain in the Potteries, ensuring ideal conditions for Waddington's gang of mud-larks. But he still put a call into the fire brigade to ask them to flood the pitch with a few more gallons of water, something he later admitted to Banks, at the time a Leicester player.

One correspondent, presumably unaware of Waddington's favourite act of subterfuge, blamed heavy rain for turning 'the near naked pitch into a mud-heap'. The broadcaster Bryon Butler, covering the match on this occasion for the *Daily Telegraph*, commented, 'Mud covered the Victoria Ground and only a little green triangle in each corner reminded us that the pioneers of the game intended that it should be played on grass.'

It was stinging criticism of Waddington and his groundsman but neither took any notice in the years to come as Stoke endeavoured to eke out the most from home advantage.

For most of the game Stoke dominated, only to be thwarted by Banks and his Leicester defenders. Dobing hit the post. Viollet returned a ball punched out by Banks on to the crossbar. Banks made a series of saves described in the press as 'dynamic'. He had only a few weeks earlier being criticised for a below-par performance for England against Scotland at Hampden Park.

His Fleet Street detractors in the Victoria Ground press box welcomed his return to form. 'If it had not been for the brilliant work of Banks, Stoke surely would have been in front,' wrote one of them. His 'brilliant work' was less welcome to Stoke fans and players. Just as the England goalkeeper appeared unbeatable in the face of the Stoke onslaught, he proved he was human after all. Stoke took the lead, Banks making a mistake thanks in part to the wretched state of the pitch.

Banks ruefully explained in his autobiography, 'Such greasy conditions are always troublesome for a goalkeeper. The ball tends to skid off the surface at an alarming speed, which makes judgement difficult.' He recalled finding himself in such a predicament diving to save a shot from the Stoke full-back Bill Asprey. 'I thought I had the ball covered but it shot up and it was all I could do to claw it away from goal,' Banks remembered.

Keith Bebbington gratefully pounced on the loose ball and scored. Given their domination of what was described as an 'ill-tempered' game, Stoke should have won. They failed to do so thanks to a fluke equaliser. A clearance from Eric Skeels rebounded off Leicester's Terry Heath into the path of Dave Gibson who flicked the ball into the net. It left Leicester as favourites for the return leg, one which would leave Waddington cursing his luck.

This time he had no control of the state of the pitch. He had no control of injuries to his players either. Before kick-off, he was forced to leave out his first-choice goalkeeper Lawrie Leslie and bring back Bobby Irvine. Then with the game in the balance with half an hour still to go his recent signing Calvin Palmer was carried off on a stretcher.

Stoke had just equalised after conceding a Leicester goal as early as the third minute of the game. Jimmy McIlroy, never afraid to play a long ball, put Dennis Viollet in the clear to score. Stoke had the upper hand and were playing attractive attacking football. But Palmer's injury, in the days before substitutes were allowed, effectively handed the initiative back to Leicester. Waddington could only impotently look on from the stands.

Gibson restored Leicester's lead, somehow heading the ball through a narrow gap between Irvine and his near post. In the closing minutes, Howard Riley made it 3-1, the game lost for Stoke. To their credit, Stoke managed to score a second in injury time, Scottish centre-half George Kinnell ambling forward to find the target. It was too late.

Waddington and his players endured a night of frustrating failure, the first real setback in his mission to bring tangible success to a century-old club without a mention in football's major honours list. He was left to rue his luck. His opponents celebrated the first major honour in their club's history instead, though the influential

Bryon Butler disparagingly dismissed the competition as 'soccer's consolation trophy'. Butler, for all his doubts, did however lead the campaign for the winners to be given a European place and for the final to be staged at Wembley, a call for which Waddington would be forever grateful.

This entertaining clash between Stoke and Leicester on their respective end-of-season mud-heaps helped to boost cries for a showpiece League Cup Final. Football League secretary Alan Hardaker declared, 'The stillborn babe has suddenly become a bouncing infant.'

Stoke, under Waddington, played their part in breathing life into the competition. But Banks's Leicester were the winners. He proudly recalled, 'As individuals we were delighted. But even more so for the club and its supporters.'

Less than a decade later Banks would share similar sentiments after winning the same trophy with a different club, thanks to a swift and audacious bid from the unlikeliest of suitors.

After releasing Jimmy O'Neill following promotion, the position of goalkeeper became troublesome for Waddington. His relationship with O'Neill's immediate successor, Bobby Irvine, broke down even before it began. In an emergency deal, he had signed Lawrie Leslie to go between the sticks. Irvine stayed to fight for his place, playing in the League Cup Final, but despite being a decent goalkeeper Waddington felt Irvine had temperamental failings. This for him was finally confirmed when the Irishman picked a fight with Leeds United's Allan Clarke and ended up being sent off. It cost Stoke the game and Irvine was out the door.

Harry Gregg, Manchester United's Northern Ireland goalkeeper and hero of the Munich disaster, came in through the door for a brief spell, though mainly in a coaching capacity. This was merely a short-term fix. Waddington, in contrast to many of his peers, obsessively sought a reliable goalkeeper. He explained his philosophy to anyone caring to listen, not least Peter Coates, the Stoke City chairman who guided the club into the Premier League in 2008.

'I always remember one of his pearls of wisdom. He was talking about goalkeepers,' Mr Coates told me. 'The way he looked at a goalkeeper was the same as a striker. If a goalkeeper made ten, 12, or 15 saves more than the average goalkeeper could make it was no different than strikers with 20 or more goals a season rather than the average striker with ten.'

Goalkeepers, in Waddington's view, were undervalued. As he endeavoured to establish Stoke in the top flight of English football in the 1960s, hiring a top-class goalkeeper was a long-term priority.

At one point, he cast his eyes abroad, hoping to sign the Swedish international Sven Larsson. He had been lined up to play in a friendly at the Victoria Ground against Moscow Dynamo on a trial basis. Waddington applied to the FA for permission to field Larsson and it agreed. But just an hour before kick-off the FA contacted Waddington to tell him not to select the Swede.

The FA's behaviour infuriated Waddington. 'After all the advance publicity I felt that the crowd would feel cheated so we went ahead and played Sven, who performed well for us,' Waddington recalled. 'Subsequently the FA brought a charge against us for playing a keeper without going through the proper registration procedures and fined us £100.'

It also meant the deal for a new goalkeeper fell through, and indeed any bid for a foreign player was bizarrely off limits. However, the search was soon called off as one of Dennis Wilshaw's' young protégés, John Farmer, eventually settled into the role. His impressive performances for Stoke earned him England under-23 caps. Alf Ramsey, the England boss, seemed impressed. Waddington, while recognising Farmer's promise, was less sure. Then, quite bizarrely, the England full international goalkeeper became available, less than a year after he had lifted the World Cup.

Banks felt that his place as first choice at Leicester was safe. A promising teenager called Peter Shilton had emerged as his understudy. But neither Banks nor anybody else in football thought he would usurp England's number one, a man ranked by football's world governing body FIFA as the best goalkeeper on the planet.

Strangely, the Leicester manager Matt Gillies and his board of directors felt otherwise. Financial pressures had already led to the club deciding to sell centre-forward Derek Dougan, a cult figure among fans. Those same pressures led to the decision to sell the prized asset of Banks.

A cheeky transfer request from Peter Shilton also played its part as he demanded first-team football otherwise he was off. Much to Banks's bewilderment, he was put on the transfer list by Leicester instead of Shilton. His manager told him his best days were behind him. Banks remembered being 'dumbfounded' and 'shell-shocked'. He went home on being given the news with a 'dreadful feeling of betrayal'.

Surely though the managers of the country's top clubs would come knocking on Leicester's door requesting the signature of the world's best goalkeeper? There was no need to form an orderly queue. A few, including Liverpool, Manchester United and West Bromwich Albion, made tentative enquiries. Only West Ham United made a firm offer but just as Banks thought he might be joining his England World Cup-winning team-mates Bobby Moore, Geoff Hurst and Martin Peters at Upton Park, it was withdrawn. The West Ham manager Ron Greenwood opted instead to sign Kilmarnock's Scottish international Bobby Ferguson.

Waddington quietly monitored events. Opportunity beckoned. It was time to act by putting in an audacious bid for Banks.

'I contacted Leicester manager Matt Gillies and I was amazed that I had a clear field as we quickly agreed a £50,000 fee. I was confident of clinching the signing,' Waddington recalled.

The deal was verbally struck over a weekend with Banks away on England duty. The various parties agreed to meet at Leicester's Filbert Street on the Monday morning. Despite agreeing a deal with Gillies, Waddington, true to the mantra of never trusting anybody in football, treated his Leicester counterpart with suspicion. He was right to do so.

Gillies had been back on the phone to rival managers once again touting Banks's availability and warning them of the bid from Stoke. Gillies admitted as much as soon as Waddington sat down in his office. Waddington told the story, 'I was sitting in Matt's office, I heard the unmistakable tones of Bill Shankly on the phone. All credit to Matt Gillies, who could probably have collected a bigger fee. He told Bill that no other club would be allowed to make contact before I had talked to the player.'

Perhaps Gillies felt embarrassed. Shankly built up a legendary reputation as a loud and abrasive figure in the game. He had been so loud in his telephone call with Gillies that Waddington could hear his disparaging comments about Stoke. 'You don't want to let him go to Stoke City. What good can they do him?' Shankly ranted. But despite Shankly's protestations, Gillies gave Waddington the go-ahead to meet Banks.

Accounts of the meeting from the two men in subsequent years slightly differ.

In both stories though the pair are not just complimentary but praiseworthy of each other. For Waddington it was a matter of persuading Banks to come to Stoke rather than the more glamorous alternative of Shankly's Liverpool. He said he told Banks, 'The first thing I want to tell you is since our discussions on Friday there have been a number of clubs, top clubs, chasing you. They want to see if they can sign you. He said, "What have you done? Have you changed your mind?" I said, "Changed my mind about what?" He said, "About signing me." I said, "No, I haven't." I said, "Look, that's the way I am. I want to be fair. I don't want you to come up to me in a couple of weeks' time and say 'Tony, why didn't you tell me Liverpool have come in for me'."'

According to Waddington, Banks told him it was too late for Shankly and Liverpool. He would be signing for Stoke, happy to move to the Potteries.

From Banks the account is less straightforward. He recalled, 'Stoke, a mid-table First Division side, were hardly the most fashionable club of the day, but I'd played against them often enough to know they were a good side with the potential to be even better. I told Matt [Gillies, the Leicester City manager] that I would be interested and he immediately arranged for the Stoke manager Tony Waddington to come to Filbert Street to discuss terms. I had no idea what wages Stoke City were offering but as Leicester were the worst payers in the First Division I didn't expect to take a drop.'

Money, as ever in football, did turn out to be a problem even before he had the chance to meet Waddington, not from Stoke but Leicester.

Much to Banks's dismay, indeed anger, he was refused a loyalty bonus by the Leicester board, not a penny. Banks had not asked to leave. He had been told to go so he was entitled to some financial compensation. As far as Banks was concerned his club had acted dishonestly and in a fit of petulance called the deal off. If necessary, he would play in the reserves. According to Banks he had yet to meet Waddington to discuss terms. Rival bids from Liverpool or anyone else were not on his mind, just the loyalty bonus and his determination to stay put at Leicester if not a penny was forthcoming.

Banks described how he broke the news to Waddington. 'I left Matt's office in a dark mood and found Tony Waddington sitting in the main foyer. "I'm sorry Mr Waddington but the deal's off," I said and proceeded to tell him why,' Banks wrote in his autobiography. 'His face betrayed no emotion at the news. He simply stood up and said, "Leave this to me" before sweeping into Matt's office without knocking. Five minutes later he marched out. "Two grand all right?" I told him that would be fine by me. "Good!" he said. "Then let's do the deal and get out of here."'

It was a classic piece of wheeler dealing from Waddington, something he himself kept quiet. Banks was impressed but there was something of a twist.

A couple of years later Banks chatted about how he was settling in at Stoke on a pre-season tour in the Netherlands with one of the club's directors, Dr Gordon Crowe, a good friend of the chairman Albert Henshall and indeed Waddington. He told Dr Crowe how happy he was at Stoke and revealed he felt the transfer would not have gone through if it were not for Waddington persuading Leicester to come up with his loyalty bonus. The good doctor's reply was abrupt.

'Did he hell? We paid you that!' commented Crowe. Apparently in negotiating the deal, Waddington had found Gillies just as awkward and intransigent as Banks had done earlier. Out of frustration, he spontaneously offered Leicester an additional £2,000 on top of the £50,000 transfer, with the extra money to be passed on to Banks.

It was an offer made without the clearance of the Stoke board. Waddington reasoned that his directors would back him. He was right. Banks fondly summed up the deal. 'That was typical of Tony Waddington, he was a great guy and one of the most underrated managers in football,' commented Banks. 'Tony realised the importance of a good goalkeeper to a team and I'd like to think he believed the board's money was well spent.'

Waddington certainly did. He reasoned, 'If you're looking for players during my particular time, it would not really be fair to single out any one particularly as outstanding. But of course there are little exceptions to that. It goes without saying that Gordon Banks has got to be one of them. Gordon was a tremendous professional and absolutely fantastic goalkeeper.'

Stoke fans agreed. They were delighted and stunned to hear that the world's best goalkeeper had signed for their club. Banks's new team-mates thought much the same. It was a brilliant transfer coup from their manager, one to rank with the return of Matthews some six years earlier.

Waddington was impressed by the way his prized signing had settled into the Stoke side. He shared his vision of bringing silverware to a club starved of success. 'He came into the dressing room at Stoke and everybody knew him of course,' Waddington remembered. 'He just said, "Well you all know me. I've not come here just to sit back and enjoy myself. I think this club are going to win things and I think this club is good enough to win things. I don't want anybody to think I've just come here to mess about." That's how he played. And, he was tremendous.'

Banks was equally fulsome in praise of Waddington. He wrote in his autobiography, 'Some say that Tony was ahead of his time in recognising the value of a good goalkeeper. To my mind it was more a case of other managers being behind the times. Whatever, I loved the man. He always tried to sign the gifted players who would entertain the supporters; always believed that football at its most inspirational and creative has a place in the best of all possible worlds.

'His first priority was to his players, his second to the supporters who paid their hard earned cash to watch us. He never forgot how important the role of football was in the lives of working people, as evidenced by his marvellous description of football as "the working man's ballet".'

With Banks ensconced in goal, stood behind some of the most uncompromising defenders in English football, Waddington now had the platform for a team of creative players to challenge for the honours he craved. It was also important Banks, for all his fame, treated himself as just one of the lads. He was able to contribute to Stoke's unique brand of team spirit.

7

Team Spirit

HOW does a football manager encourage team spirit? In Tony Waddington's case the answer was simple. Just keep a bottle of the stuff maturing in the chairman's whisky cabinet during the course of the week to be opened up on the day of the game. It seems unthinkable in the Premier League era of sports psychologists and bio-scientists. But half a century ago, a tot of whisky just before going out to play seemed a perfectly reasonable means of boosting performance and encouraging team spirit.

Waddington said 'it was just to steady the nerves' and revealed that even Stanley Matthews, a health and fitness fanatic, had the odd drink of glucose and champagne 'as the adrenalin got to him' near to kick-off. Waddington angrily denied it was the most glaring example of an unhealthy drinking culture at his football club. 'Forget the stories that any of my players ever staggered out on the pitch,' he argued.

As for Frank Mountford, Stoke's genial coach, who enthusiastically led the whisky tasting, Waddington could not be so sure of total sobriety on his part. Mountford would go up to the boardroom about an hour before kick-off to collect a bottle of whisky from the chairman for what he euphemistically termed 'team spirit'. He then handed out a tot around the dressing room on a one for you, one for me, basis. For a more puritanical or conventional regime this practice might appear a little eccentric if not dubious. But it all helped to build up a sense of camaraderie in the Stoke dressing room as Waddington built a team he felt capable of taking on the best in the land.

Even Matthews was unable to go on forever. Once Gordon Banks arrived, another of English football's legendary figures had already gone out the door. Matthews played his last top-flight game against Fulham at the Victoria Ground on 6 February 1965 at the age of 50, even then only being picked by Waddington because of injuries to other players. Stoke won 3-1 with Matthews going off to a guard of honour from both sets of players.

Matthews felt he could carry on playing. Waddington thought otherwise. Matthews had served his purpose, both on and off the pitch. He attracted fans. He attracted other players to Stoke in what he termed a 'renaissance' for the football club. 'I exploited Stan to the maximum, not only for publicity and headlines, but in getting other players to come to Stoke,' Waddington admitted in one of Matthews's many biographies. But by the mid-1960s, along with other veteran players, Sir Stanley Matthews needed to go with Waddington thinking in the long-term, rather than the short-term, in his transfer dealings.

Just as the signing of Matthews helped to attract players, the arrival of Banks did much the same though Waddington had already hired some key reinforcements. After years of trying to lure his friend George Eastham's son to the Victoria Ground, George Eastham junior finally arrived in the Potteries. Crucially, he was Banks's room-mate on England duty and played his part in facilitating the goalkeeper's transfer.

Eastham recognised that Waddington burned with ambition, however unlikely that seemed to outsiders. In turn, Waddington admired Eastham junior, perplexed by his treatment at the hands of the Arsenal hierarchy. He recalled being in the Highbury boardroom at half-time in a game between Arsenal and West Bromwich Albion hearing the Gunners' contingent criticising Eastham 'unmercifully'. As far as Waddington was concerned he was the best player on the pitch. Given the apparent antipathy from the Arsenal management towards Eastham, he put in a bid and Arsenal gratefully sold him to Stoke. As Waddington dryly noted, 'Football is about opinions. A manager must have confidence in his own judgement irrespective of conflicting points of view.'

In the assessment of Eastham, he believed he was right and the Arsenal board, coaching staff and supporters wrong. Along with Eastham, one of the most popular players among Stoke fans of the 1960s and '70s, Harry Burrows, had arrived from Aston Villa. On the same day he put pen to paper, the Everton and Welsh international striker Roy Vernon also signed up to the Waddington project, though inadvertently this deal led to the Stoke manager dropping his first major clanger in running the football club.

The troubled negotiation with Vernon ought to have served as an omen for Waddington. After securing Burrows's signature, Waddington drove down to Swansea to meet Vernon, who was with the Wales team on international duty. Waddington recalled in his reminiscences to the *Stoke Sentinel* a night of hard bargaining, 'My talks with Vernon went long into the evening, but the Wales manager, Dave Bowen, gave permission for him to stay up late. I needed to send a telegram to the Football League before midnight to beat the deadline, but it was 11.50pm when he agreed to sign.'

Even then the forms were not completed in time to meet the midnight transfer deadline. It was one in the morning before Vernon put pen to paper, a mere detail Waddington hid from the powers that be at the Football League. Bowen told him, 'You have made one of the best signings you will ever make.' He turned out to be right. But Vernon's impressive form in his first couple of years in Stoke's red and white stripes led to Waddington, much to the dismay of Stoke City, selling his impressive young striker John Ritchie. It was a move Waddington quickly regretted.

A serious injury to Ritchie influenced Waddington's decision to sell him as much as the form of Vernon had done. In a game with Blackburn, the centre-forward clattered into the opposition goalkeeper, suffering a chest injury. Stoke's club doctor and board director, Gordon Crowe, feared he might have suffered a punctured lung and a prolonged stay in hospital ensued. At one point Ritchie was sent abroad for treatment and appeared to be making a sound recovery. But the medical specialists warned Waddington that Ritchie might suffer a relapse at any time, putting his long-term career in doubt.

Once a transfer offer came along, Waddington decided to sell. Sheffield Wednesday's manager Alan Brown had already made several bids for Ritchie, mainly because he always seemed to cause his defenders a host of problems. Once the negative medical assessment of Ritchie's long-term prospect came through, and with Vernon ensconced in Stoke's forward line, Waddington agreed to let him go across the Pennines for a £75,000 fee but admitted there was not much logic to allowing one of his most popular players to leave. He was right. There was outrage among the fans. Even Ritchie didn't seem keen on the transfer. He refused to move house and stayed put in the Potteries. Waddington observed, 'I suppose he never left us in spirit.'

Once Stoke's fortunes rose with Banks and his robust defenders making Waddington's side difficult to beat, Sheffield Wednesday went into decline. The club put Ritchie on the transfer market. A relieved Waddington said, 'He did his job for Wednesday but at a time when they were not doing well as a team and when the opportunity came to get him back in 1969 I did not hesitate.'

Just to sum up his relief and joy after taking some severe criticism for selling Ritchie in the first place, he likened it in the

Stoke Sentinel to 'the return of Stan Matthews all over again'. He further boasted, 'We had sold Ritchie for £75,000, a figure that would be ten times that amount today, and bought him back for £25,000. He had cost us just £2,000 from Kettering initially so we made a profit on him.'

Ritchie had been restored to the Stoke frontline in the summer of 1969. He also had a new popular strike partner, another of Waddington's finest signings, Jimmy Greenhoff. As for Ritchie, he described his return to Stoke City as the 'happiest day' of his life. He was a Stoke man, a Tony Waddington man.

In Greenhoff's case, Waddington's instincts in assessing an out-of-favour player proved key. He was advised to stay clear of the forward because he was viewed by scouts as lazy. Sceptics also wondered at the wisdom of signing centre-forward David Herd, a Scottish international, from Manchester United. Surely this was another veteran with his best days behind him? In both cases, as will be explained later, Waddington ignored the negative advice. He desperately needed decent strikers. He was going to back his judgement and go out and buy a couple of them.

Perennial relegation scraps influenced his thinking. Despite strengthening his side, Waddington and Stoke endured a couple of torrid seasons, flirting all along with the drop. Vernon suffered from persistent injury and with Ritchie gone, the goals had dried up. Only Gordon Banks and the emerging local lads in defence, John Marsh, Micky Pejic, Denis Smith and Alan Bloor, stopped a flood of goals going in at the other end. Banks consistently lived up to the merit of Waddington's conviction of top-class goalkeepers being as valuable as prolific strikers.

Defensive heroics from Banks and company saved Stoke from relegation season after season. The most torrid of all these seasons just happened to be his first at the club, 1967/68. Stoke's bizarre start to that campaign served as a portent of troubled times ahead and their future skipper went on strike.

After losing the opening game of the season away to Arsenal 2-0, Stoke were held to a 1-1 draw at home to Sheffield United. Next up at home they faced one of the title favourites, Manchester City, Peter Dobing's former club. It was with just hours to go before kick-off that the player dropped the bombshell that he was going on strike. In fact he threatened to pack in the game altogether. The *Stoke Sentinel* reported, 'He has walked out with his insurance cards and told officials he has finished with soccer.'

A flustered Waddington hid behind Football Association regulations to explain away a contract dispute with a player he had until then treated as a friend. He told the *Sentinel*, 'Dobing asked for certain demands when we were discussing a new contract. These demands were against the regulations of the FA, so he promptly asked for his cards and we have given them to him.'

The statement left angry fans baffled. Just to add to the intrigue, Waddington sympathetically revealed, 'In all fairness to Dobing, he did telephone us from Crewe an hour before the game saying that if we were stuck for players he would offer to turn out.'

He was not needed as Stoke won 3-0. Waddington would have been happy at the result but as an inveterate public relations man not the notoriety brought to his football club as a result of Dobing's behaviour. *The Guardian* observed, 'Stoke turned out to be the most troublesome place in the League. Dobing, last year's top scorer, refused to play and was given his cards. Then the crowd taking their cue from an ill-tempered match provided what was described by Stoke officials as the worst outbreak of hooliganism at the ground for several seasons.'

Nine people were taken to hospital and more than two dozen fans were arrested. The beautiful game had turned ugly, Dobing and the unruly Stoke fans cast in the role of villains. A bizarre match-fixing scandal aside, Waddington enjoyed a trouble-free start to his managerial career at Stoke. By the late summer of 1967, his dream job threatened to turn into a nightmare.

While many supporters could be forgiven for wanting to see the back of Dobing for his prima-donna antics, Waddington decided to draw on his diplomatic skills to keep the player. He negotiated a new contract and persuaded irate supporters that it was all just a little misunderstanding. In response one fan theatrically turned up at the club's offices in the presence of the local paper to hand in his season ticket, worth the princely sum of £6. He did so in protest at how the club in his view had swept the 'Dobing walkout saga' under the carpet.

Waddington ignored the critics and persuaded his board to come to terms with Dobing and offer him a new contract. Frank Mountford was one to praise Waddington's man-management skills in dealing with petulant players. He explained, 'To give Tony credit, he was very astute. If you did try to argue with him, you'd never get the better of him. I liked the way he was able to handle players such as Peter Dobing.' In praising his former boss, Mountford noted, 'You could never fall out with him.'

Only years later did Dobing reveal quite possibly the true reasons for him going on strike and temporarily resigning from the club. Matt Busby's Manchester United had made an offer for him and Dobing told the *Lancashire Telegraph*, 'This was a chance to play with some of the greatest footballers of our time, the likes of George Best and Bobby Charlton, but Stoke simply said, "No, you are not going anywhere."'

Without any sense of irony, Dobing made the revelation while criticising current Premier League footballers for being greedy. 'In those days the clubs had all the power but now it is ridiculous, the players hold all the cards and what is happening in the game has become obscene,' Dobing reasoned. Whatever the circumstances, Waddington managed to keep his troubled skipper at Stoke. He was right to do so. Dobing, once he returned to the fold, turned out, along with Banks in goal, to be the club's and Waddington's saviour.

For the first few weeks of the 1967/68 season any unrest in the dressing room, thanks to Dobing walking out, did not appear to have a detrimental effect on the club's form. Indeed, team morale and spirit, tots of whisky aside, were relatively good. This was demonstrated spectacularly in a bizarre game at Upton Park against West Ham United. The trip to London doubled up as an unplanned wedding party for director Dr Gordon Crowe. Waddington explained, 'Gordon Crowe rushed in and said, "Drop what you are doing. You are going to be the best man." I managed to find a couple of hours to fulfil my duties before we set off for London and I suggested that he and his wife Margaret might as well start their honeymoon at the Russell Hotel.'

Perhaps the night before the game the players toasted the happy couple with a little too much enthusiasm. Preparations prior to kick-off became a little haphazard, especially after John Marsh lost a contact lens, a regular occurrence for the full-back.

The desperate search for Marsh's eyewear meant that the players were late out on to the pitch, much to the annoyance of West Ham's normally mild-mannered manager Ron Greenwood. He stormed into the Stoke dressing room to find out what was going on. Waddington recalled, 'Ron Greenwood came into the dressing room to find everyone on hands and knees peering for Marsh's contact lens. Not surprisingly Ron looked amazed and remarked, "It is time you were going out." Suddenly Marsh straightened up and said, "It's been in my eye all the time. It just slipped out of place." We were three goals down at half-time.'

Waddington further reflected, 'I suppose Ron Greenwood must have thought, "The way Stoke prepare for games, it is no wonder we are on top." He must have been even more amazed at the result, for Peter Dobing and Harry Burrows each scored twice in the space of nine minutes and we went on to win 4-3.'

It was a remarkable comeback that ought to have resulted in a resurgence in form. Instead, it resulted in a dip.

By the end of the season Stoke were facing relegation with title-chasing Leeds United arriving at the Victoria Ground. Pessimistic fans feared the worst but Dobing, the man condemned as a pariah at the beginning of the season, had other ideas and produced a masterclass to save Stoke and Waddington's job. No side had scored more than two goals against Leeds that season but Dobing, in a virtuoso display, helped himself to a hat-trick.

His first goal came just after the half-hour, latching on to a pass from George Eastham before scoring from an acute angle. Just before half-time he made it 2-0, hammering a low left-footed shot into the net. As the players went in for the break, Waddington must have been disappointed that his team had failed to build a more decisive lead.

Any fears were justified. Leeds, under Don Revie, were desperate to secure a first league title and fought back admirably. Of all ironies, their first goal came from a man to be signed by Waddington, a player destined to become a Stoke legend, Jimmy Greenhoff. Jackie Charlton then scored the equaliser, leaving Stoke fans and their manager fearing the worst. But a defensive howler from Charlton allowed Dobing to complete his hat-trick.

Leeds pressed for another equaliser with, much to Waddington's annoyance, the referee adding seven minutes of injury time. Another goal failed to materialise, Banks defying Mick Jones, Billy Bremner and his future team-mate Greenhoff. One Fleet Street correspondent hailed it as a 'famous victory' for a side even 'friends had given up as hopeless relegation cases'. Salvation was in sight for Waddington and Stoke.

Despite the heroics against Leeds, successive away defeats to Everton and Fulham meant Stoke's top-flight status was in the balance as Waddington and his players arrived at Banks's former club Leicester City. It was Banks's first match back at Filbert Street since being shown the door to make way for Peter Shilton. Quite bizarrely, the kick-off was put back to 7.30pm to allow Leicester's fans to go along to Grace Road to watch their county cricket team play the touring Australian national side.

It meant that, as the teams trotted out, Stoke knew they only needed to secure a point to stay in the First Division. Banks, who had just missed England's game with Spain some days earlier with flu, came off his sick bed to perform heroics in goal. As the game progressed, however, Leicester's interest declined. They were safe in mid-table. Stoke were able to hang on for a goalless draw.

At the end of the game the *Stoke Sentinel* reported, 'There were hugs, handshakes and high fives all round when the final whistle blew.' Waddington told the newspaper, 'I just could not go through it all again.'

He backed his goalkeeper. Who wouldn't? Far more bravely he kept faith with his defenders from the youth ranks, reinforced by the arrival of Northern Irish international defender Alex Elder from Burnley. He needed a goalscoring centre-forward to make up for the departure of John Ritchie and Roy Vernon's constant battles with injury. At the 1968 European Cup Final at Wembley, opportunity knocked.

As Bobby Charlton and company brought Manchester United the honour of becoming the first English side to lift the European Cup, their former youth team player Waddington looked on with admiration. The triumph came a decade since United lost players in the Munich air disaster. The manager Matt Busby almost lost his life too.

At Wembley, a lifetime's ambition had been achieved for Busby. Waddington, not just a former player but a fan, celebrated the success with Busby and his team.

He also took time to chat to David Herd, who had played in the earlier rounds but failed to make the United starting XI for the final. Waddington described himself as being 'fortunate' to be invited to United's victory celebrations. For him it was also an opportunity for some transfer dealing.

'David had just been given a free transfer and I went ahead to sign him that evening,' Waddington revealed. 'I was still looking to plug the gap left by John Ritchie and as a short-term investment I could scarcely have signed a better replacement. He was a goalscorer of the old brigade – no frills, but possessing a tremendous shot and good in the air. He was signed to get goals.'

Sadly the following season proved as traumatic as the last, Stoke again narrowly avoiding relegation. At one point centre-half Denis Smith played in attack alongside Herd, an act of seeming desperation. Smith recalled in his autobiography, 'This wasn't as crazy as it sounds as whilst in the youth and "A" teams I had been played up front now and then and once scored in seven consecutive games. Waddo, I think in desperation as much as anything, tried me there when he had run out of other options.'

Once the season was over another striking option became available. There were signs of progress despite a relegation struggle and England's number one goalkeeper enjoying more matchday practice than he might like. It would be a decade before Waddington would go through the agonies of a relegation struggle again. Recruiting Jimmy Greenhoff in the summer of 1969 to the forward line proved pivotal to further fuelling Stoke's revival.

On scouting players, Waddington had a rule. He reasoned it was 'not just a question of going to watch players – it is hearing the talk after a game and getting involved in conversations'. Those conversations led to his interest in Greenhoff after hearing that the former Leeds player had become embroiled in a wage dispute at his new club Birmingham City.

Waddington's assistant Frank Mountford put Greenhoff in the same category as Dobing as potentially difficult to deal with. Waddington was the ideal man to handle him. 'I could not really believe that Greenhoff was being made available,' remembered Waddington. 'I had a chat with Maurice Lindley, the chief scout at Leeds, and asked him about the player. Maurice suggested he was lazy and would not put himself about. That was far from my view having watched the player, so I backed my own judgement, even though it was Stoke's first six-figure transfer fee.'

Greenhoff signed for £100,000. Aston Villa had put in a rival bid but Birmingham would not countenance losing him to their biggest rivals. Everton, who 12 months later would go on to win the league championship, also put in a bid.

Greenhoff, though, was persuaded by Waddington to sign for Stoke. 'Waddo came over with Albert Henshall and I got the call to go to St Andrew's as there were a couple of fellas interested in signing me. I wasn't told who. So I went down,' recalled Greenhoff.

He added, 'I must admit Stoke weren't my first choice at the time but we had a chat and I asked if he'd start to look at putting a younger team out at Stoke. I didn't want to be bought to do the running for other players. I wanted to play my own game. Waddo said that he would and we shook hands on the deal.'

Despite last-minute overtures from Everton, Greenhoff honoured his agreement with the Stoke manager. He noted that the make-up of the Stoke team was becoming much younger. In his view, Waddington, who always bristled at the suggestion of only recruiting old players, honoured his part of the bargain. He would remind Greenhoff and others that the only old player he signed was Stanley Matthews. So Greenhoff travelled to the Potteries to join up with his strike partner John Ritchie, and one of Waddington's brightest young signings, Irishman Terry Conroy.

Dublin cattle dealers do not normally fit into professional football's scouting network. Waddington found one who did. The cattle dealer alerted him to a talented prospect by the name of Terry Conroy. The scout worked part-time for the north Dublin club Home Farm. In the early 1960s, he persuaded Waddington to go on tour to Ireland and take in a game against Home Farm. A teenage Conroy played and impressed the watching manager, showing himself to be a player for the future.

At the time of this tour, Conroy was serving an apprenticeship in the printing trade. His father, himself a printer, insisted that he completed his apprenticeship rather than gambling on a professional career in England. So Conroy stayed in Dublin with Waddington's friendly cattle dealer keeping an eye on his progress until an eventual move to Irish League side Glentoran.

Again Waddington had a friendly scouting spy to monitor Conroy's fledgling progress, George Eastham senior. He was manager of Glentoran's rivals Ards and alerted Waddington to the possibility of him missing out on the young player. Fulham had bid for him and it seemed that the fine young prospect was off to London rather than the Potteries. Waddington immediately headed for Belfast.

Conroy was going nowhere without the approval of his father. He set off for Dublin by train, noting on the newsstands that the *Belfast Telegraph* was emblazoned with the headline, 'Conroy signs for Fulham'. He had not signed for anybody. On Conroy's return to Belfast, Eastham was lying in wait and intent on scuppering the Fulham deal. He collared Conroy, then introduced him to Waddington. As Conroy put it this was an example of a 'classic old style illegal tap-up'.

There was just one snag. Conroy's dad still needed to approve any deal so it was back on the train to Dublin. 'Waddo had a silver tongue and he turned on the charm all the way home. Somehow you wanted to be with Waddo,' Conroy fondly remembered. 'By the time I got off the train I was convinced Stoke was the place I wanted to go.'

Given Waddington's penchant for a drop of the hard stuff, he found it easy to convince Conroy's father of the wisdom of his son playing for Stoke. 'He proceeded to clinch the deal by accompanying me home, ingratiating himself with my father with whom he spent the night knocking back half a bottle of whiskey,' Conroy revealed. 'By the time that was done he had my father eating out of his hands.'

The only issue, of course, was Waddington's failure to go through the formal procedure of making a transfer deal thanks to his act of subterfuge with Eastham. A call duly went into Glentoran with a £10,000 bid for Conroy. Manager Billy Ferguson informed Conroy of Stoke's interest, blissfully unaware of Waddington's drinking session with the player's dad at his Dublin home.

Conroy kept quiet about the 'tap-up' from Waddington. He had made his mind up but there was one other factor in him moving to Stoke rather than just Waddington's charm. He explained, 'The final clincher was the fact that the club had signed World Cup-winning goalkeeper Gordon Banks just the week before. Stoke City was indeed the team for me. The fates had conspired to make it so. I was off to the Potteries.'

It was the spring of 1967, a couple of years before Conroy was able to claim a regular place in Stoke's starting line-up. But by the summer of 1969 after something of a struggle Waddington finally had a side capable of challenging the top sides in the First Division.

Conroy had been a welcome addition to the team, a popular character on and off the pitch. As Denis Smith outlined, 'Waddo had by now introduced another young talent into the team, Irish international winger Terry Conroy, a player with a mercurial change of pace and the whitest, palest legs you've ever seen. With TC, as he became universally known, alongside the experience of George Eastham, Peter Dobing and John Ritchie, we had blended into a formidable side with a strong will that was very difficult to beat.'

In turn Conroy recognised the value of Smith and his defensive colleagues in a revised version of Waddington's Wall. He mused, 'Behind them, of course, should any marauding forward be lucky enough to make it past all four with his limbs intact, lurked the one and only Gordon Banks. This was some team that Waddo was putting together, a changing of the guard. The all-local back four knitted together beautifully and gave us creative types the platform to play from and they also gave Waddo full confidence to allow his talented attacking players a free rein.'

Banks summed it up, 'The Stoke squad combined the products of a good youth policy, such as Alan Bloor, Eric Skeels and Denis Smith, with Tony Waddington's astute signings of experienced pros with a few good years left in them. The former were long-term prospects while the latter naturally came and went. This curious mixture of stability and transience enabled the team to survive quite comfortably in Division One without ever threatening the elite bank of clubs challenging for honours. But all that was to change in 1970.'

He was right. For all of the travails in the late 1960s, Banks, Smith, Greenhoff and Conroy in their reminiscences reflected the bullish nature of the Stoke City dressing room of the time, those player views also echoing the opinions of increasingly optimistic fans of the football club. They were all ready to help Waddo to complete his mission to bring major footballing honours to the Potteries, a working-class area steeped in the game of association football.

Everyone at his football club – the players, the coaching staff, the board and of course the fans – were on board with Waddo's unlikely grand presentation of a 'working man's ballet'.

They were about to dance in triumph but only after suffering agonising failure. Not even a tot of whisky would help.

8

Outgunned in the Cup

FROM perennial relegation strugglers to challengers for major honours, Stoke City began the 1970s as a club transformed. Tony Waddington had built a team capable of giving a more than satisfactory performance of his working man's ballet. Thanks to Waddington, Stoke were about to enjoy the most successful period in their history, a joyful and agonising rollercoaster for players and fans alike.

Key to the transformation was not just the playing personnel but his backroom staff. The coaching team he gathered around him to work out on the training pitch and in the Victoria Ground gymnasium was described by visiting national sports journalists as 'skeletal' when compared with other First Division clubs. Office staff numbers were also kept to a minimum.

To sum up his and the club's philosophy when it came to employing staff, Waddington took a dig at what he saw as the footballing aristocrats of Arsenal. 'We don't have a clerk of works like Arsenal, we have a groundsman. And that's the difference,' he commented, perhaps with a degree of bitterness towards them.

For his coaching team, Waddington put a premium on skills training though curiously never expected any of his coaching staff to tell his players actually how to play football. They didn't need to. 'Tony would like to play a lot of skilful football. He would like to play pure football,' commented Alan A'Court, a former Liverpool player who Waddington recruited as a coach from his old club Crewe in 1969. He added, 'Tony cared for the players off the field as well as on and I think the players responded in that way. I think what helped him and what I noticed considerably was when I came [to the club] in 1969, the first thing that struck me was the skill and ability of the players he had around him.'

For all the tales among fans of a drinking culture at Stoke City, A'Court insisted Waddington put fitness as well as skill at a premium. 'If players are training daily they cannot maintain the endurance routines if they are drinking heavily the night before,' the Stoke manager angrily retorted to gossip about his players' social activities.

For pre-season training, he brought in British international middle-distance athlete Roy Fowler to supervise gruelling cross-country runs, sweating out any excesses from the night before. Fowler revisited the club during the course of a season to ensure training went beyond a kick-about in the gym or the training pitch next door to the Victoria Ground car park.

Working as Waddington's assistant coach, Frank Mountford brought continuity from the Matthews era, indeed from Stoke's title-challenging team of the 1940s, as well as the whisky bottle on matchdays. His expertise with the so-called magic sponge and a bucket of water was less appreciated by the players. Terry Conroy summed him up, 'He [Mountford] had a dry sense of humour and we loved him, but he could be pretty rough when he came out on the pitch to "treat" you. His gruff bedside manner left something to be desired and he certainly didn't have MD after his name.'

Mountford also appeared less than impressed with some of Waddington's coaching innovations. As a rule Waddington liked to sit in the directors' box to assess the action. He was not one to sit pitch-side or stand on the touchline gesticulating. Instead, he installed a phone line to the dugout to give his instructions for Mountford to relay to the players. What followed is the stuff of folklore among Waddington's former players.

Jimmy Greenhoff remembered being out of the side and sitting in the directors' box alongside his manager, who was becoming increasingly irate, and phoned down to Mountford. According to Greenhoff, Waddington shouted into the phone, 'What's up with Eric Skeels? Tell him to get a move on. Tell him to get stuck in.'

Waddington was unaware Skeels had broken a bone in his foot. Mountford had no idea either. No amount of shouting made a difference to Skeels's performance. In frustration, Waddington kept phoning down to Mountford. Eventually his trainer's patience snapped. Instead of answering the phone, Mountford chucked it into his bucket of water. He later explained, 'People talk about me being on the phone at a game. I couldn't fall out with him so I just put the phone down and that was the end of it. But I do sometimes think I made a mistake throwing the phone in the bucket. Whether Tony agrees with it or not I don't know.'

Clearly the pair chose never to discuss the matter. But Waddington did respond in his interview with the *Stoke Sentinel*'s Peter Hewitt a decade after leaving Stoke. Waddington said, 'The tale is told that Frank became so exasperated with my constant demands that he threw the phone into a bucket of water. I prefer to think he would have come upstairs to see me personally if he had any personal thoughts on the matter in hand.' There was mutual respect between the pair. But Mountford was relieved of his phone duties.

Even then Waddington felt he wasn't quite getting his message across so resorted to radical action. Most managers would give up their seat in the directors' box to go down to the dugout and either yell out instructions or talk directly to one of them in a break in play. Waddington stuck to using the phone. A'Court remembered, 'A player had got injured and the player laid there for three or four minutes. Tony rung down and said, "Alan, I want to have a quick word with George," because George was playing on the wing.

'He was right in front of us by the box. I shouted across, "George! Telephone!" and he comes off and he's on the phone to Tony. And Tony was passing his instructions on. I thought, well, anything goes in professional football!'

The referee didn't notice Eastham enjoying a chinwag with his boss on the phone at the side of the pitch. Somehow the incident did later come to the attention of the FA. There were to be no more phone calls to players during the course of a game.

In his quest for more professionalism among the backroom staff, Mountford, aside from answering the phone, was also relieved of his medical duties as bearer of the fabled 'magic sponge'. It was better for him and A'Court just to concentrate on the football.

Fred Street arrived at Stoke after what Waddington called one of his most 'audacious transfers'. The club had no qualified physiotherapist, relying on the NHS at the City General Hospital under the direction of Dr Gordon Crowe. As a result, Waddington turned to Arsenal manager Bertie Mee, himself a qualified physiotherapist, for advice. Mee nominated Street, a remedial specialist in London, as the best. Much to Waddington's and no doubt the Stoke players' relief, Street agreed to move to the Potteries. He was hailed by Waddington as an 'immediate success'.

The physio also unwittingly found himself at the centre of a series of fractious FA Cup semi-finals between Stoke and Arsenal, first with Waddington's Potters, then with Bertie Mee's Gunners. Both ties left a sour taste in the mouths of Waddington, his players and disconsolate Stoke fans, whose dreams of FA Cup glory, in their view, had been cruelly taken away. Their dreams were shattered by an elite club with as Waddington dismissively observed, a 'clerk of works' rather than a 'groundsman'.

Ironically, a league game between those sides at the beginning of the 1970/71 season served notice to the football world of Stoke's credentials as a serious challenger for honours. As Gordon Banks observed, 'At the start of the decade the Stoke team had a much more settled look about it. The home-grown talent had matured and blossomed while the older players such as George Eastham and Harry Burrows were still good for a few more years. Tony was still buying experienced pros, but in Jimmy Greenhoff and John Ritchie he had invested in two players who were in their prime rather than on their way out.'

For the visit of Arsenal, Banks was absent. Thanks to a bus strike many of Stoke's fans were also absent. They missed what turned out to be a treat for Waddington. Arsenal turned up at the Victoria Ground in scintillating form, meeting levels of play which would eventually lead them to the league and cup double that season. They had thrashed West Bromwich Albion 6-2 the previous week and just knocked Lazio out of the Inter-Cities Fairs Cup, the precursor to the UEFA Cup and eventual Europa League. In contrast, Stoke had just been booted out of the League Cup by Millwall.

Somehow Waddington's men managed to rip up the form book. John Ritchie opened the scoring with a classic centre-forward's header, towering over defenders to flash the ball into the net. Just before half-time he put Stoke two up after robbing a dozing Arsenal defender of the ball and then going on a mazy run past three other defenders before firing past Bob Wilson.

Terry Conroy recalled in his autobiography, 'That performance epitomised our [Stoke's] free-flowing football of the period.' His stunning third goal ended the game as a contest. 'I received the ball in the outside-right position, played a one-two with the middle of my right foot with Peter Dobing and then hit the return pass first time from about 25 yards out. It flew in. Funnily enough it was one of those shots which could have gone anywhere but it arrowed right into the corner.'

Jimmy Greenhoff scored a fourth by chipping the ball over the hapless Wilson. Alan Bloor completed the scoring with, for him, a rare goal. Conroy recalled, 'The day was special because of the fact we stuffed Arsenal 5-0 and could have scored ten. That's how good we were that day because we played some unbelievable football and everything went for us.'

Full-back Mike Pejic, perhaps taking into account the traumatic FA Cup encounters with Arsenal to come, rather sanguinely recalled, 'If you look through time, teams who win the title usually have a blip at some stage and this was obviously Arsenal's. But that shouldn't take anything away from how well we played. We were fluent throughout the match, worked the ball well and created a load of chances. I don't remember any stage of the game when we were under pressure.'

Centre-half Denis Smith took as much pride in his team's defensive as attacking performance. 'As good as we were that day in attack, we were equally strong handling Arsenal's strike force,' Smith reasoned. 'Bluto [Alan Bloor] and I had one of our best games together that afternoon keeping John Radford and George Graham quieter than church mice. Strong at both ends of the pitch, we were now a formidable side.' It was a day of triumph, although Arsenal were about to wreak revenge, not once but twice.

Stoke had not reached the semi-finals of the FA Cup since the late 19th century. Even quarter-final appearances were rare but under Waddington this dismal run was about to end. His team's 1971 FA Cup run began by avenging the League Cup defeat to Millwall earlier in the season. In the fourth round it took a second replay at the neutral venue of Old Trafford to see off Huddersfield Town with Greenhoff scoring the winning goal in a 1-0 victory.

During this marathon tie, Denis Smith fractured his ankle. Remarkably, with Waddington's encouragement, Stoke's legendary hard man played on. 'I was desperate to play. Waddo was keen for me to play too and he was a past master at getting performances out of players that should have been lying on the treatment couch rather than taking the field,' Smith recalled in praise of his manager. 'If you were carrying an injury he would take you off for a chat and tell you "you're all right". He was quite incredible like that.'

Buoyed by his manager, Smith played on through the pain barrier for the rest of the season. Next up in the cup was Ipswich Town and again the tie went to a replay. Despite playing seemingly on one leg, Smith scored the winner.

For the quarter-final away to Hull City, Waddington's men encountered a gruelling test from a lower-division side, one to challenge their resilience. On a snow-covered pitch, the opposition tore into them. Ken Wagstaff scored twice and as the game approached half-time Stoke, failing to cope with their rampant hosts, appeared to be going out of the cup with their hopes of silverware dashed for another season.

Then Conroy intervened, dancing around the Hull goalkeeper to make it 2-1 as the half-time whistle blew. Back in the dressing room Waddington demanded his players give the ball to Conroy more often. The tactic worked as Stoke conjured up what Smith described as one of the club's best halves of football under Waddington.

John Ritchie equalised and then scored the winner amid deep controversy with Conroy and John Marsh cast as a pair of villains by furious Hull fans. Stoke had been wrongly awarded a throw-in. Marsh took it before his opponents could even begin to protest and Conroy raced with the ball towards the byline before crossing to Ritchie to head home the winner. The game ended 3-2 to Stoke; joy for the Potters' fans and utter despair for Hull's faithful.

Conroy, the man who inspired the comeback, recalled the triumphant atmosphere on the train back to Stoke, 'The train was packed. Waddo bought us all champagne and also invited many of the supporters to join in. The atmosphere was unbelievable. We were on a high and this was one of the most joyous train journeys of my life. It was a very special time as the fans were able to mingle with us and tell us all about the emotions they had been through.'

Here was an example of Waddington acting as a man of the people. He may have had the demeanour of a stuffy Home Counties bank manager, but recognised the importance of football to the average working man and woman, acknowledging the immense value they placed in their club as a vital part of the community. Greenhoff in an interview with the Stoke City fanzine *Duck Magazine* commented, 'We always came out before away games with any spare tickets for the fans. Waddo insisted on it and we were happy to do it. He especially made the point on the longer journeys to the likes of Norwich, Ipswich and the London matches. It was a big thing to Waddo. We socialised a lot with the fans. We always had lunch as a team in the social club [across the road from the Victoria Ground main entrance] and fans would be in there too. It was great.'

Conroy fondly recalled, 'Going back over that era the club had a great identity with the people within the town. Tony was an unbelievable PR man where he could reach into the interests of the public. Every day he would have a story in the *Evening Sentinel* where he would be signing some international player or whatever. And, he created conversation in the Potteries in the streets and 95 per cent of people in the town were Stoke City supporters.'

Cup fever gripped the Potteries and fans dared to dream of the club making a first trip to the twin towers of Wembley. They listened to the semi-final draw to hear Stoke being paired with Arsenal, opponents the Potters had demolished earlier in the season. Despite that result, Arsenal, as title challengers, were favourites. Waddington, however, fancied his club's chances.

In preparing for the match, which was to take place at Hillsborough, home of Sheffield Wednesday, he decided to spirit his players away in what he considered to be the 'tranquil setting' of a nearby hotel at Matlock Bath in the Derbyshire Peak District. 'It was important to calm down nerves and ease the pressures,' reasoned Waddington. 'We had a thermal spring at the hotel, which was an ideal place. Many of the players had grown up during the Stan Matthews days, so they were used to the publicity and media attention.'

He also packed away a video of the 5-0 victory over Arsenal to remind his players they were more than a match for their title-chasing London opponents.

In contrast Arsenal travelled to Germany only to suffer defeat to Cologne in the Inter-Cities Fairs Cup. They hoped for not just the double of the league title and the FA Cup but an historic treble with a European trophy, only for those dreams to be dashed.

They were also haunted by that 5-0 defeat earlier in the season, wary in particular of the aerial threat from Ritchie. Defender Peter Simpson admitted in the build-up to the game, 'If there is one thing our defensive system lacks, it is height. We can't just grow overnight so we have to concentrate on coping with it. But there are players who can exploit it, and, if any Stoke man is going to damage us, it must be this Ritchie.'

Simpson insisted he was confident Arsenal would win but being dumped out of Europe just days before an FA Cup semi-final hardly served as a morale-booster.

The *Daily Telegraph*'s football correspondent, Donald Saunders, mused on the morning of the game against Stoke, 'Young Kennedy, Rice and George, in particular were under great emotional stress and may not have had time to build themselves back up for another supreme test.'

Even so, he still made Arsenal favourites while noting Waddington as 'Stoke's shrewd manager' who had produced 'a highly effective blend of youth and experience this season, despite a cruel crop of injuries'.

One of the key men missing was the captain Peter Dobing. He had broken his leg against Ipswich a few months earlier. As a result Waddington gave the captaincy to the player with the most 'big-time' experience, Gordon Banks, much to his World Cup-winning goalkeeper's surprising annoyance. Banks insisted only an outfield player could captain a football team, not the goalkeeper. He likened it to asking a desk-bound general to lead an army.

It was a battle of wills, a test of temperament for both men. Banks told the *Daily Mail*, 'When manager Tony Waddington asked me to take over [as captain], I thought it would be impossible to lead from the back. I felt I was not involved enough, but during the first couple of weeks it worked in the opposite way. I found I got too wrapped up in the action. When a referee gave a questionable decision, I found myself haring up the field to see him.

'So I went back to Mr Waddington and volunteered to hand over the captaincy. But he told me that if I could keep calm then it would be an example to the rest of the club. Well, I've managed to do that since and I've really begun to enjoy the responsibility.'

Waddington's astute handling of his reluctant captain worked and Banks, by far and away Stoke's biggest star of the day, was going to lead his team out in the semi-final of the FA Cup.

Prior to going out on to the pitch, Waddington instructed his players to hassle the Arsenal players from the start, disrupt their opponents' rhythm, and ensure the game was played at a high tempo. They duly obliged and their first goal came, with a touch of fortune. The ball cannoned off Denis Smith from a Peter Storey clearance and straight into the back of the net. Then Ritchie made it 2-0, not with one of his trademark headers but as at the Victoria Ground several months earlier by pouncing on an Arsenal defensive error. This time Charlie George was caught dozing, his weak pass latched on to by Ritchie who rounded Bob Wilson to score.

'We went in [at half-time] two goals up and I know people say this, but it should have been five,' Ritchie ruefully remembered. For Waddington there was a decision to make. Hindsight points to him possibly making the wrong one. Terry Conroy had been struggling with illness all week. Was it time for him to make a substitution? Waddington decided against doing so. He explained, 'We led 2-0 at half-time with one of our best performances under a great deal of tension. Terry Conroy was struggling as a flu virus hit him and I had to make a decision whether to bring him off as I had full-back Jackie Marsh available. I decided that Terry was still a threat and might prevent Arsenal from attacking too much on their left flank.'

It was a gamble. It did not pay off but only after some last-minute controversy and heartbreak.

For all their dominance, Stoke, as Ritchie indicated, had spurned several glorious chances to put the game out of sight. They could not afford to concede an early second-half goal but that's exactly what they contrived to do, Storey rifling a shot past Banks.

Even then Stoke looked to be comfortably holding on until deep into injury time. What unfolded in those closing moments was what Smith described as a 'chain of events' which left him shaking his head with disbelief. With Stoke fans roaring for the final whistle to be blown, Mike Pejic was penalised for a foul on Storey, a harsh decision in the view of the Stoke players.

George Armstrong took the free kick with the ball appearing to be sailing comfortably into the safe hands of the world's best goalkeeper. Inexplicably, Banks dropped the ball. He was furious, not with himself but the referee. 'In jumping to collect it, I was bundled over by a marauding yellow shirt. I thought the referee, Pat Partridge, would award us a free kick for the foul, but I looked up to see him pointing to the corner flag.'

The marauding shirt belonged to George Graham. Smith observed, 'As plain as the nose on your face, it should have been a free kick.' Smith admitted that in the resulting scramble from Banks spilling the ball he had then handled it. The hapless Partridge found himself simultaneously castigated by both sets of players, Arsenal infuriated by Smith's handball and Stoke incensed by the foul on Banks a few seconds earlier. There was still time on the referee's stopwatch for a corner kick, another bone of contention for Waddington's players.

Perhaps still fuming at the controversial series of refereeing decisions, Stoke lost concentration. Three Arsenal players jumped higher than them as the ball came in and Frank McLintock was able to direct it towards goal. John Mahoney had been deputed to guard Banks's right-hand post but he had wandered across the goal, leaving a gap. If he had stayed put, it would have been a simple clearance. Instead the unfortunate Mahoney was forced to emulate Banks and pull off a save by turning the ball around the post, but the referee immediately awarded a penalty for handball.

His room-mate Conroy went up to console him. Conroy revealed years later how Banks and Mahoney had clashed that morning in a dust-up during a five-a-side game at the team hotel. Waddington loved his players to work out with such sessions. On this occasion he looked on with horror as the Welsh midfielder thumped the England goalkeeper in the face. Waddington intervened to calm things down with his fired-up players. It was fine to show passion, but not demonstrating it with an impromptu boxing match on the morning of the biggest game in the club's history.

Apparently it took three decades for the pair to apologise to each other, doing so at an old boys' reunion. By then Banks could wryly comment on the last-minute penalty award thus, 'John Mahoney did a passable impression of me.'

Storey, an international team-mate of Banks, stepped up to take the penalty. He stroked the ball into the net with the goalkeeper hardly moving, almost standing like a statue. Banks moaned that Storey 'mis-hit' his penalty and as a result it 'threw me completely'. Storey, of course, disagreed. He told reporters at the post-match inquest, 'I looked around. It had all gone quiet. So I told myself, "Stop hanging about. In the next minute you'll be a hero or a mug and there's only one way to find out." Then I remembered it was Banks and, of all people, I knew he'd have rumbled that I usually aim to the goalkeeper's right. That made up my mind. It had to go to his left. So I ambled up and belted it.'

It was the last kick of the game and Arsenal had rescued a replay in deeply controversial circumstances with a 2-2 draw. To Waddington and his players it felt more like a defeat.

He waited in the dressing room for his disconsolate players. 'The lads were in total despair in the dressing room afterwards. I tried to reassure everyone that we were still in the cup, but the feeling remained that it was not going to be our year. They realised a great opportunity had slipped by,' he mournfully recalled.

These sentiments have been echoed by his players. 'Our Wembley dream had been snatched from us in the cruellest of circumstances,' Smith concluded. Conroy, who played well despite not being fully fit, described the scene, 'The dressing room was like a morgue after the match. I have had a few disappointments in life but nothing has ever really come close to that.'

Banks, the stand-in captain, railed, to anybody who would listen to him, against the performance of the referee. 'I have never been so disappointed,' declared Banks in his post-match comments. 'Not because of the result but because Pat Partridge, the referee, did not give us a free kick when I was charged in the back. He awarded a corner to Arsenal instead and that led to the penalty.'

Years later in his autobiography, Banks put the disappointing result down to a lack of experience. Captain Peter Dobing and playmaker George Eastham were both missing from his line-up. 'Perhaps owing to a lack of big-match experience among many of the side, we began to panic. We didn't display the calm authority required to play the ball out of defence. We conceded possession too often and Arsenal were not the sort of side to give it back again without a fight,' Banks calmly reasoned. Waddington needed to pick his players up. Immediately after the Hillsborough game he told reporters, 'We were 30 seconds from the final. Now we must pull ourselves up again for Wednesday night.' It turned out to be an impossible task.

For the replay at Villa Park, Stoke looked a shadow of the team which faced Arsenal in their earlier encounters. Graham gave the Gunners an early lead, one they never appeared in danger of relinquishing. Just a couple of minutes after half-time Ray Kennedy scored to make it 2-0. The game was all but over, as were Waddington's dreams of leading out Stoke City for an FA Cup final at Wembley for another year.

His team's performance was variously described by the national press as 'brave' and 'battling'. Sadly, for all the patronising platitudes, the performance was also ineffective and Arsenal's defence remained resolute. There was to be no reversal of fortunes. Waddington commented, 'Arsenal did well to pull [the goals] back on Saturday, when they overcame the same problem we faced tonight. Perhaps they did better than us in the end because they have more experience of this sort of competition.

'I feel sorry for my players. They are all terribly disconsolate and upset. They did so well at Hillsborough, but this time they just fell short of reproducing that form.'

Arsenal went on to complete a league and FA Cup double. Their cause was helped by beating Stoke 1-0 at Highbury, the league fixture originally being scheduled by strange coincidence for the day of the fateful FA Cup semi-final at Hillsborough.

Manager Bertie Mee also came calling for one of Waddington's backroom stalwarts, physio Fred Street. As Mee had recommended him in the first place, it was no surprise. Waddington reluctantly let him go, little realising they would soon be reunited in another series of fractious cup games between the two clubs. In the meantime, Waddington needed to lift his players through the summer for another campaign. He needed to draw on the chastening experience of going out of the FA Cup with cruel misfortune.

Smith described the defeat as a 'crushing blow'. He added, 'I ask myself how history could have been different if we'd gone to that cup final and beaten Liverpool, earning further global exposure and lifting the small club complex which has always plagued Stoke City supporters? But we'll never know.'

Smith further noted that even Banks, a World Cup winner but also twice an FA Cup losing finalist, found it difficult to come to terms with this particular loss. Banks, in his autobiography, noted how Arsenal had grabbed their lifeline 'like a drowning man'. For the replay, they were simply the better team.

Conroy, in assessing Waddington's approach to preparations for the semi-final replay, observed, 'There was no possibility of lifting us for that game and we never really turned up. Our minds were still dwelling on the "what ifs". We had come so close to winning the FA Cup. It hurt.'

Waddington accepted that he was powerless in trying to lift the mood among his players. 'They realised a great opportunity had slipped by and we never seemed to get our game together in the Villa Park replay,' he moaned.

The pain of the manager and his players was shared by the fans, indeed by the entire community. A disconsolate air hung over the Potteries, an emotional cloud rather than the familiar billowing smoke once belching from the factories. How do you learn from a crushing defeat? It is the most important lesson in sport.

Waddington, as he stood in the Villa Park press room to reflect on the exit, commented, 'We learned a lot tonight.'

As both he and Banks acknowledged, one of those lessons, an odd one given Waddington's previous track record as a manager, was the need to supplement a talented young team with seasoned campaigners. One of those campaigners was George Eastham, a member of England's 1966 World Cup-winning squad signed by Waddington shortly after their Wembley triumph. He had, with Waddington's blessing, put his playing career on hold for a coaching stint in South Africa. Thanks to the crushing disappointment of seeing Stoke failing to reach the 1971 FA Cup Final, Waddington realised he had make a mistake and Eastham was recalled. It proved to be a wise decision.

9

History Makers

LICKING their mental wounds, Waddington, his players and their disconsolate fans would have been forgiven for resigning themselves to Stoke City's fate as the trophy-less paupers of the professional game of football. Waddington's zealous pursuit of sporting glory appeared, to pessimistic observers, doomed to fail. Then on one glorious sporting weekend years, indeed decades, of sporting pain came to an end.

Tens of thousands poured out of their houses on to the streets to welcome home their heroes in a deep outpouring of joy throughout the Potteries. Even those with little interest in football decked themselves out in red and white. Waddington had delivered on his promise. He had led his team out at Wembley. The director of a 'working man's ballet' had finally orchestrated a major triumph by winning the League Cup.

Waddington vowed that he and his players would learn from the cruel lesson they were taught by Arsenal. They did so less than 12 months later, lifting the League Cup after a gruelling and thrilling campaign.

For the opening tie against Southport, then a Fourth Division side, Waddington rested players, risking as so many managers do in the League Cup being accused of not taking the competition seriously.

His decision almost backfired. Southport proved tougher opposition than expected, but thanks to a winner from Jimmy Greenhoff Stoke scraped through 2-1. In the next round, Oxford United, a mid-table Second Division side at the time, also turned out to be stubborn opponents and Greenhoff again scored, but a late goal from Oxford's John Evans ensured a replay at the Victoria Ground. Back on home soil, Stoke won comfortably with goals from John Ritchie and the promising young midfielder Sean Haslegrave, a player later to catch the eye of Waddington's old friend Brian Clough.

Manchester United being pulled out of the hat to meet Stoke in the last 16 set up a series of titanic clashes between the two football clubs. They met seven times in the 1971/72 season; the obligatory two league games, twice in the FA Cup and three times in the League Cup. United were a team in form, going into the tie as First Division leaders. Four years on from their European Cup triumph, they remained formidable opposition. The prospect of toppling one of the elites of the game appealed to Stoke players and fans alike as it might have helped to erase painful memories of losing out to double winners Arsenal in the FA Cup.

At Old Trafford they nearly succeeded, Ritchie scoring before Alan Gowling grabbed a late equaliser for United. For the replay, more than 40,000 packed into the Victoria Ground to see how Waddington's men might fare against Best, Law, Charlton et al. They went home disappointed. Despite the game going into extra time nobody, for all the attacking talent on the pitch, managed to beat Banks or one of his long-suffering rivals for the England goalkeeper's shirt, Alex Stepney. Waddington and Matt Busby gathered at the end of the game for a coin toss to decide the venue for a second replay. The Stoke manager called correctly and once again, Stoke had home advantage.

This time around more than 42,000 turned up for what local hero Denis Smith called a 'passionate night' of football. Smith, a player Waddington happily described as 'a rough diamond', missed the first replay with a back injury. Crucially he was passed fit to play in the second. It was just as well as he and his defensive partners were about to face their sternest test, from one player on absolute fire.

As he did so often, George Best tormented Stoke's defenders. He was such a bête noir that Waddington even cheekily tried to sign him after the game, more of which later. A fierce right-foot shot from Best struck the roof of Banks's net to give Manchester United a deserved 1-0 lead at half-time. They should have been winning by more but it was time for Waddington to change the habit of a lifetime. He needed to make a tactical substitution.

The use of substitutes was relatively new at the time and only one was allowed during the game. Managers therefore were reluctant to pull off players in favour of another one too early for fear of injuries. On this occasion Waddington decided he needed the experience and playmaking skills of George Eastham, who went out for the second half instead of John Mahoney in a decision that transformed the game.

Delighted Stoke fans viewed it as a 'masterstroke' from Waddington as Eastham, at the grand old age for a footballer of 35, began to dominate the midfield. Best still posed a threat but Stoke's own forwards began to cause United's defenders problems thanks to the promptings of Eastham, who laid on the ball for Peter Dobing to score the equaliser on 70 minutes. Just as the crowd began to think there was about to be another period of extra time, Eastham took a corner to be met with a header from Ritchie, the ball flashing into the net.

The ground erupted and there were just a couple of minutes left on the referee's stopwatch, which Stoke saw out to complete a famous victory. More were to come.

'Our manager Tony Waddington played a key part. He played every ball with us. He lived for football,' reflected the winning goalscorer in tribute to his boss. Ritchie went on, 'It was a titanic struggle over the three games, very evenly matched. I think our fitness and stamina finally won it for us. We were United's equals in those days and a good game was guaranteed, though they had a heavy cross to bear. Everybody wanted to beat them.'

As for Stoke's tormentor in chief, Ritchie remarked, 'George Best was brilliant in the final game, putting us under pressure for long periods.'

Years later, Waddington revealed he found the disconsolate Best sat alongside Willie Morgan in the foyer of the Victoria Ground's offices waiting for the coach home. He offered them a drink. Best asked for a cola, Morgan a bottle of wine. The wine was refused but a couple of cans of cola proffered. More remarkably the prospect of Best moving to Stoke was also discussed.

According to Waddington, United's boss Frank O'Farrell had told him he was having trouble with Best. One of the most talented players ever to grace a football pitch began to show the temperamental flaws which would eventually see him lost to the game. 'He [O'Farrell] seemed to be ruling him out of his plans. We got together and talked of a possible deal on an exchange basis,' said Waddington.

'The player he really wanted was Denis Smith. There was no way I was releasing Denis, not even for George Best. But we carried on talking about other possibilities. Chiefly because Frank was ready to sell Best he was dismissed. Matt Busby took over the reins again and my proposed deal never got any further.'

Maybe a move from United to Stoke to be taken under the wing of Waddington, a convivial and sociable boss, would have helped to extend Best's career. In contrast, given Waddington's alleged liberal attitude to players drinking, such a move may have been even more disastrous for a chronic alcoholic. Waddington held counsel on his thoughts on the implications of the transfer. For Waddington and Stoke it most certainly would have been a stunning coup, one arguably bigger than bringing Stanley Matthews back to the club.

The draw for the quarter-final paired Stoke with Third Division Bristol Rovers. Once again Waddington and his players began to believe their dreams of a Wembley final may come true. As Waddington put it, they were 'steaming towards Wembley'.

It was another away trip but they saw off their lower-league opponents easily. Stoke raced into a 4-0 lead before easing up and ending up 4-2 winners. Smith, who was one of the scorers, suffered a concussion after a clash of heads and didn't remember a thing about the game. For weeks to come he lost his sense of balance, forcing Waddington to leave him out of the side. He was still absent when West Ham turned up at the Victoria Ground for the first leg of the semi-final, though Waddington still harboured hopes of fielding his 'rough diamond'. Smith felt ready to play.

Smith recalled, however, in his autobiography that he fell victim to Waddington's network of spies. Stoke fans quite happily picked up the phone and called the Victoria Ground to warn the Stoke boss of any 'errant' activities on the part of his players. In fairness those fans, rather than simply operating as 'Waddo's spies' and party-poopers, had the club and its players' welfare at heart.

Yet again Waddington's centre-half was an injury concern and the manager's legion of unpaid scouts had been the bearers of bad news. Waddington decided to ask after his health. As Smith recalled, Waddington told him on the phone, 'I know you've been in Stone [a market town, south of Stoke-on-Trent] because I've had several fans phone up telling me that you were swaying around as you walked down the street and that I shouldn't pick you because you're not right.'

Smith, himself, had not noticed a thing. If ever there was proof that Waddington was running a community club this was it. Concerned fans had delivered their verdict. For all their admiration of their centre-half, he needed to be left out and Waddington did just that.

The marathon League Cup semi-final of 1971/72 between Stoke and West Ham turned out to be one of the zaniest series of games in the history of football. Very few observers had witnessed anything to match it up until then and given the abolition of replays in the League Cup, it's unlikely to be matched in the future.

The players must have been sick of the sight of each other, even though in some cases they were friends.

At a foggy Victoria Ground Greenhoff set up the opening goal for Dobing. But West Ham slowly came back into the game with Clyde Best giving Stoke's promising young centre-half Stewart Jump nightmares. He appeared unable to cope with the Bermudan striker's physicality. First of all Best won a penalty after being fouled by Jump, Geoff Hurst triumphantly lashing the ball past his old World Cup-winning mate Gordon Banks into the net. Then just after the hour, Best lashed a ball, teed up by Harry Redknapp, in for the winner.

One Fleet Street old sage, taking his cue from the celebrating West Ham players, wrote, 'West Ham can start rehearsing for a day out at Wembley. Stoke surely can't burst their League Cup bubble now.' He was a little premature in his prediction. This tie had a long way to go.

Quite rightly, Waddington's counterpart Ron Greenwood was a little more cautious. 'We won't be thinking about Wembley until we have beaten Stoke again,' the West Ham manager told reporters. No doubt he was chastened by memories of Stoke's remarkable comeback at Upton Park a few seasons earlier from being 3-0 down at half-time and emerging 4-3 winners.

If Greenwood needed a reminder, it inconveniently came in a league match at Upton Park against Southampton just a few days before the second leg against Stoke as from 3-0 up at half-time, West Ham drew 3-3.

Stanley Matthews resigns for Stoke City on BBC Sportsview *with Tony Waddington and his anxious chairman, Albert Henshall along with Blackpool assistant manager Eric Hayward. 18 October 1961 (PA Images)*

Stoke City's promotion-winning squad, 1963. Back row (left to right): Len Graham (Trainer), Eddie Clamp, Bill Asprey, Jimmy O'Neil, Tony Allen, Tony Waddington (Manager) Middle row: Stanley Matthews, Dennis Viollet, Eddie Stuart, Jackie Mudie, Jimmy McIlroy, Don Ratcliffe Front Row Seated: Keith Bebbington and Eric Skeels. (PA Images)

Tony Waddington and Stanley Matthews welcome four former Stoke-on-Trent schools footballers to the Victoria Ground. From left to right; Waddington, Bill Bentley, John Marsh, Matthews, Mike Starkey and Mick Bernard. Marsh and Bernard went on to play in Stoke's League Cup-winning team. (PA Images)

Waddington leaves Burnley FC's ground Turf Moor after negotiating the transfer of the Clarets' Northern Ireland international Jimmy McIlroy in January 1963. (Mirrorpix)

As Tony Waddington prepares for his first season as a First Division manager, sheep graze on Stoke City's Victoria Ground pitch. 2 August 1963. (PA Images)

Tony Waddington welcomes John Mahoney, a future League Cup winner with Stoke City, to the club on 9 September 1967. (Mirrorpix)

Waddington accompanies his injured captain Peter Dobing to an FA disciplinary hearing in December 1970. He gave Dobing the captaincy despite the player briefly going 'on strike' in August 1967. (Mirrorpix)

Tony Waddington leaving an FA disciplinary hearing at the Dominions Hotel, Lancaster Gate, London on 24 February 1971. (Getty Images)

Waddington's reluctant captain. Gordon Banks leads out Stoke City followed by Mike Pejic at Hillsborough, Sheffield for an FA Cup semi-final against Arsenal, 27 March 1971. (Getty Images)

Heartbreak for Waddington and his Stoke players as Arsenal are awarded a controversial penalty deep into injury time during their FA Cup semi-final against Stoke City (in white) at Hillsborough, Sheffield, 27 March 1971. (Getty Images)

Leading out his Stoke City players for the 1972 League Cup Final at Wembley. (Mirrorpix)

Stoke City's Terry Conroy (number 7) celebrates with his team-mates after scoring the opening goal of the 1972 League Cup Final against Chelsea. (Getty Images)

Stoke City goalkeeper Gordon Banks makes a last-minute point-blank save from Chelsea's John Dempsey to ensure a 2-1 victory for Waddington's team in the 1972 League Cup Final. (PA Images)

Tony Waddington and Stoke City League Cup-winning team, March 1972 (Left to right): Mike Bernard, Alan Bloor, Mike Pejic, Jimmy Greenhoff, Gordon Banks, John Mahoney, Tony Waddington (Manager), George Eastham, John Marsh, Terry Conroy, Peter Dobing, John Ritchie, Denis Smith. (PA Images)

Tony Waddington pictured at the Victoria Ground, Stoke, on the morning of a UEFA Cup tie against Ajax of Amsterdam. (Mirrorpix)

Stoke City directors inspect the damage from the collapse of the Victoria Ground's Butler Street Stand roof. 7 January 1976. (Staffordshire Sentinel News and Media)

Gordon Banks and Tony Waddington in the Victoria Ground directors' box shortly after the Stoke City goalkeeper announced his retirement from the game because of an eye injury. (PA Images)

Tony Waddington pictured shortly before his resignation as Stoke City manager, March 1977. (Getty Images)

As for Stoke, they remained bullish despite their defeat in the opening leg. Waddington knew his team could play a lot better. He reminded them that only one goal was needed to get back into the tie. Back then there was no away goals rule in the League Cup, nor a penalty shootout if the sides were level after extra time. There was the chance to take the tie away from London to a neutral venue. They took the chance, thanks to the brilliance of Banks.

As the clock ticked down to the 90th minute, the score remained 2-1 on aggregate to West Ham. But, Stoke's players sensed anxiety among their opponents and memories of their own battle to cling on to a narrow lead to secure the dream of a Wembley final came to the fore. This time they were able to channel their emotions positively, keeping up the pressure on West Ham, and the Hammers finally snapped.

A cross floated in by Terry Conroy found John Ritchie and he trapped the ball before smashing it into the net to take the tie into extra time. The contest seemed destined for an inevitable replay until with just a couple of minutes left, Mike Pejic and Banks got into an almighty defensive tangle. The ball fell loose to Redknapp, who looked certain to score until Banks rugby-tackled him. The referee awarded the penalty and Stoke's dreams of Wembley appeared to be ending yet again in last-minute heartbreak.

But Banks had other ideas. He gambled that Hurst would smash the ball to his right, although the striker actually fired it down the middle. 'I was flying through the air with both arms pointing skywards,' recalled Banks. 'Geoff had hit the ball so hard that I couldn't afford to have "soft" hands. I tensed the muscles up in my arm and wrist and, to my great relief, watched the ball ricochet off my hand and over the bar.' Banks had pulled off yet another wonder-save and it was off to Hillsborough for a replay.

After the drama of Upton Park, that turned out to be something of a non-event thanks largely to Banks for Stoke and a defensive masterclass from Bobby Moore for West Ham. Once again the tie went into extra time with neither side able to score and after five and a half hours of football, they couldn't be separated, meaning a toss of a coin between Waddington and Greenwood to decide the choice of ground for the replay.

Waddington won and chose his old stomping ground of Old Trafford. He could have opted for Villa Park in Birmingham, 40 miles south of Stoke. Instead he settled for a trip 40 miles further north just, as he saw it, to make like as difficult as possible for West Ham and the London club's supporters.

Hillsborough had been packed to the rafters with Stoke fans, leaving Greenwood regretting his decision to agree to a northern venue. Waddington wanted to eke out any possible advantage, including having the choice of location for a replay. He correctly relied on Stoke supporters turning up in greater numbers than their rivals. They were more able to make the trip up the M6 to Manchester to turn Old Trafford into a home from home. But for all that support, West Ham remained favourites.

Stoke's players visibly wilted in the game at Hillsborough. 'To say my players are tired is an understatement,' groaned Waddington to the media. 'Some of them played when they weren't fit. We're not a club that has £170,000 players [multi-million pound players in modern terms] in reserve. We're stretched to the limit.'

Along with fitness problems, Stoke's players also gave Waddington a disciplinary headache. The man who insisted he always wanted his team to play silky football consistently found himself in the FA dock for a string of offences on the part of his players. He had to explain away to an FA disciplinary committee the worst record in the First Division. 'We are not the kind of team which goes out to kick lumps off everybody. That's not our style,' protested Waddington. 'We are not proud of our record this season but I don't think it should harm our reputation. It must be remembered that we are coming up to our 40th game this season, and some teams haven't reached 30 yet.'

He went on to blame over-zealous refereeing. 'The change of attitude of referees is such that it has now become an occupational hazard that the more games you play the more bookings you are likely to get.'

Somehow he received a sympathetic hearing. John Marsh, Terry Conroy and John Mahoney all faced long bans but instead they were put on a form of footballing probation. They were allowed to play but any further misdemeanours would see them spending a long stretch sitting up in the stands.

All three, along with Waddington, were about to take their place in football history. He described the FA's leniency as a 'big breakthrough'. Supremely confident of eventual success over West Ham, Waddington then told the press, 'A few times before we have been on the brink and failed. I think my players will have that bit extra driving them forward because they know only too well what rewards are at stake.'

His players didn't let him down in what turned out to be a football classic between Stoke and West Ham for the prize of meeting Chelsea at Wembley in the 1972 League Cup Final.

'One of the greatest footballing nights of all time', is how the *Daily Mail*'s Jeff Powell described the epic encounter at Old Trafford. *The Observer*'s Hugh McIlvanney described it as 'one of the most exhilarating matches even Old Trafford has ever seen'. *The Sun*'s Peter Batt commented, 'I have always resisted the temptation to describe any match as the most exciting I have seen, but this was the exception. This really was the greatest.'

Everyone present at Old Trafford on the night of 26 January 1972 agreed. It was a stunning and pulsating exhibition of football, one full of immense skill, courage and controversy. Powell further remarked that even the sight of the England captain Bobby Moore going in goal and saving a penalty 'seemed scarcely out of the ordinary'.

Moore put on the green jersey, in an era before substitute goalkeepers were allowed, after Bobby Ferguson had been injured in a collision with Conroy. It led to angry scenes both on and off the pitch between the players and the management teams. Greenwood scowled, 'One minute Ferguson had collected the ball and there was no danger. The next minute he was concussed. You can draw your own conclusions.' To this day, Conroy insists the clash was accidental.

Just a few minutes after the incident, Moore was facing a penalty. Mick Bernard stepped up with Moore parrying away his spot-kick, only for the fortunate Bernard to score from the rebound. Even then there was added drama. 'After I had put the rebound in referee Pat Partridge told me Moore had moved and there were two defenders in the box as I took it,' explained Bernard some years later. 'He went over and had a word with his linesman and I was ready to take it again but thankfully he signalled a goal!'

Despite being down to ten men with Ferguson still being treated in the dressing room, West Ham quickly equalised, a shot from Billy Bonds deflecting off Smith and ending in the net past a wrong-footed Banks. Once Ferguson was restored to the pitch, his team went into the lead with a spectacular volley from Trevor Brooking but deep into eight minutes of first-half injury time, Dobing equalised for Stoke to end a breathless 45 minutes of football.

Much to the Hammers' angst, Conroy scored what turned out to be the winner just after half-time, his shot skidding under the body of the groggy Ferguson. West Ham staged a spirited fightback but Stoke held on to a famous win.

Waddington hailed it as a tremendous game of football that 'nobody deserved to lose'. His frustrated counterpart appeared less than gracious in defeat, accusing Waddington and his team of lacking sportsmanship in their treatment of Ferguson, 'The attitude Stoke adopted towards Ferguson in the second half when he was still hopelessly groggy was not what I would describe as sportsmanship. The boy is sitting in there now, just staring in front of him. He just doesn't know where he is. He can't remember coming to the ground, taking part in the match, and doesn't even know what the score is.'

Quite remarkably, perhaps as a sign of less than enlightened times in terms of player welfare, Greenwood received a sympathetic hearing from the national press exercising a pro-London bias. Never mind that he ignored the advice of the Manchester United club doctor by sending a concussed player back out on to the pitch. It was all somehow the fault of Stoke, Waddington and his players.

Waddington, presumably wanting to be seen as magnanimous, refused to become involved in a war of words. Instead, he left it to his captain Dobing to defend his team's integrity. 'It's ridiculous to suggest we tried to take advantage of his injury,' insisted Dobing. 'I told the West Ham trainer to take all the time he needed to get the boy right. The only time we ever tried to put pressure on a goalkeeper was when Moore was in goal.'

For all the bleating and moaning, Waddington's Stoke players were through to Wembley to face Chelsea. They had made the 'big breakthrough'.

Reflecting some days later on a monumental night of football, David Miller of the *Sunday Telegraph* and *The Observer*'s Hugh McIlvanney were among the few Fleet Street critics to give Waddington credit. McIlvanney went along to the Victoria Ground to meet and congratulate the Stoke manager, describing him as the 'miracle worker' of the English Midlands. He did so while commenting in his inimitable style, 'Stoke's first team have accumulated fewer trophies than a blind big-game hunter.'

Waddington concurred by telling McIlvanney, 'Any pots we've got here have been collected by the youngsters. We've had a bit of success at youth level and that kind of thing. But apart from taking the Second Division championship in 1963 the first team have kept clear of the prizes.'

Assessing the impact of Waddington on Potteries football, McIlvanney argued, 'Now after a decade as manager he is as confident as such a modest pleasantly muted personality can be that Stoke are on the brink of history.'

Miller praised Waddington while criticising his West Ham counterpart. He regretted that Greenwood, 'one of the game's clearest thinkers', had let his 'normal dignity' slip by criticising Stoke's alleged unsporting tactics. Warming to his theme, he noted, 'Tony Waddington has not bought a player for three years and has only twice ever spent more than £30,000, for Banks and Greenhoff. Yet the tradition of skill which Waddington has established in a decade – and by which miraculously Stoke have survived – beginning with the evergreen Matthews and carried on by McIlroy and Viollet is now maintained by Dobing and Eastham, two of soccer's most gifted and unrewarded craftsmen.'

Both those men, along with Waddington, were finally about to be rewarded but not without one or two problems along the way, including another almost inevitable trip to meet the men from the FA disciplinary committee.

Just a fortnight before the League Cup Final, Waddington struggled to field a team thanks to injuries and suspensions. For a game against Tottenham Hotspur he was missing five of his first-team regulars. Marsh, Ritchie, Dobing, Eastham and Mahoney were all suffering from niggles. Waddington also feared that Mike Pejic and Mike Bernard might be unavailable for the biggest match in his club's history after going into the referees' notebooks once too often. Fortunately the FA once again proved lenient and they were given the all-clear to play at Wembley.

To ensure he was able to fulfil the league fixture against Spurs, Waddington asked for a reserve game against Leeds to be called off so he could bring in reinforcements. 'We have barely enough players for one match, let alone two,' groaned Waddington. 'Some players may have to play, even though they are not fit.'

Taken on face value, Waddington and his players were struggling. It was not ideal preparation. In reality, whether by accident or design, by missing the Spurs league game they were all earning some vital rest ahead of what would be, for most of them, the biggest game of their lives.

As with the build-up to the FA Cup semi-final against Arsenal almost 12 months earlier, Waddington spirited his players away into five-star comfort. 'I booked the team into a hotel in the Surrey countryside at Selsdon Park complete with a nine-hole golf course. It was a perfect retreat to allow the players to relax,' he reasoned.

They arrived at Selsdon Park fresh from beating Hull City 4-1 in the fifth round of the FA Cup. The prospect of what for then would have been a unique FA Cup and League Cup double loomed. In contrast Chelsea had suffered a humiliating FA Cup exit at the hands of Leyton Orient. Stoke were the in-form team. Yet very few pundits gave them a prayer of lifting the League Cup. For the footballing soothsayers, Chelsea remained firm favourites with Stoke nothing more than plucky underdogs.

After contacting the captains of various First Division clubs, *The Sun* would have been grim reading for any members of Waddington's squad prone to pessimism. From their defeated semi-final opponents West Ham, Bobby Moore predicted, 'We know only too well what a good side they [Stoke] are. But if anyone can get past their tight defence to score it's Peter Osgood, of Chelsea, and I think there's a good chance of that happening in the final. Chelsea's experience in recent years against teams like Real Madrid will be the decisive factor. It could be a close thing but Chelsea must be rated the favourites to win by the odd goal.'

His view was almost unanimously shared. Billy Bremner of Leeds United commented, 'I'd love Stoke to do it because Jimmy Greenhoff is a great friend of mine. But I'm sorry to say that Stoke have very little chance. I back Chelsea to win 3-1.'

Howard Kendall, who would later move to Stoke as a player-coach, offered, 'There won't be a lot in it but Chelsea have been so impressive recently that they must win.' And Mick Mills of Ipswich Town, later to become one of Waddington's successors as Stoke City manager, confidently predicted a Chelsea win. 'I must plump for Chelsea because they are such a consistent side,' he reasoned. 'Stoke have one or two youngsters who may get nervy and let them down, but Chelsea are used to the big occasion.'

Arsenal's skipper Frank McLintock, mindful perhaps of how his side brought heartbreak to Stoke only months earlier, offered diplomatically, 'I wouldn't like to bet on it. Stoke and Chelsea have players who can make goals but I think Chelsea will have the edge in midfield. Yet I have a lot of respect for Stoke and admiration for their manager Tony Waddington.'

Only Bobby Moncur of Newcastle United gave Stoke a chance. 'I would like to see Stoke win because they've never won anything,' he sympathetically commented. He added, 'They stand a very good chance because they are that much more determined. Chelsea are favourites and the pressure will be more on them.'

There was no such sympathy from the powers that be at Waddington's boyhood club Manchester United. 'Chelsea are such a good side that they must start off as favourites,' Bobby Charlton declared. Remembering, no doubt, the agony of going out of the competition to the Potters, Charlton went on, 'Stoke are quite capable of beating any of the top teams on their day. But Chelsea have much more experience of the big cup games and I can't see them slipping up.'

Waddington's old mentor Matt Busby shared this view, though openly declaring he wanted Stoke to win. 'My heart says Stoke but I admit it is an emotional choice,' the legendary manager told *The Sun*. 'I would dearly love to see this marvellous club pick up their first major honour.' But he concluded, 'It will be close. I have to take Chelsea to win.'

None of this doom and gloom from most of his peers unnerved Waddington. He remained supremely confident of taking his place in footballing history. 'A great deal hinges on the occasion and the reaction Wembley brings especially from the younger players,' countered Waddington. 'Some kind soul sent me a newspaper cutting in which Don Revie says we can do it and he's not a bad judge. If we can find the right balance we could leave all the tipsters with red faces. Wembley may be new to most of my team but we have been around a bit, including the youngsters.'

Frankly, when it came to answering criticism of his side Waddington could not win. On the one hand some critics felt his team lacked experience and was too reliant on youth. As a direct contradiction, others felt he relied too much on his older players, notably Dobing and Eastham. Even Banks, still the world's best goalkeeper, was mystifyingly singled out as an 'old-stager'.

'The idea that I sign the oldest players available is a joke, one that doesn't offend me. I have always gone for quality and if a man had enough of it age did not worry me either way,' reasoned Waddington as he outlined his footballing philosophy to *The Observer*.

'I have always believed in playing good football, believed that the way you win is as important as winning itself. I have tried to find men who would do a job for me, and I have been lucky so far. But I can't deny that I'm happy to have so many gifted young players in the side today. There should be a bit of football played at Wembley in the League Cup Final. Chelsea can certainly play and I think people will believe me now when I say that we can too, even if we are still looking for an honour to prove it.' All that was about to change.

On Saturday, 4 March 1972, Waddington became the first man to lead a Stoke City team out at Wembley. His team talk had been cursory. 'Tony was not a great tactician. His genius lay in his ability to put a good jigsaw puzzle together,' recalled Denis Smith, damning his former boss with faint praise.

'He'd be able to slot the pieces in the right places by selecting the right players in the squad and the right starting XI to go out there on the pitch. He was no rousing speechmaker. He would simply say, "Go out and be solid. Don't allow them too much room, and keep the ball by giving it to the likes of George [Eastham] and Peter [Dobing] early on. You know your jobs. Enjoy it."'

The plan worked like a dream with both those veteran midfield players involved in the opening goal after just five minutes. Dobing flung in the ball from a long throw with the Chelsea goalkeeper Peter Bonetti only able to punch it away to the feet of Eastham. He chipped it immediately into the penalty area, ensuring absolute chaos. First Smith mis-kicked with the ball hammering into the turf then ricocheting off first Chelsea's Peter Osgood, then Mick Dempsey. To the horror of the Irish defender, it ballooned up into the path of his impish international team-mate Terry Conroy. 'It was the greatest fluke of all time,' joked Conroy. His headed goal had given Stoke an early lead and any pre-match nerves were immediately eradicated.

Bizarrely, Conroy's goal helped every player to settle apart from the scorer himself. Banks noticed him beginning to doze. Even in international matches, Banks revealed that he had experienced top-class players going into their metaphorical shells after scoring a goal so he was not going to allow it to happen on this occasion. 'Seeing Terry start to coast, I shouted to Jackie Marsh to get upfield and snap him out of his stupor,' recalled Banks. 'A few well-chosen words from Jackie did the trick and Terry was soon back to his old self.'

Conroy acknowledged he had temporarily switched off. He explained in his autobiography, 'I looked up at the scoreboard, which had only just been introduced at Wembley then. I saw the words "Conroy 4". That stunned me. I had scored at Wembley. My name was literally up in lights, my dream utterly fulfilled. Roy of the Rovers stuff.'

As for the verbal rocket from his full-back, 'The problem was that we had almost the whole game still left to play. I was in something of a daze for quite a few minutes after that and only came around when Jackie Marsh literally shook me out of it.'

All 11 Stoke players needed to be on their mettle. Chelsea gradually came back into the game and as the clock ticked down to half-time, Stoke were grimly hanging on. Yet again though, in an echo of their agonising FA Cup clash with Arsenal, they conceded a late equaliser as a scuffed shot from Osgood, who was lying on his backside, somehow evaded Banks.

The sides went into the changing rooms at half-time with the scores level at 1-1. Chelsea were buoyed by the equaliser but for Stoke it was a sickening blow. Waddington needed to lift spirits, preferably without the legendary drop of his trainer Frank Mountford's whisky.

There was no panic from the manager. 'I think he was happy with the first-half performance,' recalled Marsh. 'Waddo just said, "Keep on playing your football like you have been doing in the first half," which we were renowned for anyway.'

Just to add to his woes, Marsh yet again lost one of his contact lenses during the course of the second half. He explained, 'Garland nudged me in a challenge and I could not focus very well with my left eye for the light was fading a little. I told the referee, but he explained he could not hold up the game so I played on until Frank [Mountford] brought a new lens.'

Marsh's travails proved to be a temporary inconvenience. Of more concern to Waddington was Jimmy Greenhoff after he suffered a bad shoulder injury. 'I did my shoulder after 20 minutes and I should have come off,' Greenhoff recalled. 'But what do you do? No way was I coming off that early, as it's a cup final plus you always think you can do better than whoever is on the bench.'

Waddington and his backroom staff feared that Greenhoff had suffered a dislocation. He told the *Stoke Sentinel*, 'I had to make the decision whether to send Jimmy back on or bring on John Mahoney. Jimmy decided to give it a go and we planned to throw everything at Chelsea, which I feel took them slightly by surprise.'

For all the attacking pressure, it was not until around a quarter of an hour left to play that Stoke were able to regain the lead, the injured Greenhoff playing a key role.

Football fans love a football romance. They do believe in fairy tales and one played itself out on the Wembley pitch in the form of Waddington's working man's ballet with a man he brought out of semi-retirement in the lead role, George Eastham. 'George has a sense of the dramatic. He should have been a film director,' Waddington surmised.

Eastham's winning goal, his first in competitive action for more than two years, came from a move prompted by Dobing. His cross-field pass found Conroy, who, once he had been awoken from his stupor, had tormented Chelsea's defenders all afternoon. Out on the left wing he was given 'acres' of space to run at David Webb, to tease him, float past him, and cross the ball for Ritchie to nod down into the path of Greenhoff. Bonetti was only able to parry away Greenhoff's half-volley, straight towards Eastham.

Momentarily, Dobing was in his way. But Eastham shouted to him to leave the ball and he prodded it into the net with the outside of his left foot. Cue ecstasy among the Stoke travelling support. 'What is all the fuss about me scoring? I just happened to be there on the spot when the chance came,' Eastham commented with more than a touch of understatement. For Eastham, Stoke and Waddington, destiny beckoned.

The break in play for Chelsea to restart the game allowed Mountford to calmly jog on to the pitch with Marsh's replacement contact lens. With Stoke back in the lead and just a quarter of an hour left to play it was also time to take off the injured Greenhoff. It turned out to be the most uncomfortable ten minutes of Waddington's life, watching his team see out the game, being battered black and blue by his agitated injured striker sitting next to him.

Greenhoff, despite the severity of the injury, told Waddington as he sat down he would never talk to him again if Stoke went on to lose the match. 'For the rest of the game he would be kicking and nudging me frantically on the bench', Waddington remembered. 'I thought he would go on to put his shoulder back into place, and he was almost hysterical when Mike Bernard made his famous back-pass that Chris Garland intercepted. Gordon Banks, assured as ever, turned away the shot.'

That dramatic last-minute intervention ensured that Stoke won their first major trophy despite Bernard, to his horror, almost throwing the game away. Opting to pass the ball back to Banks and supposed safety, Bernard failed to spot Chelsea's Garland lurking with intent. Bernard set up Garland with a glorious chance to equalise. Only the alertness of Banks stopped him.

'I saw what Mike was trying to do and I could see that Denis Smith was too far away to intercept, so I knew I had to get out there quickly,' Banks told journalists, who were admiring yet another of his wonder-saves. 'Garland was forced to shoot and I managed to block the ball as he shot.'

There was just time for a Chelsea corner, which resulted in a foul on Banks. He took the free kick before the final whistle sounded and those draped in red and white erupted in a euphoric wave of jubilation, not just in the stadium but throughout the Potteries. Waddington's men were history makers.

'I thought it wasn't on before the game, after the game, during the game, and so on. Until the game was over you've got to take it all in and hope that things work out,' Waddington told Jimmy Hill for ITV Sport in his post-match comments. He then reflected on his bugbear, Stoke City, 'the club who never win anything'. He told Hill, 'You just said this thing about 100 and odd years. The oldest cliché in the game is "it's a funny game" as you well know.

But I think it's almost become a fact that "Stoke City haven't won a thing in over 100 years" has nearly knocked that one into the hat.

'I hope what will not happen from now on is that people will turn around and say well Stoke have only won the League Cup in 100 and odd years. Let's forget about 100 and odd years. As far as we are concerned it's a great day for us.

'I think it's a great day for football too in lots of ways. As an example Mr Mears [Brian Mears, the Chelsea chairman] has just come in to congratulate me and what he said sums it all up. He said congratulations Tony, it couldn't happen to a nicer club. And, that's very important because we have a relationship with a lot of people in the game, with everybody in the game. I think what happened today was good for football as well as good for Stoke City.'

In articulating the pride he felt in the club and Potteries football, he signalled his intent to win more trophies. It was a bold ambition and turned out to be one too far.

As a decade earlier with his promotion-winning side, Waddington declined to join in the pitch-side celebrations, leaving it to his players to take the applause of the delirious Stoke fans. He was also at pains to thank his board of directors, modestly giving them credit for the triumph rather than himself. 'It may sound corny but I mean it,' Waddington told journalists. 'They know what it's like to have breadline gates, to be £100,000 in the red and to have their supporters screaming for their blood. It all happened in the bad old days but they still got on with the job, kept on grafting and the public of Stoke owes them a tremendous debt.'

Almost half a century later, Waddington as the manager is more likely to be given credit for the club's revival rather than Albert Henshall and his board of directors of the 1960s and 1970s.

Banks, at the time, was happy to give Waddington credit for helping win his first and ultimately only domestic honour. 'I signed [for Stoke] simply because the club were ambitious without being ruthless and because Tony Waddington was utterly honest with me,' he enthusiastically noted. 'They wanted to go places but in their own way, with their own style. They treat players like human beings, not robots who come out to play on matchdays.'

For the victory parade the following day, it appeared the entire community had turned out to welcome the team home. The streets around the city of Stoke-on-Trent were full. Red and white scarves, flags and even the odd old-fashioned rattle were in abundance. Even those with little interest in football turned out as the players brought joy to the wider community of north Staffordshire.

Aboard the rather clapped-out single-decker open-top bus, celebrating with their team-mates, were Meir lads Denis Smith and Alan Bloor. They both held the League Cup aloft at the front of the bus as it wormed its way down Sandon Road and through the heart of their home district on the southern edges of the city.

Smith described in his autobiography how he and Bloor were both in tears as they spotted relatives and friends among the sea of faces with thousands cheering and waving. Smith reflected, 'What an incredible thing football is. There was such a strong connection between these young fellows who kicked a ball around for a living and these thousands of people who struggled to make ends meet, scraped around for a living and were filled with such unconfined joy.'

Against this joyous backdrop, Waddington could not resist raising one matter which consistently perturbed him; the relative paucity of the Victoria Ground crowd on a matchday in contrast to the vast numbers celebrating League Cup victory. It averaged around the 20,000 mark even during successful seasons, the ground only packed to the rafters for key games. At the town hall reception Waddington quipped to the tens of thousands celebrating, 'I hope to see you all at our next match.'

He also hoped for more success. Only the prospect of winning more trophies would bring in the crowds and generate the revenues needed to compete with the best teams in the land.

One of those feats was once again immediately in sight – the FA Cup. Waddington and his players were optimistic they could return to Wembley within weeks of their League Cup triumph. Sadly, though, after the ecstasy they were about to suffer more heartbreak and despair.

All had seemed well for Waddington and football fans in the Potteries in the early spring of 1972 but it was all about to turn sour with a series of cruel twists.

10

The Man in a White Coat

FATE conspired to re-unite Stoke City and Arsenal in the FA Cup, generating an encounter full of yet more controversy and outright rancour. Even the temperament of Stoke's outwardly mild-mannered manager was about to be sorely tested thanks, in Waddington's view, to the seeming incompetence of match officials.

A League Cup triumph at Wembley in March 1972 turned out to be the pinnacle of his managerial career. Little did he realise, as his players were about to meet their north London bogey team, that the seeds of decline were about to set in; failure to progress in Europe, a mounting bill in wages and transfer fees and especially to Waddington's horror the shock loss of his World Cup-winning goalkeeper. Stoke lined up against Arsenal after yet again knocking Manchester United out of a cup competition. At Old Trafford a goal from Jimmy Greenhoff put them within minutes of knocking the Mancunians out at the first time of asking. That was until inevitably George Best intervened, flicking the ball past Banks and into the net for the equaliser.

Walking off the pitch, there was a feeling of frustration among Waddington's players. For the first time, against United and on their home turf, Waddington and his men sensed they were the better team. They were confident of winning the replay with their old nemesis Arsenal waiting to play them.

For the replay, their defensive warrior Denis Smith was yet again an injury doubt and remained so until Waddington indulged in some impromptu and unorthodox physiotherapy. Smith had been driven to the ground and an anxious Waddington went out to meet him. 'He [Smith] seemed to be stuck for a moment but then suddenly got out of the car and I thought he moved remarkably well,' recalled the manager. 'Denis said, "It's no use." I replied, "You got out of the car well enough. Get back in and come out again." He remarked later something seemed to click as he got out of the car. We had him doing warm-up exercises in the dressing room, something he could not have managed a few hours earlier, and he would give it a go.'

There were no complaints this time around from Waddington over the size of the crowd as more than 49,000 optimistic fans packed into the Victoria Ground, sensing more cup glory.

Once again Best proved more than a handful and his attacking genius was only matched by the brilliance of Banks in goal. Best got the better of him to score the opener only for Smith to go marauding upfield to score the equaliser, taking the game into extra time amid a febrile atmosphere.

Terry Conroy popped up to score the winner, his last significant contribution of an eventful season. TC, as he was known among the players, suffered throughout his career with knee injuries. After another appointment with the physio, he was ruled out of the semi-final against Arsenal, a significant blow to Waddington's plans. Nevertheless, he had the personnel to win, players confident of reversing the frustrating and painful result of 12 months earlier.

In the build-up to the 1972 FA Cup semi-final, Waddington became mired in controversy. Just six days before they were due to meet Arsenal, Stoke played relegation favourites Nottingham Forest in a league match at the Victoria Ground. Arsenal's manager, Bertie Mee, went along on a scouting mission. It was a wasted visit as Waddington selected his reserve team, risking the ire of the Football League and Forest's relegation rivals. Only John Marsh, of the League Cup-winning team, turned out.

According to Waddington, nearly everyone else, not just Conroy, was either injured or suspended. He insisted, though few believed him, that only Banks had been rested. Dismissing the critics, Waddington declared the team 'to be the fittest available to me in the present circumstances'. As a gruelling season was drawing to a conclusion, his players were carrying knocks. They also needed rest before another tilt at securing a trip to Wembley. Stoke lost 2-0 to Forest; league points seemingly sacrificed in the quest for cup glory.

Waddington's men returned to Villa Park, the scene of their agonising FA Cup exit 12 months earlier, in bullish mood. 'It's incredible how little tension there is in the club,' piped up Mike Bernard, any mental scars from nearly giving away the League Cup now banished. 'Nobody bothers to talk about the match. We've had too much experience for that. I don't think Arsenal will give us a lot of trouble. They won't be the force they were last year when they beat us in the semi-final replay.'

Centre-forward John Ritchie weighed in with some similar sentiments in a ghost-written column for *The Sun*. 'So much has happened to Stoke since our last trip to Villa Park. We have won the League Cup and now have our eyes on the FA Cup. This time we can get our own back on Arsenal. As a team we are better equipped. The last 12 months have seen us develop considerably while Arsenal – in my opinion – have slipped,' he commented.

Waddington acknowledged the upbeat mood among his players though admitted he had not forgotten the 'traumatic experience' of a year earlier. He revealed he had never seen so many grown men so dejected, so upset, many of them in tears. 'I felt I had let them all down,' confessed the boss. This time around he promised the fans a different outcome. Stoke were improving. Arsenal were in decline as far as Waddington was concerned. This turned out to be an overly-optimistic assessment of the state of the two sides.

Stoke's players inexplicably froze once again at Villa Park, perhaps having been over-confident. Waddington offered an alternative theory, condemning what he saw as their opponents' over-physical approach, not that any of his players were shrinking violets. The game turned on an injury to the Arsenal goalkeeper Bob Wilson, who tore his cartilage as he landed after jumping to field the ball. Up until then Arsenal dominated the game with Stoke fortunate to only be a goal down.

Foolishly the Arsenal coaching team allowed Wilson to carry on, hoping he might be able to run the injury off. The plan backfired and actually allowed Stoke back into the game, Arsenal conceding a soft equaliser, an own goal from Peter Simpson. As Wilson carried on hobbling, Peter Dobing missed a great opportunity to score the winner, hitting the post instead.

Eventually the struggling Wilson was hauled off with centre-forward John Radford going in goal. Even then Stoke, once again facing a stand-in goalkeeper in a cup semi-final, failed to take advantage. Radford pulled off a couple of fine saves from Greenhoff and Smith as the game ended in yet another draw, Arsenal this time around perhaps ruing their luck more than Stoke.

It was time for another replay, to be played at Everton's Goodison Park, but not before Waddington uncharacteristically revealed his disdain, indeed contempt, for his opponents.

'Waddington attacks Arsenal tactics, Stoke accuse: Intimidation!' 'Will it be a kicking match? Waddington hits out at Arsenal tactics.' These were just a couple of the headlines splashed on the back pages of national newspapers as the teams prepared for what turned out to be a fiercely controversial replay.

Waddington expanded on his excuse for Stoke's lacklustre performance at Villa Park. His players were stopped from playing football. 'We like to play football against everyone, but now, unlike before, we have the resilience to face what amounts to intimidation without folding up,' fumed Waddington. 'I think we made that point on Saturday. It was a lot like the League Cup semi-final with West Ham. Arsenal were out to stop us playing football. But we are well equipped to deal with this sort of thing if it happens again. I can't put it more diplomatically than that.'

Given Waddington had consistently built teams with his wall of hard men in defence and at least one steely character in midfield, his threat appeared clear rather than implicit. It was fighting talk, almost boxing-style trash talk, totally out of character for the normally urbane Waddington. It set a sour tone. There would be more angry words to follow.

On the same day Waddington ranted and raved to the gentlemen of the press about Arsenal's 'intimidating' tactics, those football writers announced that they had voted for Gordon Banks as their Footballer of the Year. George Eastham came third in the poll. 'What makes it so pleasing is that when Gordon came to us in 1967 he said he was coming to help Stoke win a major honour. We are pleased to have helped him with that one,' commented Waddington once he had calmed down after his coruscating appraisal of Arsenal. Fleet Street's decision to recognise the achievement of Stoke's most famous player of the day did little to lighten the mood in the camp. It was about to be a tumultuous night on Merseyside.

One member of Waddington's 1970s 'wall', Mike Pejic, missed the Villa Park tie through suspension. He was now back. There were doubts over the fitness of defenders Bloor, Marsh and Elder as well as talismanic striker Greenhoff but all were passed fit. Waddington hinted at a safety first policy in the absence of Conroy.

If necessary his side would try to take the tie to a second replay, provisionally scheduled to be played at Coventry City's Highfield Road stadium. Conroy, by then, would possibly be restored to fitness for any such game. This seemed a distinct possibility as time was running out in Stoke's 60th game of the season. At least it was until the intervention of a whistle-happy referee, a dozing linesman and a man in a white coat.

As early as the fifth minute, Stoke's players began to wonder if the football gods once again had conspired against them, the sporting deity incarnated as the match officials. They ruled that a header from Smith had been hacked off the line by Bob McNab. A press photograph soon to be pinned up on the Stoke dressing room wall by Waddington appears to show that the ball had crossed the line, and that it should have been a goal.

Stoke persevered and began to dominate. *The Guardian*'s Eric Todd wrote, 'For many years the cry was "Lucky Arsenal", as if anyone ever won anything without assistance from fortune, and on last night's performance that saying is as true today as ever.'

With George Eastham in 'outstanding' form, a flurry of goals from Stoke seemed inevitable but they were wasteful. One eventually came from the penalty spot. The ball fell to Greenhoff, who tried to round Geoff Barnett, only for the Arsenal goalkeeper to tug his ankle and bring him down. Greenhoff took the penalty himself and scored, giving Stoke the initiative and seeing them seemingly cruising to victory.

The cliché goes that 'football is a game of two halves', to be specific two contrasting halves. This most certainly applied in this particular cup tie as Arsenal were reinvigorated after the half-time break and Stoke were aghast at the behaviour of the officials.

Arsenal went on to win thanks to two highly contentious goals. Firstly, referee Keith Walker incensed the Stoke players and management with the award of a penalty. George Armstrong went to ground after what neutral observers viewed as the softest of touches from Peter Dobing. In those days diving for penalties was virtually non-existent in English football but to Dobing's amazement Walker pointed to the penalty spot.

To the referee's credit, he tried to justify his decision to the media, something now banned in the era of professional refs. Walker told the *Stoke Sentinel*, 'Dobing deliberately hit the Arsenal player in the small of the back.' Dobing countered, 'There was no pushing on my part.'

Banks said the tussle between Dobing and Armstrong, from his vantage point, looked like 'six of one and half a dozen of the other'. From baffled reporters sat up in the Goodison Park press box there was a sympathetic hearing for Dobing and Banks. 'From where I sat it seemed that Dobing and Armstrong were jostling each other for possession in Stoke's box when the referee halted play. For a moment or two neither side seemed to know why the whistle had been blown,' commented Donald Saunders of the *Daily Telegraph*.

'Nine times out of ten this offence would have escaped the ultimate penalty but the referee pointed to the spot,' said *The Guardian*'s Eric Todd. From *The Sun* came the verdict 'decidedly dodgy'. Protests from Dobing and his team-mates were swept aside and Charlie George stepped up to equalise. Memories of the agonising day at Hillsborough 12 months earlier began to filter back for Waddington, his players, and increasingly agitated fans.

If the Stoke manager thought he had reason to grumble before the game, the next infamous passage of play would leave him incandescent with rage afterwards. It became the stuff of legend among his followers for years to come. Alan Ball picked out George, who in the opinion of everyone in the ground was standing at least a couple of yards offside. Everyone apart from referee Walker and his assistant Bob Matthewson, that is.

Stoke's defence momentarily hesitated, seemingly waiting for the linesman to raise his flag, an error of judgement on their part, and Matthewson, to their astonishment, waved play on.

George took advantage, crossing for John Radford, who was up in support ahead of the back-pedalling desperate Stoke defenders, to comfortably score what turned out to be the winner.

Stoke were out of the cup and their manager, players and fans were left raging in a collective fit of fury. For years to come they never forgave the match officials, nor their Arsenal opponents.

At the time, Stoke's players vehemently protested and urged referee Walker to talk to Matthewson. He agreed. 'The linesman had been well placed, and we were all confident the correct decision would soon be forthcoming,' remembered Banks in his autobiography. 'The pair exchanged a few words and I was stunned when the referee then turned and pointed to the centre circle. Goal to Arsenal.'

Smith described the decision as 'farcical, ridiculous and shocking to the point of being numbing'.

Once again, Walker defended the decision but not without any great conviction. 'There was a player on the far side of the ground who I am told put the Arsenal man onside,' commented Walker.

'Mr Matthewson is an experienced referee. I accepted the signal [to play on] from him.'

There was one important snag with Walker's argument as far as Waddington was concerned. It was the wrong signal. There was no hiding his rage after the game, no sign of any diplomatic niceties. 'What was the penalty for? And how many yards offside was George?' he ranted. 'Arsenal never made a chance until the death and they would never have scored unless they had got that penalty.'

His chairman, Albert Henshall, no stranger to referees as one of their sternest critics, described the level of officiating as 'diabolical'. He added almost with a sense of pride, 'I think I shall be in trouble. I had a real go at the referee and linesman after the game.'

The referee declined to take the opportunity to sanction Waddington or Henshall. 'I know how disappointed people feel at times like this,' the hapless referee commented in a masterclass of understatement.

For polite neutral observers the poor level of decision-making had been 'mystifying'. As for the man from the local daily paper, the *Stoke Sentinel*'s correspondent Peter Hewitt pointed out Matthewson had been 'so hot all night on even hair's breadth decisions' until he allowed George to play on. It seemed a remarkable aberration.

As Walker pointed, out his linesman was an experienced and respected Football League referee in his own right. It was an unforgivable mistake from a man normally out in the middle rather than running the line. In those days, First Division referees often took on the role of assistants for how piece matches such as semi-finals and finals.

Inevitably Matthewson would soon turn up at the Victoria Ground to referee a Stoke game, perhaps not the wisest decision on the part of the Football League. Smith took the opportunity to collar the errant official. TV pundits had speculated that the hapless Matthewson had mistaken a salesman walking along the touchline in a white coat as a Stoke player. On the night Stoke wore an all-white kit. It seemed ridiculous. Smith discovered it turned out to be true.

'When I next saw that linesman I felt compelled to ask him to explain himself and he owned up and apologised for his mistake,' Smith wrote in his autobiography. 'He had indeed mistaken the seller on the far side of the pitch for one of us. I was so taken aback I couldn't bite his head off. It was just too ridiculous to take in.'

For Smith and his crestfallen manager the apology was welcome but no consolation. As he stalked the corridors of Goodison Park immediately after the game venting his fury, Waddington came across his old friend, the Arsenal physio Fred Street. Twelve months earlier Street was in the Stoke camp, sharing their agony. Now he wanted to go into the Stoke dressing room to sportingly offer sympathy to his former players.

Remarkably, Waddington, viewed by many in the game as a mild-mannered and easy-going individual, at first refused to give him permission. Composing himself and perhaps feeling a little embarrassed he then told Street, 'I would wait a little while if I were you. The boys are a bit violent at the moment.'

They might well have asked their former physio to find an acquaintance of his in a white coat with ophthalmic qualifications to attend to the medical needs of the referee and his linesman. Their sense of anger was summed up by Gordon. 'Our dressing room was like a morgue,' he mournfully recalled. 'It [linesman Reg Matthewson's decision] proved to be a very costly mistake for Stoke City, one that generated not only bitter disappointment but bitter feelings.'

Years later, Waddington calmly recalled the most tempestuous night of his career, one which turned out to be his last opportunity to go within one match of reaching a Wembley final. 'It was a reverse situation from the previous season, but the gods seemed to be against us again in the replay at Goodison Park when Arsenal's 2-1 winner by John Radford came from a blatant offside run by Charlie George,' he ruefully recalled.

'Everyone in the ground saw it except linesman Bob Matthewson and referee Keith Walker. We played in our white strip that night and apparently Matthewson had been distracted by a white-coated ice cream seller on the far touchline. He thought Charlie George had been played onside when he was yards in the clear.'

Even the job description of the man in a white coat ended up as a source of mystery for Stoke fans. For some he was not an ice cream seller, but a programme seller. Others claim he was selling peanuts. It is all treated in hindsight with resigned amusement.

Waddington failed to see the funny side. He had been robbed of the chance of leading his side to an historic cup double. It would have almost certainly been seen as emulating the achievement of his old friend in winning the league championship that same season.

THE MAN IN A WHITE COAT

Brian Clough had succeeded in bringing a title to Derby County, a sleepy provincial football club. Waddington dreamt of a cup double for his own underachieving club in the Midlands. Those dreams were shattered thanks to a linesman's defective eyesight and a mystery man in a white coat.

11

The Crash

FOR all the frustration and disappointment of failing to follow up a League Cup triumph by lifting the FA Cup, Tony Waddington no doubt used the summer of 1972 to still proudly reflect on taking his place in his club's history.

He will be remembered as the first and so far only man to lead the Potters to a major honour. Stanley Matthews, for all his brilliance, never helped to bring a major trophy to Stoke City. Indeed, as earlier commented upon, he walked out with the club on the brink of claiming a league title.

Waddington was convinced his side would be able to further re-write the record books by bringing the Football League championship to the Potteries. In the meantime, his club was about to embark on its first foray into European competitive football, the UEFA Cup, courtesy of winning the League Cup.

To be successful in both quests, he, given limited playing resources, needed all of his top-class international players. Little did he or anybody in the English game of football predict that he was about to lose his most iconic player of the era in the cruellest of circumstances; his goalkeeper Gordon Banks.

Banks proved pivotal to persuading another World Cup winner to come to the Potteries as Waddington sought to strengthen his squad for a European adventure and league title bid. 'When we were together in the England squad I was forever "selling" Stoke to Geoff Hurst. I firmly believed Stoke had a team good enough to win the First Division title,' Banks enthusiastically noted.

'I kept telling Geoff if he wanted to top up his collection of trophies with a championship medal he could do no worse than a trip to the Potteries.'

Hurst's signature was duly snapped up, only for critics to accuse Waddington of signing a great player but in their jaundiced view another 'has been'. Hurst proved them wrong. He was a more than useful acquisition. 'I always bought players to do a specific job and I felt Hurst could teach us a few techniques from his vast experience,' Waddington reasoned. 'He had a supreme natural temperament, fully in control of his mental pressures. He never allowed a missed pass or goal to affect his approach. He was able to keep his standards on a level plane and consistency was his strength.'

The signing of Hurst followed a familiar pattern in Waddington's modus operandi. This was no 'old man' seeing out his footballing days. As with Wolves's championship winners, Dennis Wilshaw and Eddie Stuart, and indeed Matthews in the 1960s, Hurst was there not just to make a valuable contribution on the pitch but to also help to bring along younger players off it. Waddington went into the 1972/73 season intent on emulating the achievement of Brian Clough down the A50 at Derby in the previous season of winning the First Division. Yet his side made a shaky start to the campaign and to compound matters their European adventure was harrowingly cut short.

He had a couple of World Cup winners in his side but even with their presence Stoke failed to overcome what many of their fans took to be an average German team in Kaiserslautern. All seemed to be going in Stoke's favour after the first leg at the

Victoria Ground with a 3-1 victory thanks to Terry Conroy, Hurst and John Ritchie.

The Germans had grabbed an away goal but Stoke had been the far better team and they travelled to Germany confident of making further progress in the competition. Instead it turned out to be a miserable thrashing and a harsh lesson in the dark arts of European football. In a bad-tempered encounter they found themselves 2-0 down at half-time, meaning Kaiseralautern led on the away goals rule. Stoke pressed for their own away goal with Waddington sending on substitute Ritchie for defender Alan Bloor. It was to no avail and the Germans went into a three-goal lead with Ritchie only lasting on the pitch for a few minutes after getting himself sent off.

During a break in play for an injury, one of the German defenders gave him a sly dig in the ribs. Ritchie retaliated with a punch and his opponent collapsed on to the ground. The referee had not seen the original blow but did see Ritchie's punch, and that was enough for him to be dismissed.

From then on the game further deteriorated into a kicking match, boot on players as much as the ball, and it ended 4-0 to Kaiserslautern, giving them a 5-3 victory on aggregate. For Waddington and his players it was a chastening experience, their lack of familiarity with competitive continental football being ruthlessly exposed by their opponents. 'We thought that we had a good enough lead for the second leg, but our inexperience in Europe showed over there in Germany,' recalled Conroy. 'They were full of tricks, and it was all new to us.' Just a few weeks later worse was to follow.

Far from challenging for a league title, Stoke's inconsistent form meant they were hovering above the relegation zone as they travelled to Anfield to face Liverpool on 21 October 1972. Any frustration building up among the players thanks to their erratic form spilled over in this game and even Banks lost his temper. First he was penalised by the referee, Roger Kirkpatrick, for taking too many steps with the ball in his hands as he lined up a clearance. From the indirect free kick Emlyn Hughes hammered the ball into the net to equalise following an earlier Stoke goal from Jimmy Greenhoff.

As the game drew to a close Kirkpatrick intervened again, playing an advantage to Liverpool rather than awarding a foul, then pulling play back for a free kick. Banks raced out of his goal to remonstrate with Kirkpatrick. His team-mates were also livid and they lost their composure as well as the game. Liverpool took a quick free kick and Ian Callaghan scored the winner.

Little did Stoke's disgruntled goalkeeper know as he walked from the Anfield pitch, but it turned out to be his last game at the famous old ground. It was his last game of competitive football.

Waddington insisted he always remembered the weekend when Banks suffered his tragic car accident, down to the detail of the rows with the referee at Anfield. Defeat there meant 'the weekend had not started too well for him', reflected the boss.

On the following morning Banks travelled to the Victoria Ground for treatment on a minor injury picked up against Liverpool. Waddington had gone with his family to the Welsh resort of Abersoch for a weekend break. It was disrupted by a phone call informing him that his star player was in the North Staffordshire Royal Infirmary. Driving home from the ground, Banks overtook another car on a bend of the Whitmore Road in Trentham, on the outskirts of Stoke-on-Trent.

'Not exactly the best place to overtake, but I was keen to be at home with Ursula [his wife] and her Sunday dinner,' Banks recalled in his autobiography. 'I pulled out to pass and suddenly found myself on a collision course with an oncoming vehicle. I slammed my foot on the brake as a prickle of adrenalin rushed across my forehead. There was an almighty bang. There was the sound of glass shattering. Then there was nothing.'

Waddington drove back to the Potteries as surgeons operated on Banks, hoping to save his sight, as shards of glass from the car windscreen had become embedded in his right eye. His car had slewed across the road as he tried to avoid an oncoming van, which crashed into a hedge. Its occupants mercifully only suffered minor injuries.

Banks spent an hour and a half in surgery for treatment to his injuries. At the time the chances of saving the sight in his eye were put at 50-50. Stoke's medical officer, Gordon Crowe, joined Waddington and Banks's wife at the hospital but the omens were not good. 'They will not be able to tell whether his sight has been affected or not for a few days,' Dr Crowe told journalists. 'He must have gone through the windscreen.'

Waddington, as he gave interviews to the national media, remained determinedly optimistic for his goalkeeper, a man he recognised as possibly his 'greatest signing'.

For Banks it was, of course, a personal tragedy and caused a premature end to a wonderful career. For Waddington and Stoke it was an immense and ultimately fatal blow to their sporting ambitions. Waddington recognised in later years that, but for what he called 'that tragic day', Banks's 'intense fitness dedication' would have allowed him to carry on playing for another decade. He would never have needed another first team goalkeeper.

'Banksy's loss hit us badly,' remembered Denis Smith. 'It was a major, major blow.' It was one, in the opinion of Smith, a fan as well as a player, the Stoke team of the 1970s struggled to recover from. Indeed, as supportive and as admiring of Waddington as his former players are, many are quite critical of how he went about replacing Banks. This included the eventual decision to sign Banks' England successor, Peter Shilton.

Frankly, it was a nigh-on impossible task to find 'another Gordon Banks'. He was considered by many in English football at the time to be the world's greatest ever goalkeeper. News of his

THE CRASH

injury dominated national newspaper headlines and led television and radio news bulletins, nationally as well as internationally. Waddington found himself at the centre of a media maelstrom as Banks recuperated in hospital. National newspaper front pages carried updates on the health of a World Cup-winning goalkeeper while the back pages declared Stoke City a club in crisis.

Bizarrely, Waddington, a manager who placed more importance than his rivals on the value of the man in goal, did not have a fit professional goalkeeper to call upon. His England under-23 custodian, John Farmer, whom Waddington had just put on the transfer list after conceding nine goals in two games as a stand-in for Banks earlier in the season, was suffering from torn ankle ligaments. Ken South, from the youth team, had just been told to pack in the game thanks to a serious knee injury. The only man available was 20-year-old Welsh amateur international Grenville Millington, who was on trial from Cheshire League side Witton Albion. 'Our chief concern was for Gordon and his family, but we had to pull ourselves up from this tragedy,' insisted Waddington.

Given Farmer's injury, he needed to recruit and fast. Fortunately Waddington's standing in the game was such that other managers gave him a sympathetic hearing. West Bromwich Albion agreed to waive the registration of their FA Cup-winning keeper, John Osborne, who had recently announced his retirement after falling out of favour. Stoke's manager declined the kind offer on the grounds that Osborne had 'not played for months'. Everton offered to release one of Banks's former England international deputies, Gordon West, on loan. Again Waddington declined.

The player he seemed destined to bring to the Victoria Ground was Aberdeen's Scottish international Bobby Clark. Aberdeen agreed a British record fee for a goalkeeper of £100,000, though did not want him to sign immediately. 'I've heard nothing from Aberdeen. But I asked for a transfer at the start of the season and obviously I'm still interested in the move. I'd love to go to England and Stoke would be fine,' Clark enthusiastically told the press.

Waddington welcomed Clark to the Victoria Ground, embracing him on the pitch for the benefit of newspaper photographers. Yet remarkably the deal did not go through; a mystery at the time, but one Waddington cleared up years later. 'I agreed with Aberdeen to sign Clark, but they wanted him for a vital game the following week,' Waddington told the *Stoke Sentinel*. 'I sent director Alex Humphreys who had been a goalkeeper in his playing days on our books, to check on Clark, but the player did not impress in a poor performance. We did not go ahead with the deal to the consternation of Aberdeen.'

Nobody had the heart to tell the Aberdeen manager that in the opinion of a part-time Stoke keeper from the 1940s, Scotland's first-choice was not good enough to play English First Division football.

Instead, the then Scotland manager Tommy Docherty advised Waddington to sign Mike McDonald, his Scottish under-23 number one, and McDonald duly arrivals in Stoke from Clydebank for a fee of £25,000.

Waddington's short-term problems had been solved with the signing of McDonald and the retention of Farmer, a local lad well regarded in the dressing room. Their manager still held out hope Banks would fully recover. 'We are given to understand that Banks could be quite optimistic, and that the sight of the right eye could possibly be all right,' Waddington told the press. 'But if it is not, with his left eye perfect, I myself feel convinced that he will play again for Stoke, and there is no reason why not for England. Now he has to be kept quiet and has to relax. He appreciates he is lucky to be alive.'

His chairman Albert Henshall was similarly upbeat and optimistic saying, 'His eyesight will be impaired, but we are hoping that with the treatment, he could be back in future in the Stoke goal.' It was not to be, at least not in a competitive game.

THE CRASH

Stoke went into the season with championship and European aspirations. They ended it without their star goalkeeper and just about staving off relegation. During the following summer, Waddington took his players on a pre-season tour of Israel, then Australia and New Zealand, hoping for a reversal in fortune and to regain the momentum from lifting the League Cup and those epic battles with Arsenal for a place at Wembley in the FA Cup Final.

It was while on tour he knew he had to make a call on the future of his most famous player. Banks had made a comeback in friendly games, even including one as an outfield player for a Stoke junior side against a Sunday league pub team, the Red Cow in Werrington, a village in the Staffordshire Moorlands.

A decision needed to be made on his competitive future. Waddington, for all of his public optimism, had severe doubts. Banks himself recalled the difficult conversation with his manager. 'Tony Waddington allowed me a six-month period of adjustment,' he said. 'I commenced with light training and gradually built up my programme over the months. My eyesight was checked periodically and I underwent numerous tests to see how I coped with the speed, flight and direction of the ball.'

This was put to the test in Israel. 'I had the players hitting shots at him from 30 and 40 yards,' Waddington revealed. 'It opened up the chief problem after losing the sight of his right eye that he could not adjust quickly enough. There was always going to be a blind area where he would be in trouble. There was a time when we thought Gordon could overcome his injuries, but that tour brought it home to everyone that his distinguished goalkeeping career was over.'

Banks commented in his autobiography, 'Tony asked the $64m question, "Can you play on?" It was the question I had been asking myself for weeks. It had lain there at the forefront of my thoughts, ticking away like a time-bomb. I could avoid answering it no longer. "Tony, you've been a great boss," I told him. "You've always been honest with me and I've got to be honest with you. I think you know as well as I do what the answer is."

'Tony slowly nodded his head. "I've seen you in training. Personally, I think you can still do us a job," he said. "I could," I told him, "but not the job I used to do. I don't want that, Tony. If I can't meet the standards I set for myself, I'm going to have to call it a day."'

The only job Waddington thought Banks could now do was as a coach. 'It was typical of Gordon that he never complained about his misfortune and quietly accepted what had happened,' lamented Waddington.

His offer of a coaching role was accepted but Banks was in for a shock. 'Tony gave me a job as a coach to Stoke's youth team with a brief to offer specialist coaching to young goalkeepers,' remembered Banks. 'The first day I gathered my young charges I was dumbfounded. Of all the apprentices on the club's books there was not a single goalkeeper! The lad who took the jersey was a part-timer who trained two evenings a week.'

Presumably an embarrassed Waddington did not bother to inform Banks of his trials and tribulations with the goalkeeping department in the immediate aftermath of the fateful car crash. Nobody had come along to replace the unfortunate Ken South on a full-time basis and there was just the eager amateur Grenville Millington turning up to train on a Tuesday and Thursday night.

Given Waddington's mantra of valuing top-class goalkeepers as much as prolific strikers, his own boyhood footballing hero in Frank Swift being one, it was a curious, though admittedly temporary, chink in his managerial armoury.

As for Banks, Waddington was forever effusive in his praise. There was in his opinion no goalkeeper to match him. There were many moments the 'Banks of England' had saved Stoke City, too many to recall, from the Hurst penalty save at West Ham to the dive at Chris Garland's feet in the last minute of the League Cup Final to ensure victory at Wembley.

Waddington explained, 'Most goalkeepers tend to dive at a player's feet with their eyes shut. Gordon would always have his eyes open and his anticipation was so great that he would often start to move before the ball was even played.'

All this was a result of supreme natural talent and also immense dedication to his art. Waddington understandably wanted him to pass on his work ethic to younger players, once some wannabe goalkeepers could be uncovered in the Potteries. Eventually some were found. There were also some more than handy young outfield players for Banks to help to mentor. Almost told with a mischievous chuckle, Waddington commented, 'He [Banks] coached the club's youngsters to the same level that he would have trained himself, which meant his schedule really hurt.'

As Waddington gave up on fielding the best goalkeeper in the world, he realised a more fundamental rebuilding job needed to be done after an unexpected relegation battle. Nervous fans, just a year after his Wembley triumph, even began to heckle Waddington, openly venting their frustration at witnessing a rapid and unexpected decline in their club's fortunes. They met his decision to leave out Welsh international midfielder John Mahoney from a relegation clash at home to West Bromwich Albion with derision. Waddington sent Mahoney on to the pitch at half-time, joking afterwards he had responded to his club's '21,000 selectors'. Stoke won 2-0, effectively banishing any fears of relegation.

Nevertheless, it wasn't just Banks's loss being felt but the absence of other experienced players too. League Cup-winning captain Peter Dobing was forced to retire. George Eastham was nearing retirement, joining Banks as part of Waddington's back-room staff. Fans' favourite Harry Burrows departed to Plymouth Argyle to end his playing days. But there was still the core of a decent side and there was also, once pre-season touring was over, a rather unusual trophy to win in the guise of the Watney Cup.

Those tours abroad had always been boosted commercially by the presence of Banks, as with Matthews a decade earlier. They drew in the crowds. Waddington understood long before the era of names on the backs of shirts the marketing value of players.

The late John Ritchie, in a club video tribute to Waddington, recalled the trip to New Zealand and a wager with his manager. Stoke visited Dunedin, a city as with the rest of the country more renowned for rugby union. But even in a city where rugby was a religion everyone had heard of Banks, if few had heard of Stoke City, Waddington or Ritchie. Banks had yet to announce his retirement so played on the tour, helping to generate interest among curious sports fans.

'We went out determined to have a good game, still sleeting and snowing, we played this little team and we gave them a real pounding in the first half,' Ritchie fondly remembered before his untimely death at a relatively young age.

'The crowd were getting a little bit restless so Tony Waddington had a wonderful idea. He thought, "What if we put Gordon Banks in the other goal?" It was announced to the crowd. They were delighted.'

It was a great marketing ruse, public relations at its best. As for the bet, Ritchie explained, 'He bet me $100 I would not score any more goals against Gordon. We finished up winning eight nil and I got all eight.' Waddington never paid up but Ritchie forgave him. Indeed, he was amused by the cheek of his boss.

As for the unusual trophy, this came in the form of a pre-season competition sponsored by a brewery and in an era with relatively little televised football it was bafflingly showcased by the BBC's *Match of the Day*. It was contested between the two highest-scoring teams in each of the four divisions, apart from those involved in Europe or being promoted or relegated. Remarkably, Stoke qualified as being among the First Division's top scorers despite being embroiled in a relegation battle.

Throughout the summer, the club had kept news of Banks's imminent retirement quiet. Waddington, despite agreeing it was time for Banks to hang up his gloves, even indicated that he might play in the opening game against Fourth Division side Plymouth Argyle.

'Gordon did well in several friendlies on our close season tour of New Zealand and Australia, but there is still a fair bit to do,' Waddington teased. 'He cannot see out of his right eye and we still have to work on trying to solve situations that this creates. Perhaps he is the only goalkeeper in the world who could possibly get back under these circumstances. With anyone else, retirement would have been automatic.'

Fans turning up at Home Park in Plymouth hoping to see the England goalkeeper make his comeback were, of course, left disappointed and John Farmer played instead. He performed superbly, ensuring Stoke won 1-0 with Geoff Hurst scoring the crucial goal.

Afterwards, Waddington toyed with the press as he was quizzed on the future of Banks. He simply told journalists that he would give them a definitive answer before the start of the league season, which was just a couple of weeks away. Asked whether Banks would be transferred to allow him to play at a lower class of football, Waddington responded, 'Either Gordon will play for us, or stay with the club in another job. There will be no stepping down the league.'

Stoke's progress in this rather curious competition gave Waddington the chance to give Banks a grand send-off at the Victoria Ground in front of his home fans. They thrashed Bristol Rovers 4-1 to set up a televised final against Hull City.

On the morning of the game, Banks finally revealed he was retiring at a pre-match press conference held with his manager sat alongside him. Waddington requested that the media leave Banks and his wife alone as he adjusted to retirement. He was also at pains to point out it was a difficult decision for both men. Holding up a finger against a thumb to illustrate a fine margin, Waddington said, 'Gordon was not much from playing First Division football again.' Banks mournfully responded, 'It was a difficult decision but my manager and I agreed it was the only one I could make.'

Instead of going out on to the Victoria Ground for a 'cup final' appearance, Banks sat out the game alongside Waddington in the directors' box, taking the applause of appreciative but saddened fans. His loss to the club, its supporters and Waddington was immense.

Their mood improved thanks to Stoke and Waddington claiming another trophy, one lifted on their home ground. Farmer, now Stoke's first-choice goalkeeper after several seasons as an understudy, had little to do as the League Cup-winning defence easily policed their Second Division opponents' strikers. At the other end, Jimmy Greenhoff put in a performance Waddington considered worthy of an England call-up, but it never came.

Greenhoff scored twice to ensure a 2-0 victory and Stoke became the proud holders of the Watney Cup, which they still possess today as the competition was scrapped after the final.

For Waddington and company there were more important competitions to focus on, to recreate their cup campaigns, and finally take a shot at a league title. They needed to do so after being robbed of the services of the world's best goalkeeper thanks to injuries suffered in a car crash on a Staffordshire country road.

12

A Footballing Bromance

'STOP pussy-footing, Hudson!' yelled the woman sat behind me in the crowd as Tony Waddington's latest signing danced around his Liverpool opponent in a mesmeric version of a 'working man's ballet'.

Ever since taking over as Stoke City manager, Waddington regularly sought a playmaker to weave his magic in front of an uncompromising wall of defenders. Usually it had been a wily old fox such as Stanley Matthews, Jimmy McIlroy, Peter Dobing or George Eastham, the latter pair having departed to retirement and coaching after their League Cup-winning heroics.

Now there was someone different, not a veteran of the beautiful game but a young player in his prime. Eastham even disparagingly joked of one of his Chelsea opponents after scoring his winning Wembley goal, 'I didn't see young Alan Hudson scoring.' His manager differed in his opinion of the precociously talented Londoner. Just a couple of years later Waddington pulled off an audacious transfer coup by signing Hudson, a player Stoke fans immediately took to their hearts, the one impatient fan behind me on his debut being an exception.

Admiration of manager and player alike was mutual. After trudging off the Wembley pitch in a losing cause, Hudson reflected on the contrasting merits of the Stoke and Chelsea managers. His boss, Dave Sexton, had, in his view, let Chelsea down tactically. Waddington, despite some of his own players' reservations over the extent of his tactical nous, had done the opposite and had got the better of his managerial opponent.

Hudson wrote in his loving tome, *The Waddington Years*, 'I must mention the ability of the opposition manager on that day. I believe that with Terry Conroy so dangerous out wide our manager should have looked back at the roasting David Webb was given a couple of years earlier in those wide open spaces in front of the twin towers against Leeds United.

'On that day it was Leeds United's Eddie Gray. On this day it was the turn of Terry Conroy. I blamed our manager. He had gotten away with it in the 1970 FA Cup Final but this time we paid the price for him overlooking the subject.'

Conroy's rampant runs finally paid off by setting up the winning goal for Eastham. Now Conroy was to become a team-mate, a man for Hudson to feed along with Jimmy Greenhoff. Waddington's signing of Hudson, making him the playmaking replacement for Eastham and putting him in the number ten shirt vacated by his League Cup-winning captain, was a statement of league title winning intent. Yes, Waddington had lost Gordon Banks and other senior players, but he intended to respond by rebuilding his team with star signings, making it one capable of bringing the league title to the Potteries for the first time in the club's history.

Yet in signing Hudson many in the game felt he was taking a risk. He was an immensely talented player unquestionably, but the midfielder's critics viewed him as temperamental, a flamboyant playboy wasting his talent. Waddington thought differently. It did not worry him that the opportunity to sign Hudson and his team-mate Peter Osgood only arose when the pair spectacularly fell out with Sexton. The bust-up dominated the back pages of national newspapers in the early weeks of 1974, light relief from the three-day week, and political turmoil dominating the front pages.

On New Year's Day Sexton dropped the pair for a game at Old Trafford. He also left out the goalkeeper Peter Bonetti. In Bonetti's case there was a reconciliation but Sexton made it clear that he was not going to offer up the hand of peace to Hudson and Osgood. After a training-ground meeting ended in a blazing row, Hudson and Osgood apparently refusing to train with the first team, the pair were suspended and transfer-listed.

As speculation raged over their futures, Stoke's name initially failed to appear. Queens Park Rangers, a team at the time oozing international-class players, were touted as firm early favourites for Hudson's signature, and championship contenders Derby County for Osgood. Neither move materialised. Managers at other clubs appeared wary of the players so yet again a gap opened up in the transfer market for Waddington to exploit.

As a naturally cautious operator he sought counsel from men in the game he respected, beginning with the Crystal Palace manager Malcolm Allison. As the two men negotiated the transfer of Stoke's utility player Stewart Jump to Palace, they discussed the shenanigans at Chelsea. In particular Waddington wanted to know what Allison, who was recognised himself as, to put it mildly, something of a flamboyant character, thought of Hudson. Allison was dismissive. 'Hudson! You've no chance,' Waddington recalled Allison telling him. 'Alan Hudson, he wouldn't step out of London by ten yards. You ain't got a cat in hell's chance.'

However, Allison agreed Hudson was a great player and that was enough reassurance for Waddington. He put in a bid for Hudson, and also one for Osgood, but the capture of Hudson was the priority.

To pull off the signings of Hudson and Osgood he needed to secure the support of the Stoke board. Despite a potential outlay of half a million pounds that support was forthcoming. Stoke's chairman, Albert Henshall, even ventured to the press the club would be prepared to go heavily into debt to secure the funds needed. 'Our manager [Waddington] contacted Dave Sexton [Chelsea's manager] and made a £500,000 bid for them,' Henshall told *The Guardian*. 'But at the moment Chelsea are not prepared to make it a straight cash deal, so we will just have to wait and see what happens.'

Stoke's desire 'to splash the cash' with money the club did not have must have made their bank manager nervous. He was blissfully unaware at the time, but Henshall's boast of being prepared 'to go heavily into debt' would later return to haunt him, the parlous finances of Stoke leading eventually to the departure of the club's most successful manager.

Chelsea's desire for an exchange of players rather than a straight cash deal was of little interest to Waddington and his chairman. It did not suit their ambition as at the time, money was no object. 'I am only interested in signing players and not letting anyone go. Money-wise there are no problems,' he reassured fans. He further asserted, 'If I decided to let a player go then we would be defeating our purpose of strengthening the side.'

Waddington's meeting with Hudson, hoping the Chelsea player would agree to uproot and move to the Potteries, came at a hotel on a winter's Friday afternoon. Hudson remembered being sat with Waddington on a wooden park bench outside the hotel to discuss the move, away from prying eyes. He was smitten.

'We shook hands. I remember it being cold, and sat quickly on a freezing wooden park bench,' Hudson recalled. 'I cannot remember any talk of money, just that he wanted me to take over the role of George Eastham, the player who was then the playmaker, which was more important to me than the greenback. After he rattled off the names of his previous inside-forwards, he had sold Stoke City to me and with them wearing red and white stripes I realised I was now fed up with being blue and you can take that more ways than one.' It was the beginning of a wonderful footballing bromance.

'Hudson is exactly the sort of player I've been looking for to push us right into the front rank of the First Division,' Waddington told reporters. Hudson, who had already more or less made up his mind to join Stoke after being charmed by its manager, told them, 'It looks promising. The terms are good. But you've got so much to think about, it blocks up your head.' He went off to see his wife, Maureen, discuss a move from the capital to a rural village just outside Stoke-on-Trent.

Crucially, he also discussed the move with his dad. If there were any doubts, these were banished by his father. 'I went to my father and I said I've just spoken to Mr Waddington,' Hudson remembered. 'My dad just turned around and said "sign for the man, just do it". The man is a genius. I'd never seen my father feel so proud to meet a man as when he met Tony.'

As far as father and son were concerned, Waddington had saved Hudson's career. The player was forever grateful.

'Fortunately for him and luckily for me the coast was clear, being the only manager interested in taking me and all of my troubles away from Chelsea Football Club,' Hudson wrote. 'I thought that Manchester United, with Tommy Docherty as manager, Arsenal or Tottenham Hotspur would be knocking my front door down, but it was only little old Stoke City from the backwaters of the Potteries where the Trent would soon replace the Thames.'

Hudson signed in a £240,000 deal, then a British transfer record. His impact on the banks of the Trent where it meandered alongside Stoke's old Victoria Ground was immediate. He pulled off a bravura performance on his debut against Liverpool, leaving Waddington and the Stoke fans swooning on the terraces and in the stands.

Hudson's bow came on 19 January 1974 in front of a crowd of more than 32,000 fans, a considerable boost on previous attendances that season. Liverpool, of course, were much vaunted opposition. But the Stoke fans came to cast an eye over Waddington's latest signing, not Kevin Keegan and his international team-mates. They left feeling that their side had been robbed, Liverpool equalising with the last kick of the game after an inordinate amount of injury time and spoiling an otherwise perfect day.

According to one commentator Hudson had played with 'a maturity and command that made him look worthy of the investment'. Another swooned, 'Hudson created an immediate impression – why not at £240,000 – with his brilliant distribution and faultless positional play.'

He had set up Stoke's goal for Geoff Hurst, a fierce drive rebounding off Liverpool centre-half Larry Lloyd into the path of the former England striker. Hudson went off the pitch as disappointed as his new-found fans at the 1-1 draw. Members of the Fleet Street press pack, having previously dismissed Waddington's record signing as an unreliable playboy, were mightily impressed by his performance. So too was another observer, Liverpool's manager Bill Shankly.

The ebullient Shankly sought out Waddington to congratulate him on securing his new signing. The delighted Stoke manager commented, 'I will always recall Alan's marvellous debut for us against Liverpool in 1974 when he won over the Potteries in our 1-1 draw. Bill Shankly came to me after the game and said, "I just want a quiet word with you in the dressing room." A quiet word was impossible for Bill, but he came in and paid Alan the tribute. "That was the greatest 90 minutes display I have ever seen from a player."'

It was some accolade. Hudson's virtuoso performance against the champions of England, though, had been brought out of him by Waddington. The player revealed prior to the game his manager had staged a full-scale practice match between the first XI and the reserves. Waddington handed Hudson a different-coloured shirt than everyone else and instructed his team-mates to immediately pass him the ball, and to no one else.

'He was making the point that we were going to play all our football through the midfield, and that meant me in particular,' Hudson wrote in his tribute book to Waddington. 'It was a great compliment and gave me the much needed confidence that I had lost at Chelsea, so overall it was the beginning of my love affair with him as regards him giving me complete responsibility to go out and play all over the field.'

Not everyone was happy with the arrival of Hudson, as the new signing himself noted. Mike Pejic refused to give him the ball, not just in training sessions but in matches, the left-back electing instead to keep possession and go haring down the wing. Terry Conroy, who was yet again spending time on and off the physio's table on Hudson's arrival, put this down to Pejic's 'rebellious' streak. 'He thought that Waddo was putting all his eggs in one basket and that the money could have been spent on several players,' Conroy reasoned. 'He also had a problem with the change of tactical emphasis Huddy's signing brought too, as he dropped deep to pick up the ball from the defence to start attacks.'

Conroy saw it not as a slight on Hudson but an example of the defender's battle with the management, openly questioning Waddington's tactics. Other players kept any reservations to themselves.

For all their differences, it is somewhat ironic the enforced departure of Pejic to Everton years later helped to, according to Waddington, trigger his decision to resign as manager in protest. In explaining his tactical deployment of Hudson, Waddington commented that it might have suited Stoke and the way he wanted to play the game but not Hudson's international ambitions.

Much to fans' bafflement, the England manager Don Revie only awarded him two caps. Most put this down to simply Revie's aversion to flair players. Waddington had other ideas. It was down to his deployment of Hudson in the Stoke midfield. 'I allowed him to play his natural deep-lying game,' he ventured. 'I often wonder whether the way we played him affected his England chances, but he always set up moves anywhere on the field. With a player of his talent I was not going to dictate the way he played.'

Waddington never believed in over-coaching players, certainly not naturally gifted ones such as McIlroy, Eastham, Hudson, and of course Matthews.

Prising Hudson away from Chelsea was one thing. Tempting his mate Osgood to move to the Potteries was quite another and much to Waddington's annoyance it proved impossible. Osgood sat in the stands to watch Hudson's debut, constantly pestered by anxious Stoke fans about whether or not he was going to sign for their club. As well as the supporters, he also kept an increasingly irate Waddington guessing.

The Stoke manager agreed terms with Chelsea and shook hands on a deal with Osgood but only then did Osgood reveal that he wanted time to talk to Southampton boss Lawrie McMenemy. Waddington immediately sensed the deal was off, just seconds after it was agreed.

'What the hell do you want to go there for?' Waddington asked the player. Osgood responded he had promised to inform the Southampton manager of his intentions and didn't like breaking a promise. 'If you go from here after just agreeing everything, you will go [to Southampton]. You will sign,' Waddington told him.

He had written Osgood off as a future Stoke signing and Osgood joined Southampton, the wrong move for the player as far as Waddington was concerned. He felt the addition of Osgood to his squad would have greatly enhanced their chances of winning the league title.

Osgood did go on to win the FA Cup with Southampton. He also helped to relegate them. In thinking that Osgood's arrival at Stoke would help to bring them not only more cup success but the league title, Waddington reasoned the England striker would make a perfect attacking foil for Greenhoff and Ritchie. Missing out on the signature clearly rankled him for years to come.

In Hudson he had had a sympathetic hearing. 'I think he [Osgood] reneged on the deal for all the wrong reasons by saying that they were not football reasons, but domestic,' asserted Hudson. 'Southampton were closer to his home and a part of the world that suited his lifestyle. They were the wrong reasons. Football comes first and foremost. I was annoyed with Peter Osgood, not because we were friends, but because once I realised that Tony Waddington was so very special to play for I knew that my mate would have been a revelation in front of the Boothen End. He would have possibly gone down as their greatest player ever.'

As it turned out, Hudson proved himself to be without doubt one of Stoke's greatest ever players, in one of its greatest ever teams, one on a par with the league title challengers of the late 1940s. After going toe to toe with the reigning champions Liverpool, a further sign of the 1970s side's growing potential came in a game against champions-elect Leeds United.

Leeds arrived in the Potteries hoping to equal a record going back more than a half century, the longest unbeaten run in the First Division of 29 games, set by Burnley in 1920/21. Stoke, boosted by the arrival of Hudson, were themselves in fine form, unbeaten for nine league games and slowly but surely climbing up the table.

The match, yet another bad-tempered affair involving the two clubs, began badly for Waddington's men. Denis Smith fouled Billy Bremner just outside the penalty area but before the Potters were able to organise their defence, Bremner took a quick free kick, chipping the ball into the net with goalkeeper John Farmer barely moving.

'Billy fell to the floor as if he had been shot, but as I was telling referee Homewood what a little sod Bremner was, up jumped the Scot to place the ball down for the free kick on the edge of the area and smack his shot past John Farmer,' recalled Smith. 'He'd well and truly done us. My protests fell on deaf ears.'

Minutes later, Allan Clarke put Leeds two up and the game had hardly begun but already looked over. But a hamstring injury to Leeds midfield playmaker John Giles on 20 minutes swung the encounter in Stoke's favour. Waddington's assistant Alan A'Court noted, 'Obviously Leeds without Giles were only firing on four cylinders instead of five.'

Growing in confidence, Stoke surged forward, winning their own hotly-contested free kick on the edge of the penalty area. Greenhoff slid the ball to Pejic, who promptly hammered it into the net. The Leeds defenders' inability to cope with John Ritchie then led to the equaliser as his craning header knocked down the ball for Hudson to score. The sides went into the dressing room at half-time level at 2-2 with Leeds rattled.

For the delighted Stoke fans, it seemed difficult to believe from how the game was panning out that their side began as underdogs with their opponents clear favourites not just to win on the day but also to claim the league title. Stoke dominated with Leeds's defence having to play in front of a goalkeeper carrying an injury. David Harvey's handling became more and more erratic as he hobbled about with his left foot and ankle heavily strapped up.

Yet Stoke, despite their ascendancy, struggled to score the winner until it eventually came after successive corners taken by Jimmy Robertson, a fresh signing of Waddington's from Spurs. His third was met by a diving header from Smith, which turned out to be the crucial goal, but once he scored the game deteriorated with both sets of players not only arguing with each other but the referee.

Don Revie reacted furiously after the final whistle. Some Stoke apprentice put their heads round the door of the dressing room to tell the celebrating first-team players of Revie's cup-throwing antics in the away changing area.

Revie's mood was darkened by the knowledge, unbeknown to the winning scorer at the time, that an offer to sign Smith had been rejected by Waddington. Leeds had put in a world-record fee for a defender back then of £250,000, but it was turned down flat.

Waddington's verdict on the game? 'Leeds need no sympathy. They are a very good team. The bare figures will at least confirm that for posterity,' he commented. Leeds went on to win the title, the last domestic honour for Revie before he took over from Sir Alf Ramsey as England manager. In turning down the bid for Smith to replace World Cup-winning centre-back Jack Charlton, Waddington once again made it clear to his rivals he had title-winning ambitions of his own.

Stoke were no longer to be treated as a backwater club down on their luck.

Sir Alf sat in the crowd of more than 39,000 watching Stoke humble Leeds. Alongside him sat Terry Conroy, nursing his latest injury and admiring the quality of the football being played by his mates. 'Waddo was purring about how we were playing,' recalled Conroy. 'Our success was based on the fact that the manager trusted us to go out and play. We played off-the-cuff cavalier football. Team talks if we had them at all, were cursory. Waddo wasn't a great rabble-rousing speechmaker.'

Instead, in Conroy's view, Waddington trusted his players to deliver. 'It's that simple', he asserted. 'He put the team together and let us get on with it. It was then up to you to play well enough to select you the following week.'

Putting faith in his players paid off, Stoke winning nine of their 18 games with Alan Hudson in the side in the latter part of the 1973/74 season. 'For the rest of the season we felt we could beat anybody. Those were happy days,' summed up Hudson. It was enough to secure fifth place in the league, banishing memories of their shaky start to the season, and securing a return to European football.

For this adventure, Waddington recruited a surprise helper, a man he unwittingly helped to get the sack. He was the man who scored against Stoke on Waddington's managerial debut back in the 1950s, 'old big head', Brian Clough.

13

Title Challengers

'CLASS is permanent, form is temporary' is the regular clichéd mantra glibly quoted by sportsmen, sportswomen and their fans, but there is plenty of sense in the sentiment.

One factor only occasionally mentioned is luck. Tony Waddington quite often felt down on his luck as it deserted him with excruciating regularity. Notwithstanding a few unlikely cup victories, lifting a major trophy in the guise of the League Cup despite not being given a prayer by pundits, the sporting gods often conspired against him and his team. They had done so in the FA Cup against Arsenal, not just once but twice. They did so as Waddington's side embarked on their first and only serious challenge for the league title.

English football in the 1970s enjoyed genuine competition among a host of teams, including Stoke. To compete with the best in the land his players, regardless of their undoubted talent, needed luck on their side, especially with a relatively small squad embarking on a gruelling league campaign. To be successful one key vagary in the roulette of team sport comes into play. It is avoiding serious injury, putting the best possible starting formation on to the field.

Waddington, in the club's first championship challenge in decades, ended up cursing his luck, quite possibly, though he never admitted as much, as his own decisions, especially in the transfer market.

It was the summer of 1974 and everyone connected with Stoke City felt bullish – fans, players, the board and of course a man by now seen as one of the venerable leaders and elder statesmen in the game of football, manager Waddington. The fixture list threw up some intriguing early challenges and on the club's return to European football, the UEFA Cup draw meant a daunting tie. Ajax of Amsterdam, aristocrats at the time of European football, were on their way to visit the city of pits and pots.

For the opening fixture of the league season, Waddington's men faced the team humbled by them only months earlier as Leeds United were to visit as league champions. Leeds arrived with a new manager in charge, a man revered by football fans across England, but crucially not the Football Association big-wigs and apparently the players he inherited from the previous manager Don Revie. Brian Clough was to meet up with his old mate Waddington.

Pre-season had been fruitful if eventful. A tour to Cyprus coincided with the Turkish invasion of the island, Waddington describing his team's departure home to England as 'beating a hasty retreat'. He also acquired a new player while on tour to Cyprus, the Sheffield United winger Geoff Salmons.

At the time he described Salmons, a player costing £200,000, as the 'missing piece in Stoke's jigsaw'. He told the press, 'Salmons has always caused us a lot of trouble when we played Sheffield United. I am delighted to sign what is a rarity these days, a left-sided midfield player.'

Later he would have reservations despite Salmons becoming something of a fans' favourite. 'I saw him as a replacement for George Eastham, who was forced to retire. Salmons was a great character who never quite took the game seriously enough,' Waddington remarked when reflecting on his managerial career.

'Salmons had pace, skill and a great left foot but never really settled in as well as I had envisaged.'

However, for the season-opener against Leeds he settled in quite nicely along with the rest of the team.

Few realised at the time how much disarray there was within the Leeds camp with the arrival of Clough, the country's most charismatic manager. A less-than-charitable Charity Shield match at Wembley the previous weekend provided a clue with the club's skipper Billy Bremner being sent off along with Liverpool's Kevin Keegan for engaging in a punch-up.

The next clue came on the opening day of the league season, a 3-0 thrashing at Stoke. It took most observers by surprise, but not Waddington. 'The forecast is bright for smooth Stoke,' concluded *The Guardian*. It noted, 'Stoke took the league champions to pieces, wrapped them in three neat parcels, and despatched them, care of Brian Clough, to Elland Road for analysis.' 'Shocker, Clough clobbered!' commented the *News of the World*. In a nod to the Leeds captain's travails the *Daily Mail* offered, 'Hudson outshines "no bite" Bremner.'

Waddington's side, with Hudson imperious in midfield, was a match for any team in the land, including the reigning champions. 'We played well enough in the first half to be three goals up yet Stoke deserved to win,' Clough lamented. Leeds had been in the game at half-time, finishing stronger, Farmer in goal for Stoke keeping the score at 0-0.

Fans sat behind Waddington even urged him to take off John Ritchie, the centre-forward looking to be a mere spectator. By the end of the match they were no doubt relieved that the manager ignored the advice of what he wistfully termed 'the fans' selectorial committee'.

Hudson ran riot in the second half, setting up goals for John Mahoney, Jimmy Greenhoff and Ritchie. 'We fancied ourselves to win this one,' Hudson dryly commented post-match. 'It was a ding-dong first half. We had the first 20 minutes. They had the next. But we dominated in the second half.'

Stoke thrashed the champions 3-0 and made top-class international players such as Bremner and his Irish team-mate John Giles look average. They played some scintillating football yet far from plaudits coming Waddington's way, instead he was about to suffer brickbats.

These happened to be dark times in English football. The England national team was absent from that year's World Cup in West Germany and fans went on the rampage as soccer hooliganism struck at epidemic levels, the English 'national disease' leaving its scars both at home and abroad. On the opening weekend of the 1974/75 season supporters clashed at railway stations and football grounds across the country. In the capital newly-relegated Manchester United's hooligans were to the fore, clashing with Arsenal followers at Euston station before later going on to fight running battles with yobs supporting Leyton Orient.

Football's failure to acknowledge the hooligan problem infuriated the sport's critics. Comments such as, 'Our fans are a bit of an embarrassment to the club at times but we would rather have them as an embarrassment than not at all,' the words of Manchester United boss Tommy Docherty, hardly helped. Much to his bafflement, Waddington joined Docherty in the dock at the court of critical opinion.

To counter the spectre of hooliganism, teams needed to play a more entertaining brand of football, critics of the game reasoned. They demanded better behaviour from players, a show of more respect to each other and the referees. Only then, given an alarming drop-off in attendances, the theory went, would casual fans come back to the terraces and help revive a game suffering, for the doom-mongers, an alarming slump in popularity.

Opening-day attendances at English league matches for the 1974/75 season were down by 43,000 at just under 600,000 but Stoke's fixture against champions Leeds bucked the trend. Waddington's entertaining brand of football, with his playmaker Hudson leading the opposition a merry dance, left spectators purring with delight. He had met the requirements to boost the image of what some feared to be a dying game. Yet bizarrely the poison pencils were being sharpened for Waddington by a curious army of detractors in the national press.

Queens Park Rangers, playing an expansive brand of football, quietly established themselves as contenders for major honours. More importantly in the court of public opinion, their 'easy-on-the-eye' style made them Fleet Street favourites.

Throughout his managerial career, Waddington, despite his undoubted public relations skills, struggled to counter a perceived metropolitan bias, a tendency to dismiss his club as nothing more than provincial upstarts. His patience with the national press was put to the test as Stoke arrived in west London to play QPR, fresh from the demolition of Leeds. His team won the game but failed the PR test. 'Stoke win two points and lose friends' raged *The Times* in reporting the 1-0 victory.

Its correspondent Geoffrey Green wrote that Stoke went home like a 'Staffordshire dog with a tail to wag, providing yet another feather in the cap of all those clever but dreary, backroom tacticians who are doing their best to ruin the game.' He groaned further, 'As it was the result was a travesty of justice, but typical of the type of modern defensive planning that has permeated and deadened much of sport.'

Years later, Green, by then an old sage, told me that as a young journalist he considered a ban from the Victoria Ground for his criticism of Waddington and Stoke City as a feather in his own cap.

Yet his criticisms were nothing in comparison to those offered in the *News of the World* by former Northern Ireland captain and future Arsenal manager Terry Neill. 'Tony Waddington, Stoke's boss, who is supposed to be a disciple of flowing, attacking football should be embarrassed with what his side served up,' ranted Neill, under the nom de plume Terry McNeill.

'Never mind the result which was patently unfair to Rangers. What is more important is what Stoke have done for football. The game is being choked to death by hooligans, and the one thing that can take the real fan's mind off the carnage is bright, imaginative stuff on the field. And what did Stoke players come up with? A performance of such suffocating boredom that hundreds were driven away before their time.'

Those leaving early at the sight of what Neill and his companions in the press box must have considered to be the re-erection of Waddington's Wall missed Geoff Hurst's last-minute winner. Stoke's fans went home delighted, so too Waddington. But the criticism irked.

Frankly it was unfair. There was no doubt a man colourfully depicting football as 'a working man's ballet' believed in entertaining those coming through the turnstiles to view the beautiful game. Neill, among others, knew full well this to be the case. As for serving up free-flowing football as an antidote to the growth of hooliganism, Waddington liked to recount the tale of a trip to the Vatican to meet Pope Paul VI. He went along with his chairman, Albert Henshall. They were there to be offered praise by the pontiff for Stoke's brand of entertaining football, an antidote to the chaos on the terraces.

Stoke had just played AS Roma in the now-defunct Anglo-Italian Cup at Rome's Olympic Stadium, winning 1-0. 'I can remember going into the dressing room at the end of the game and I thought everyone would be happy,' Waddington mentioned in an interview years later. 'They were all sat crying. It was tear gas that the soldiers had fired all over the place.'

The game had been marred by running battles between Italian riot police and Roma fans, many intent on violent political protest as much as straightforward football hooliganism. The irate 'ultras'

(Italian football hooligans) were angered by the club president's political allegiances. That was of no interest to the Stoke manager and his team as they beat yet another hasty retreat from violent conflict, this time under armed guard. Roma officials arranged the audience with the Pope as means of an apology for the traumatic experience. The pontiff, a man Waddington described as 'very knowledgeable' about the game of football, offered advice which struck a chord with the Stoke manager. It would have been brought to mind as he was being attacked in the English national press, blamed for not doing his bit to counter and curb hooliganism.

'He [the Pope] said it was particularly important that I get the message over to the players that they do nothing on the field that's going to antagonise or in any other way that's going to create problems where the younger people have got something to latch on to,' recalled Waddington of his papal audience. 'Make sure that your players are so well behaved that they don't give any kind of opportunity for young people to go out there and imitate them.'

In recalling this advice, Waddington expanded on his football philosophy, one at odds with the musings of his critics. 'I myself feel that there is too much hype put on the games in itself that then are made far too serious in every shape and form,' Waddington observed in the late 1980s. 'Football is still and should be always still a sport. And yet the way it is being conducted at times, it's like a war, like a battle. This is where football has got to look into its own particular background to find some way to stop hooligans invading the pitches and so on.'

A return to European football, this time in Amsterdam rather than Rome, won back many of the friends supposedly lost by Stoke for having the audacity to play defensive and counter-attacking football. In coming up against Ajax, Waddington and his players faced arguably the sternest test of their careers, an impossible task. Yet it was one they only narrowly and agonisingly failed to complete.

Waddington's assistant Alan A'Court recalled the encounter as a match-up of two like-minded footballing outfits. 'Tony would like to play a lot of skilful football,' he said. 'He [Waddington] would like to play pure football. Sometimes it wasn't easy to do that because you would play some sides who would try to destroy you by physical means. But when we went to Ajax we were playing against a club that was noted for attractive football.'

It meant both sets of fans were in for a treat, though not at times for a section of sceptical Ajax fans. They were already disgruntled by the controversial sale of Dutch legends Johan Cruyff and Johan Neeskens to Barcelona, so were less than impressed by Ajax struggling to see off a team many had never heard of.

As an exhibition of free-flowing football, the first leg at the Victoria Ground failed to live up to expectations. The *Stoke Sentinel*'s correspondent Peter Hewitt dismissively wrote that Ajax 'failed to please the Potteries audience with their possession tactics and spoiling offside trap, but they certainly impressed with their all-round skill and control, which was a standard above those of English clubs'.

Ajax's tactics took Waddington and Stoke by surprise, possibly because preparations for the tie had been unusually shambolic. George Eastham, by then on the coaching staff, had been deputed to go to Amsterdam to scout their much vaunted opponents. His flight out though was fogbound so he failed to make the trip and going into the game, Stoke had no scouting report on their opponents.

In an era when video footage of opponents was hardly abundant, this put Waddington's Stoke players at a disadvantage. They struggled to adapt to the Dutch side's style of play, allowing Ajax to take the lead and conceding a crucial away goal when skipper Ruud Krol hit a bullet of a shot past John Farmer. Krol had been given time and space to shoot, possibly because his opposite number Alan Hudson was not fully fit after recently suffering injury in a car crash and played with his right hand in plaster. He was also under the influence of painkillers.

Stoke needed to win but ended up playing catch-up and in the last quarter-hour Ajax backed off, allowing the Potters to take control. That paid off for Stoke as a free kick from Mike Pejic was touched on to the post and Denis Smith followed up to prod in the equaliser.

A draw at home against such a formidable side and conceding an away goal felt like a defeat to dispirited fans. But Waddington and his players learned lessons and remained optimistically determined to go through. 'We felt we knew enough about them to give them a good game over in Holland,' commented goalscorer Smith.

Ajax also unwittingly helped to further motivate the Stoke manager and his players by displaying a large degree of arrogance and complacency. Their manager Hans Kraay promised in the build-up to the return leg to field six forwards with the intention to, in his words, 'pulverise' his opponents.

His comments, which were meant to appease critical Ajax fans after the departure of Cruyff and Neeskens, left Waddington unfazed. 'Six forwards? That will suit us down to the ground but I'll believe it when I see it,' he commented. 'In our position of having to win we can't afford preconceived notions. We know a lot more about Ajax now because we were taught something of a lesson in the first leg. But we can only try to play as we have been doing and continue to aim for consistency in our approach. If we play to our capabilities we don't have to fear anybody, six forwards or not.'

Sat alongside him as he made those comments to reporters, his guest nodded in approval. Just weeks earlier Brian Clough suffered humiliation, watching his team of champions being played off the park at Stoke. It helped to expose his fractious relationship with his players and ultimately led to him being infamously sacked by Leeds after just 44 days in charge. Among the first to pick up the phone to console him was Waddington. He also offered him a ticket for a flight to Amsterdam along with the Stoke squad.

'The trip allowed him to relax,' Waddington explained. 'It is important that a man of his ability is not lost to the game,' he added. 'If by a simple invitation to Brian we keep his interest in football alive, then it must be to the good of the game as a whole.'

The gesture of inviting Clough to Amsterdam brought widespread praise for Waddington. Clough repaid him five years later by inviting Waddington to join the Nottingham Forest squad on their journey to lifting the European Cup. 'See you at East Midlands Airport. The tickets are in the post. You are travelling with us,' Clough gruffly told Waddington.

'It was quite an education for Brian insisted that I sat with him and Peter Taylor on the touchline in the final despite the fact that I had tickets for the directors' box,' remembered Waddington. He concluded, 'He was direct and honest and it was a pleasure to be in his company. He more than repaid that gesture of mine.'

Sadly Clough's presence in Amsterdam failed to inspire Stoke to victory. But they did come mightily close thanks to one of the most impressive performances in the club's history.

In a frantic start to the game Pejic and Ajax's Henk van Santen both had their names put into the referee's notebook for their own kicking match, a clash played minus the football. Geoff Hurst, easily the club's most experienced international and European campaigner, then uncharacteristically lost his cool with the referee and was booked for dissent after arguing for a corner when the Romanian official awarded a goal kick. Luck deserted him for the rest of the game as his Stoke team-mates settled down around him and began to dominate while Ajax's boast of teaching their visitors a footballing lesson proved idle.

Waddington's men, with Hudson prompting in midfield, controlled matters and as they laid siege to the Ajax goal in a desperate search for a winner disgruntled home supporters began hurling seat cushions in protest. They scarcely believed their team of European footballing aristocrats were being outplayed by a club with only one major trophy to show for a century of endeavour. Greenhoff came close to scoring the elusive goal, forcing a string of saves from Dutch international goalkeeper Piet Schrijvers before going off injured. Jimmy Robertson replaced him and agonisingly saw a goalbound shot deflected wide in the final seconds of the game but Ajax hung on to claim victory on away goals thanks to Krol's decisive goal at the Victoria Ground.

It was bitterly disappointing for Waddington, his players, the 1,500 travelling Stoke fans and thousands more sitting glued to their radio sets back home in the Potteries. Denis Lowe of the *Daily Telegraph* described the Ajax victory as 'hollow'. 'Tony Waddington and his team can take heart from a stylish performance,' he added. *The Guardian*'s Paul Wilcox wrote of a 'sense of injustice'.

But sadly, for all the hard-luck stories, Stoke failed to meet the basic requirement of scoring a goal, something Waddington fully recognised. 'When the disappointment clears you look to see something you have gained from it and we gained the satisfaction of hearing Ajax say how unlucky we were,' he reasoned. 'We are still left not scoring goals but if we needed encouragement about our football going in the right direction this performance brought it.'

His opposite number Kraay, the target of Ajax fans' derision on the night, offered curious praise. 'Stoke's tactics were a disappointment to me,' claimed Kraay. 'Not because I didn't like them, but because they took away the advantage all continental sides experience when they play English teams. English football is excellent when it is in England. But when English teams bring that football outside their country it plays into our hands. Stoke did not do this. They did not come at us so innocently and we could not get behind them like we expected.'

The credit went to Waddington. In summing up, his assistant A'Court recalled, 'When we talked to the Ajax players and the management they were very respectful to the Stoke team and officials, particularly Tony because they could see that they talked the same language.'

Unbelievably, Stoke almost knocked out the former Dutch and European champions by playing a brand of total football so synonymous with the Netherlands national team and the country's club sides of the day, but it was scant consolation. They were still defeated.

Although out of Europe and no doubt feeling down on their luck, Stoke returned to domestic competition with renewed confidence. There were major domestic trophies to be won, including the ultimate prize of the league title but the campaign, in between the ties with Ajax, had faltered largely because of an alarming goal shyness, and also because the team seemed cursed with injury, the most serious to John Ritchie. It set a bewildering pattern for the rest of the season, the entire campaign beset by injuries to key players.

Playing away to the leaders Ipswich Town, Stoke seemed capable of securing a draw or possibly a valuable away victory but in the 55th minute Kevin Beattie tackled Ritchie. It left the Stoke centre-forward laying prone ten yards from the trainers' dugout with his left leg broken. Stoke went on to lose 3-1 but the result seemed of little consequence. Ritchie had suffered a double fracture of the fibula and tibia, the career of a fans' favourite over.

Rather than blaming Beattie, a future England defender, Waddington rounded on the referee, Brian Daniels, and his bosses at the Football League. Daniels had deemed Beattie's tackle fair and waved play on as Ritchie writhed in agony with his leg broken. The match only stopped when the Ipswich coach Cyril Lea took matters into his own hands by sportingly going on to the pitch to attend to the Stoke player.

Waddington submitted to the FA a personal report on the officiating of the fixture, in which Stoke's defender Alan Dodd was also sent off. 'I cannot be charged with bringing the game into disrepute for drawing attention to these things,' Waddington ranted to reporters. 'The Football League made a serious mistake by appointing a referee living comparatively locally. Justice was not seen to be done. Mr Daniels was left wide open to any allegations of bias. I know that the Ipswich people were very unhappy about what happened.'

He chose his words carefully but the consistent suggestion of refereeing bias in favour of Stoke's opponents irked many in the game. Waddington and his chairman Albert Henshall's regular visits to the Football Association's disciplinary committee for criticising officials brought them a degree of notoriety, a blemish on their remarkable tenure in charge.

Given Ritchie's career-ending injury and Hurst coming to the end of his playing days, it seemed logical for Waddington to go out and reinforce his team with a striker. He did have an emerging talent in the forward line in Ian Moores, but the latest graduate of the Stoke schools and youth team system was lacking experience, although he earned an England under-23 call-up thanks to a couple of impressive performances on his breakthrough into the Stoke first team.

'He's been on the fringe of breaking through with Stoke for some time, but we have introduced him gradually,' Waddington told *The Guardian*. 'He is a big well-built lad, and has plenty of skill. We have high hopes for him.'

It was coded language for Moores being a future prospect rather than one for the present. Given the absence of goals across the team, Waddington needed an experienced and proven striker. He had tried and failed to lure England international Francis Lee to the club on three separate occasions. He first tried to sign him in the summer of 1967 from Bolton Wanderers but Lee went to Manchester City. By the summer of 1974, Lee was back on the transfer market. 'Before moving he rang me to say, "I am just on my way to Wolves. It is just a matter of seeing the set-up, but I am not going to sign,'" Waddington revealed. 'But before I could make a move [to sign Lee for Stoke] he had signed for Derby.'

Waddington gave up on the search for a forward and instead he once again went out to secure the signature of a goalkeeper. Just seven years after usurping Gordon Banks at Leicester City, Peter Shilton tasted his own medicine with the emergence of young Mark Wallington. Waddington, much to the bafflement of some of his own players, put in a bid for England international Shilton and asked him to follow in Banks's footsteps. In John Farmer, an England under-23 international, Stoke had a more than adequate goalkeeper. He had made way for Banks on his arrival at the club, ably deputised for him and rose to the task of once again becoming first-choice goalkeeper after the England legend's tragic car crash.

But all along Waddington had his doubts. A jittery performance from Farmer against Chelsea at Stamford Bridge quite possibly influenced Waddington's thinking. It was the second meeting of the two sides in just four days and Stoke had just thrashed Chelsea 6-2 at the Victoria Ground, a performance in keeping with their growing reputation for purposeful, attacking football, so they went to London confident of victory. It didn't materialise thanks to a last-minute goalkeeping clanger.

Three times Stoke took the lead and three times Chelsea equalised, the last goal coming as the referee was about to blow the final whistle when Farmer flapped at a cross and Ian Hutchinson equalised. Chelsea went into their dressing room delighted but Waddington felt the exact opposite.

Denis Smith recalled it as the moment that Farmer's career was effectively over. 'Waddo, fuming at another series of errors by John, decided he had to act,' Smith recalled. 'That goal cost a vital point, which would have seen us climb into third place. If we had true ambition to win the championship we could not afford any more such incidents. It was a defining moment for John. Waddo moved to bring in a new goalkeeper.'

As a result of his manager's ruthless decision, Farmer just a few months later decided to retire from the professional game at the age of just 27.

'Supporters will wonder why I did not persevere with John Farmer,' Waddington mused to the *Stoke Sentinel* years later. 'At 18 he was an outstanding prospect and played for England under-23s five years ahead of his time. I was never confident about playing young keepers at the top level. As they were learning their trade, they would always be making mistakes that could prove costly.'

Farmer, at the time of the signing of Shilton, was no longer a 'young keeper'. He was an experienced campaigner, a goalkeeper with a rapport and understanding with his defenders and they were all, Farmer included, local lads. But Waddington reasoned, 'When I bought Banks I thought I was buying time for Farmer. He was a perfectly built young man who seemed to be forever plagued with muscular injuries and it was only natural that he should lack some confidence after Gordon's accident. He needed to train with greater dedication to give himself a chance.'

The final stinging rebuke highlighted an alleged difference between Farmer and Shilton, a fitness fanatic. Waddington decided to sign up another disgruntled Leicester City and England goalkeeper.

'Peter Shilton was the obvious target for Stoke,' insisted Waddington. Only in later years would he hint he thought in hindsight the hiring of Shilton may have been a mistake. There were other team-building priorities. Waddington, true to form as a manager obsessed by the qualities of the man in the number one jersey, went for a goalkeeper. He did so for a British record fee.

Waddington refused to disclose the exact sum, merely saying it was somewhere between the £320,000 originally offered by Stoke and the £350,000 demanded by Leicester City. It meant that in the space of less than a year Stoke, a club only averaging gates of just over the 20,000 mark, had spent more than three quarters-of a million pounds on players, an astonishing outlay for the era. The Stoke directors had backed their manager, making it known they were happy to put the club 'heavily into debt'. It was up to Waddington to deliver another trophy, the league title a distinct possibility.

For all his admiration of Waddington, Alan Hudson vehemently criticised the signing of Shilton by his old boss. 'I was surprised on joining Stoke City to find John Farmer, who had been capped at under-23 level, to be such a capable goalkeeper and that is why I was shocked by the signing of Peter Shilton for such a vast sum of money,' Hudson reasoned. He recognised that Shilton was a great goalkeeper but believed by and large Farmer had not let his side down. There was no need to sign the England international. 'He was never happy at Stoke,' Hudson dismissively suggested. 'I think he thought he was bigger than Stoke.'

His old mate Jimmy Greenhoff agreed as did other players. Terry Conroy was a little less strident in his criticism. 'There was no better goalkeeper around. But was that what we needed at the time?' Conroy wrote in his autobiography. He concluded, 'I genuinely think that we wouldn't be worse off having John Farmer in goal. For whatever reason it didn't gel for Shilts. His time at Stoke wasn't anywhere near a halcyon period.'

Significantly, Smith had few quibbles with the signing of Shilton. He fully understood Waddington's reasoning. 'Given the opportunity any of us would swap a club goalkeeper for the one lauded as the best in the country, if not the world,' Smith wrote. But his praise was qualified, pointing to Shilton's frailties as a Stoke player, something he would not later display in goal for Nottingham Forest under Brian Clough as the club lifted two European Cups just a few years later. 'Great goalkeeper though Peter Shilton undoubtedly was, his three years at Stoke were probably the worst of his career,' Smith commented. He pointedly added, 'Perhaps we'd been spoilt with all those years playing with Gordon Banks.'

Though Smith had no problem with the initial decision, he recognised it as a mistake in hindsight. 'It's my belief that Waddo made a mistake with Shilts,' Smith reasoned. 'He overreacted to that one particular match [the Chelsea away game] in which John Farmer made a couple of mistakes. I'm not saying that John was the best out there, Shilton would prove to be that in time, but Shilts was not the right man for our club and our team.'

At the time though Stoke fans excitedly welcomed Shilton to the club. His arrival at the Victoria Ground showed the manager and the board meant business and it proved a catalyst for an immediate boost in fortunes. As Shilton made his debut away to Wolverhampton Wanderers, Stoke sat sixth in the table. The game was drawn 2-2 and Shilton's performance was described as 'breathtaking', although he was beaten by a last-minute equaliser from the penalty spot. A week later the Potteries club went to the top of the league table.

Shilton made his home debut on a typically wet and windy November night in Stoke against QPR, when a ninth-minute goal from Geoff Hurst was enough to secure the win as Shilton once again impressed. The result meant that Stoke were just a point behind the leaders Manchester City in third place in the league table ahead of a match at the Victoria Ground against Shilton's former club, Leicester City.

Jimmy Bloomfield, the Leicester manager, no doubt regretted selling Shilton just the week before. Mark Wallington, the man to replace him, had broken his wrist in training, leaving the club without an experienced goalkeeper so Carl Jayes, at the age of 19, unexpectedly found himself making his league debut, but it turned out to be a fine one.

Once again Waddington and his ground staff served up a mudbath of a pitch, one suiting the skills of Hudson, Salmons and Greenhoff. 'Instead of spoiling the game the mud heightened the drama, emphasising the fitness, commitment, and the skill of the modern British footballer,' extolled *The Guardian*'s correspondent. Stoke battered the Leicester goal only to be foiled by their opponents' teenage stopper and it seemed the game would end in deadlock. But in the dying minutes, John Marsh crossed to Moores, who failed to control the ball only for it to run loose to Smith, who smashed it into the net. Once the final whistle went, the excitable public announcer bellowed over the speakers, 'Newcastle United 2 Manchester City 1, so Stoke go to the top of the First Division.'

Waddington tried to dampen rising expectations in the Potteries as fans harboured serious hopes of their team winning the league title for the first time in the club's history. He warned that the league leadership would change hands week by week right up until the end of the season. No team, he believed, would put together a string of winning results. 'Such a run is unlikely,' he suggested. 'The struggle could go on right to the end of the season, and then be decided on goal average.'

And he darkly predicted, having already suffered the misfortune of losing a couple of key players, 'It is one of those seasons when you need luck as well as a good side.'

An emphatic 3-0 away victory at Birmingham City kept Stoke at the top of the table and left the fans seriously believing they had realistic hopes of celebrating championship glory. Greenhoff scored two of the goals in the first half-hour before hobbling off injured. Stoke went on to win comfortably but in what became the story of the season for Waddington and Stoke, Greenhoff's early departure meant another of his key players had ended up on the injury list. Waddington, the man stressing that luck would play a part in any title challenge, was also about to suffer the curse of winning the Manager of the Month award.

Waddington was hailed as November's Manager of the Month for 1974, winning a gallon bottle of whisky as a reward. His team, true to form in these circumstances, then went on a losing run, beginning at Leeds with Greenhoff missing from the side. Leeds avenged their crushing defeat at the start of the season with a 3-1 victory. 'We never looked like we would get taken over,' Hudson recalled on reaching the top of the table before 'Lady Luck' yet again deserted the side. 'We had a hiccup at Leeds when Greenhoff didn't play. We didn't have a full side out. If we'd had won that we probably would have gone four points clear.' Instead Stoke were knocked off their perch. They possibly had the chance to go back to the top of the table with the visit of Arsenal but blew the opportunity. Significantly, Greenhoff was still missing thanks to his broken nose.

For the first time Stoke fans also witnessed Shilton's seeming lack of understanding with his defenders. Smith noted that Gordon Banks would not only command his area, barking orders to defenders, but was also adept at dealing with through balls. Shilton was not. On this occasion Arsenal's Peter Simpson punted a hopeful ball forward to the onrushing Alan Ball and Brian Kidd. Shilton got to the ball first but failed to control it, leaving Kidd with an easy tap-in. Just before half-time, Kidd made it 2-0.

As Moores struggled with a knock thanks to some vigorous treatment from the Gunners' defenders, Waddington replaced him with the old stalwart Eric Skeels and bizarrely decided to send Smith up front to play alongside Hurst but the novel tactic failed and Stoke pressed but to no avail.

Worse was to follow at Coventry on Boxing Day when winger Jimmy Robertson was stretchered off in the first minute of a game Stoke went on to lose 2-0. X-rays showed that he had suffered a fracture just above his right ankle. After John Ritchie's enforced retirement and with Terry Conroy in and out of the side thanks to his dodgy knees, Waddington had lost yet another striking option. He had spoken of the need for 'luck' in prosecuting a title-winning campaign but it was infuriatingly absent.

In such a tight title race, just one win would put them back on track and a home game against fellow title challengers West Ham United provided an ideal opportunity. This time, with

Greenhoff back in the side along with Conroy, Stoke took their chance. West Ham went into the lead but Stoke equalised thanks to a hotly disputed penalty. The referee judged that Bobby Gould had knocked Smith off the ball in the penalty area, something the irate Hammers players considered an impossibility, but Geoff Salmons took the penalty and scored.

Stoke's winner came thanks to a stinging 30-yard shot from John Mahoney, one that goalkeeper Mervyn Day was only able to tip in off the crossbar. Hurst, maintaining his predatory skills, knocked the rebound into the net to secure the points and after a losing three-game streak, Stoke were back in the title race. It was turning into a gruelling marathon for the players, the fans and a manager constantly cursing his luck.

Against Manchester City in a televised game in early February, Stoke demonstrated their championship credentials to the nation with a consummate performance, once again dancing around flailing opponents in the Victoria Ground mud. Hudson was in his pomp, orchestrating attack after attack from midfield. Smith was as uncompromising and unyielding as ever in defence. A scything foul on the City forward Dennis Tueart prompted a ghoulish section of the Stoke crowd to sing, 'Nice one Denis, nice one son, nice one Denis, let's have another one.'

The only surprise was it took until just a minute before half-time to open the scoring with a header from Moores. Once Hudson added a second with a goal of individual brilliance in the 66th minute the metaphorical floodgates threatened to open, but Stoke had to settle for just two further goals from Hurst and Moores.

The emphatic result effectively ended Manchester City's own championship hopes for the season and put Stoke back in the title race. A 2-0 victory at Tottenham Hotspur then saw them back to the top of the First Division table.

But their joy was short-lived and once again the injury curse struck, this time in a pulsating game against Wolverhampton

Wanderers. With just five minutes to play at the Victoria Ground, Stoke were two goals down and without Mike Pejic, the left-back carried off the field with a broken leg.

He was the Potters' third broken-leg victim of the season with a fourth soon to follow, as Waddington slowly but surely kept losing key players to injury.

The manager would, though, have been comforted by the display of character shown by his men, especially Pejic, who remarkably insisted on seeing out the game despite his injury. In those dying moments, Conroy and then remarkably Eric Skeels scored to secure their side a 2-2 draw. Given the trying circumstances, it felt like a victory.

After a goalless draw at Luton, Stoke remained top at the end of February but were once again cursing their luck. Described by one press box scribe as an 'odd mixture of cudgels and callisthenics, capable of producing football which possesses an almost balletic grace', words no doubt appreciated by Waddington, they ought to have won. They failed to do so thanks to their own profligacy and once again falling victim to, in Waddington's view, some awful officiating.

Just before half-time Hudson felt convinced he had scored, nonchalantly knocking the ball over the line. It was cleared before hitting the net and the referee waved play on, eventually signalling a corner rather than a goal. 'I was ten or 12 yards out and rolled the ball into the net. It was in!' ranted Hudson. 'There was no one there, else I would have blasted it. It was two yards over the line by the time John Ryan cleared it. I was fuming.'

To add to Stoke's woes, Salmons fired a penalty wide. Stoke remained top but this was a lost opportunity. A 2-0 defeat to Middlesbrough the following week meant they lost top spot in the table and it would never be regained.

They did, however, battle on despite the constant setbacks, giving other championship contenders a 'bloody nose' on the way.

A victory over eventual champions Derby County on that club's very own Baseball Ground mudbath of a pitch revived hopes. The farmyard conditions suited the home side but the cloying mud also suited the visitors.

Derby took the lead rather fortuitously, a pot-shot falling into the path of Kevin Hector, who nipped in to slip the ball past Shilton. Stoke persevered with Salmons a constant threat on the left wing and he was rewarded with a cross spectacularly being volleyed into the back of the net by Greenhoff. Then, in the last minute, Greenhoff headed in the winner to the delight of Stoke's travelling fans, some of whom had angered Waddington and the Stoke board by fighting running battles with Derby supporters.

Waddington preferred his club to be praised for the balletic skills of his footballers rather than come under scrutiny for the thuggery of some of their fans. 'His main concern was playing the game properly,' observed Hudson. 'And by going to Derby County and playing the eventual champions off their own field after being a dubious goal down was the kind of performance he expected from his up and coming team.'

In summary, Waddington wanted the media focus to be on the dogged and admirable determination of his talented group of players as they sought to overcome adversity in what was proving to be an attritional season. He did not want the focus to be on misbehaving fans.

A victory at the Victoria Ground over fellow contenders Ipswich Town, just three days later, would have gone a long way to propelling Waddington's men to eventual glory. Instead, they lost.

Significantly they also lost yet another key player as Denis Smith, no stranger to broken limbs, became the fourth broken leg victim of the season. It was the fifth time that Smith had suffered a broken leg in his career. 'It proved to be a dreadful day for the club and for me personally,' recalled Smith.

TITLE CHALLENGERS

With less than a quarter of an hour to go, Stoke, who seemed a little jaded after their exploits at Derby, were 2-1 down and Mick Lambert threatening to race forward to score a third goal. Instead, Smith clattered him just outside the penalty area. 'I broke my own leg,' Smith explained to reporters in a post-match interview. 'I tackled Mick Lambert and it was just one of those things.'

If he hadn't have hobbled off, he would have been sent off. Given Waddington had already used up the one substitute allowed at the time, Stoke were down to ten men anyway, and Ipswich hung on for a vital victory.

For Stoke, it was a crushing home defeat, only the club's second of the season. 'It was that defeat to Ipswich when I thought we'd blown it,' Hudson later revealed. He also blamed his old mate Peter Shilton for the winning Ipswich goal. 'Shilton wanted a huge wall for a free kick on the byline so we didn't have enough numbers left to mark Whymark. I couldn't understand it. It was a sucker punch.'

Nevertheless, despite any despondency, Waddington and his players refused to give in. The busy Easter weekend fixture programme gave them the ideal opportunity to reassert themselves in one of the tightest league title battles in decades.

First up they had to visit the capital, West Ham on Good Friday morning, followed by a match against Arsenal at Highbury the following day, and on both occasions they were held to frustrating draws. Terry Conroy, restored to fitness after his enforced lay-off, came back in fresh and in scintillating form, scoring both goals in the 2-2 draw at West Ham. Frustratingly, he then hit the post when looking certain to score a winner in the 1-1 draw with Arsenal.

Despite those disappointing results, Waddington believed the title could still be won provided Stoke beat the leaders Liverpool on Easter Monday. He blamed fatigue for the failure to return from London with a couple of victories in the space of 24 hours and had less than 48 hours to prepare for what he considered to be the biggest game of the season. For the players, many of whom were renowned for playing as hard off the field as on, he ordered a brief period of rest.

Among those grounded was Hudson, a player suffering from a chronic ankle injury. Unless the game could be played on a soft pitch, he would miss out. Waddington had a simple solution and, as in the days of Matthews, he called for the local fire brigade.

There had not been a drop of rain in the Potteries for days but Waddington once again cunningly claimed that the Victoria Ground had its own micro-climate resulting in its pitch turning yet again into a bog. He kept quiet about the role of firemen until long into retirement. 'It only rained at the Victoria Ground, no rain sighted from Birmingham to Liverpool,' Hudson recalled. 'He [Waddington] had brought the fire brigade in overnight in the middle of a drought and absolutely soaked the entire pitch, not missing a blade of grass.'

Almost 46,000 fans, including a sizeable contingent making the short journey from Liverpool, crammed into the ground, creating a frenzied atmosphere. They witnessed Waddington's mud-larks run amok against the title favourites. The first goal came from a hotly disputed penalty, Liverpool's defenders claiming John Mahoney had been felled outside the area but the referee disagreed and pointed to the penalty spot, before makeshift centre-forward Conroy stepped up to open the scoring.

Just after half-time Conroy put Stoke two up. Hudson bamboozled Tommy Smith, who spent the entire afternoon flailing in the mud, and Conroy nipped in to prod the ball past Ray Clemence into the net. Greenhoff almost made it 3-0, only to see Phil Neal hack the ball off the line but it was still an emphatic victory. 'I have always insisted on the skill factor and it was there today,' commented a delighted Waddington. 'Our football was out of this world. Magnificent.'

A grateful Hudson purred, 'That day was my finest in a red and white striped shirt, in fact, any coloured shirt, and not just because of the importance of the match but the fact that the manager had planned everything perfectly.'

He repaid his manager's faith in him by competing with the goalscorer Conroy for the man-of-the-match honours.

The following weekend Conroy scored twice as Stoke beat soon to be relegated Chelsea 3-0, Greenhoff scoring the other goal. The title was in sight but only if they won their last three games, all against teams languishing in mid-table mediocrity. Frustratingly a 2-0 defeat to Sheffield United at Bramall Lane effectively ended any title hopes, ironically the same club to end Stoke's dreams of winning the league championship back in the 1940s.

Waddington and his 1970s Stoke side had run out of luck, unable to compensate for a string of injuries to key players. In hindsight some of Waddington's players felt his laissez-faire attitude contributed to ultimate failure. 'Our belief in our devil may care methods may well be why we didn't have tangible silverware to show for all that hard work,' reasoned Conroy. In assessing the final three fixtures – Sheffield United away, Newcastle United home, and Burnley away – he believed there ought to have been a team meeting to plot the future and assess tactics.

It never took place.

'Waddo's theory was that because we'd had success playing off the cuff we should stick to our guns. Looking back now – and hindsight is a wonderful thing, I know – we were the best team in the league, but we didn't go on and win the league because we didn't talk through how we were going to get three wins from those last three games. I just think that if we'd approached them in more detail, with more forensic detail and been given a bit more guidance, maybe we'd have emerged victorious.'

It was reluctant criticism of a man the Irish forward greatly admired. 'We'd run out of puff. Whether it was the injuries taking their toll or the lack of cohesion at that vital moment, who knows,' he concluded with an air of resignation.

Smith, one of those injured players forced to watch from the stands in the last couple of months of the season, felt much the same. He also pointed to the money splashed out on a goalkeeper rather than a striker as a factor. 'If we'd won those last three matches we'd have won the league by a clear point,' Smith reflected. 'Instead we picked up just the two draws and failed to score a goal. That decision to invest in Peter Shilton and not a striker came home to roost.'

Hudson's assessment of his goalkeeper was blunt. 'I felt that Shilton really let us down,' concluded Hudson. Unlike his teammates, he was careful not to question Waddington's judgement in signing Shilton in the first place.

It is harsh to suggest that Waddington and his players blew their chance of being crowned league champions in 1975. Given a string of setbacks throughout the season, it is remarkable they came so close. They did so while being recognised by most impartial observers as the best pure footballing side in the land, albeit one with a hard edge in the guise of its uncompromising home-grown defenders.

Fans looked forward to a bright future but sadly a storm was brewing, financial, political and physical. Little did Waddington realise, as he reflected on a lost opportunity to win the title, that it would mark the beginning of the end of his tenure at the Victoria Ground.

14

The Roof Caves In

A STORM was coming, heralded as potentially the storm of the century. Weather forecasters predicted widespread devastation to greet the New Year of 1976. They turned out to be right.

An Atlantic storm wreaked havoc across the Britain and Ireland. The English Midlands, with the Potteries nestling in the Pennine foothills of the Staffordshire Moorlands, bore the brunt of wild gusts of wind raging up to 100 miles per hour.

By the time the clear-up began, more than 30 people had been killed throughout the country with scores of others injured. Power lines had been brought down, rail services ground to a halt, and the cost of repairs ran into millions of pounds.

One unforeseen casualty was Stoke City's Victoria Ground, specifically its Butler Street Stand. Few at the club realised at the time the eventual bill for repairs would ultimately mean the sale of players, and cost their manager his job.

Those gales, battering the ageing Victoria Ground in the early hours of the morning on 2 January 1976, ripped the wooden barrel roof off the Butler Street Stand. As almost a footnote to its general account of the carnage left by the storm across the nation, the *Stoke*

Evening Sentinel reported that 45 feet of one of the stands had been blown away.

At first there was no sense of panic from either the board of directors or the manager. Contractors were called in and attempts were made to try to repair the damage in time for an FA Cup replay against Tottenham Hotspur, although they failed with the roof further giving way just hours before the planned kick-off, injuring one of the workers.

Tony Waddington looked on from the side of the pitch as the roof caved in. 'The roofing had, in fact, been passed by consultants,' Waddington told the *Sentinel*. 'But the wind got up just around noon and I saw it collapse.

'It was all over in a flash. I ran across the pitch yelling for anyone in the area to get clear but one of the builders did not make it. He was cut about the face by flying debris but we are happy to hear it was nothing really serious.'

The long-term implications for the manager and his football club had yet to be realised. It had already been a difficult few months for both parties but their fortunes were about to deteriorate even further. A roof collapse threatened to turn into the catalyst for financial collapse.

Waddington and his board of directors might have earlier concluded their luck was out after the narrow failure to secure the championship in the previous season. A fifth-placed finish, they believed, was enough to earn European football with a place in the UEFA Cup. They were wrong.

Both Merseyside clubs, Liverpool and Everton, had finished above Stoke in the table and under the rules in place at the start of the 1974/75 season, only Liverpool would be allowed into the UEFA Cup, under a one-club-per-city regulation kept in place since the days of the tournament's predecessor, the Inter-Cities Fairs Cup. Indeed, the Football Association nominated Stoke on the recommendation of the Football League.

Everton objected and UEFA backed the Merseysiders, insisting, regardless of the criteria being used by the English football authorities, that it had abandoned the one club per city rule. An incensed Waddington raged, 'Everton's bellyaching is hardly dignified. They knew at the start of the season about the rule and if the thing is handled fairly then Stoke must be in. We are very upset at the way this thing has been dealt with. There will be serious discussions within this club to see what steps to take if we are not included in next season's UEFA Cup.'

Waddington and his club, though, were powerless. Their final chance lay at the annual meeting of the Football League with Chelsea putting forward a formal motion to scrap the rule, much to Waddington's anger. He suggested that Chelsea, who had been relegated the previous season, concentrated on 'putting their own house in order'. He further ranted, 'The entire credibility of the [Football] League is at stake because under the conditions laid down we have qualified. It is certainly not going to be in their interest if the League do an "about face" at the end of the season on the rules they made at the start.

'The League must show strength by sticking to their nomination and we are not prepared to let this matter rest. There is a principle at stake and we are also fighting the matter in the view of concern for our supporters. They stayed with us to the end of last season because of the promise of Europe and this is also reflected in our season ticket sales.'

But it was clear that there was little sympathy for Waddington and Stoke from the directors and managers of other clubs, notwithstanding any personal concern for the health of Stoke's chairman Albert Henshall. He came off his sickbed while convalescing from heart surgery to plead unsuccessfully for a place in the UEFA Cup.

'I will always be grateful for the support and encouragement the club's late chairman Albert Henshall gave to me,' recalled

Waddington years later. 'I accompanied Mr Henshall in 1975 when he visited a Birmingham specialist to be told he needed a serious heart bypass operation. It was near the end of the season when at one stage we looked to be in with a chance of the First Division championship. The specialist took me aside and said that, as I appeared to have some influence over Mr Henshall, would I tell him that if he did not have the operation performed immediately he would not see the end of the season. Mr Henshall had his delicate operation and was still convalescing some months later when the annual meeting of the League took place in London.'

Henshall made what Waddington described as an 'impassioned' speech but it was to no avail. 'Unfortunately all his pleas failed to prevent the rules being changed. It was a classic case of a stab in the back,' lamented Waddington. It was a setback but a relatively minor one compared with the collapse of the roof of one of the Victoria Ground's stands just six months later.

Up until the New Year of 1976 Stoke had enjoyed an erratic season. A fresh title challenge appeared to be out of the question but another chance to compete in the UEFA Cup seemed a realistic target. Unfortunately for Waddington he was prevented from going out into the transfer market to further reinforce his squad. The club was heavily in debt thanks to his earlier spending, a financial outlay approved by a board claiming it was happy to go deep into the red. For all the sparkling football on offer from his players, declining attendances also meant the income stream into the club was drying up.

Waddington perceptibly realised that not just Stoke but other football clubs could not go on solely relying on gate money for the majority of their income. In responding to the FA's refusal in the summer of 1976 to sanction shirt sponsorship, he commented, 'The way the game is going to change from the point of view of players and the way it is played means that there has to be changes. Football cannot afford itself at present.'

THE ROOF CAVES IN

What Waddington badly needed to help to generate funds was a decent cup run. Once the Butler Street Stand roof caved in, such a success became a financial imperative. It did so mainly because remarkably the ageing stand, with its wooden barrel roof, was not fully insured. As Waddington explained, his board began haggling with the insurers over the cost of the repairs. 'Naturally the club had taken out "an insurance" in the event of storm damage,' he said.

'However, during the course of the repair work, another part of the stand came down. It was a bone of contention by the insurance company that the premiums covered the initial weather damage, but they would not accept responsibility for the remaining condition [of the stand]. In the end the club had to find £250,000 to replace and repair the entire roof, which added to the considerable financial problems.'

Slowly but surely, the Stoke board and their manager began to realise the club faced severe difficulties. They still hoped to simply patch up the damage but it proved impossible and the roof had to come off. Effectively, a new stand needed to be built, but the money to do so was simply not there. In a match programme the board admitted the roof collapse had 'hit us like a bomb'.

As the wooden timbers were being carted off, in one case by full-back Mike Pejic to his farm in the Staffordshire Moorlands, the Stoke board secretly plotted a fire-sale of players. Only a lucrative return trip to Wembley would give Waddington any chance of keeping his talented squad together.

Before taking on Spurs in the FA Cup, Stoke needed to temporarily find a new home. Staffordshire Police had ordered the closure of the Victoria Ground for safety reasons while demolition crews moved in to completely rip off the Butler Street Stand roof. It was hoped that the work would be completed in time for the cup tie but not an imminent league game at home to Middlesbrough.

Waddington did not want to postpone the fixture and leave his players without a competitive game before taking on the Londoners, and neighbours Port Vale offered to help despite suffering some damage to their own ground during the storm. The damage there, though, was considered relatively minor. Turnstiles and outside toilets had been damaged with bits of asbestos left strewn all over Vale Park. The threat to public health from asbestos, though recognised at the time, was not taken as seriously as it is now. It was quickly cleared up and Vale Park made ready to allow Stoke to host Middlesbrough.

Vale's club secretary Richard Dennison explained, 'Football is all about making friends and helping people. It was right that we should go out of our way to help Stoke, for the last thing they wanted was a blank weekend and fixture congestion if they want a cup run.'

It was a magnanimous gesture from fierce local rivals, albeit ones not kicking a ball in anger at each other in almost two decades. Stoke players were even allowed to train on the Vale Park pitch in preparation for what was about to become, in extraordinary circumstances, football history with Stoke playing their first league game at a 'neutral' venue, the first and only top-flight match at the home of Port Vale.

It turned out to be a dour encounter, one witnessed by around 20,000 fans, myself included, five times the average gate for the Third Division Valiants. A moment of magic from Alan Hudson with just a couple of minutes left to play proved decisive, floating past four Boro players before passing to Ian Moores to stab the ball into the net from close range.

Waddington did not hesitate in blaming his opposite number Jack Charlton for the dire fare on offer, criticising Middlesbrough's alleged defensive mindset. 'The way Middlesbrough played it was poetic justice that we should score with almost the last kick,' Waddington told baffled journalists at the post-match press conference. Both sides, in their view, had played poorly. He explained further, 'We had to be patient and it helped in a way playing here. On our own ground the crowd's frustration gets to the players, but they were so far away that we were able to keep playing steadily.'

During Waddington's final years in charge at Stoke, a curious pattern developed in criticising the fans, both those failing to turn up largely because of justified fears of crowd violence and those going along but choosing to heckle rather than cheer on players.

The Victoria Ground was a tight, old-fashioned venue allowing fans to vent their frustration as much as trying to encourage their footballing heroes. Vale Park, built in the 1950s and rather pretentiously dubbed the 'Wembley of the North', offered wider spaces between the pitch and the terraces. It perhaps explained the flat performances of both sets of players. But Denis Smith offered a more prosaic explanation, describing the match as 'a sideshow to the soap opera which was unfolding behind the scenes'. Waddington had more to worry about than the odd disgruntled fan.

Stoke were a club in trouble, one desperate for that cherished financially lucrative FA Cup run. The team had yet to get past the third round though. Even if they overcame First Division rivals Tottenham Hotspur, another high-flying club lay in wait in the guise of Manchester City. Much to the fans' delight and Waddington's relief, they managed to win both.

Neither of his regular full-backs, Mike Pejic and John Marsh, were available to the manager for the Spurs game. Pejic had been taken to hospital after being substituted at half-time against Middlesbrough with a mystery stomach complaint. His exertions from the day before in carting out the wreckage from the Butler Street Stand could hardly have helped.

Their absence meant Shilton's goal came under pressure, but this particular storm was one Stoke were able to weather. Tottenham did take the lead with a goal from Steve Perryman but Stoke soon equalised through Moores, a player about to become one of the first to be sold by Waddington in the fire-sale demanded by his board, coincidentally to Tottenham.

With just a few minutes left some unselfish play from Greenhoff gave Moores another glorious chance to score, but his shot was palmed away by a Spurs defender. Geoff Salmons scored from the penalty spot to secure victory and put Stoke in the fourth round of the FA Cup for the first time since moving on to the last of their epic semi-final encounters with Arsenal four years earlier. Could this finally be their year? Waddington was no doubt saying his prayers.

Given the bank manager and the board were about to pressurise him into his selling his best players, Waddington's effusive praise of Greenhoff after winning the Spurs replay is significant. 'The crowd here take time to accept star quality players, but Jimmy has got through to them,' Waddington crowed. 'No one can play his type of game half as well.'

He then went on to take a swipe at Greenhoff's former manager at Leeds United and the then England manager Don Revie, who much to his frustration had been ignoring not just Greenhoff, but also Hudson and Pejic for regular England call-ups. He also ignored Smith, despite trying to sign him for Leeds. 'The trouble is that when someone like Don Revie tags you it sticks,' Waddington claimed. 'It is so easy to put a label on players and the idea got around that Jimmy was not keen on getting stuck in, yet he is constantly having to take tackles from behind and still gets past people.'

It was clear that Waddington began to share his friend Brian Clough's antipathy towards Revie. More importantly given events to follow in the transfer market Waddington revealed he could in his words, 'easily have sold him [Greenhoff] for far more than we [Stoke City] paid Birmingham City many times, but I have always resisted'. As of January 1976, his captain was not for sale. Little did Greenhoff and his team-mates realise that Waddington's board had other ideas.

THE ROOF CAVES IN

A few days later Manchester City arrived at the Victoria Ground for what turned out to be an ill-tempered cup tie, ending in a row between Waddington and his counterpart Tony Book. Far from conducting a version of 'a working man's ballet', Book accused Stoke's players of resorting to thuggery.

Pejic took the brunt of the criticism, returning to the Stoke side only to be sent off for allegedly headbutting Dennis Tueart. 'There was no contact whatsoever,' Waddington fumed. He accused Tueart of deliberately taking a tumble to get Pejic sent off. In response, Book raged, 'I had a very clear view of the incident. He was struck on the bridge of his nose and has the bruises to prove it. He also had two stiches in the back of his head.'

As for Stoke's approach to the game, Book witheringly commented, 'Nearly all my players have had to have treatment for lacerations and bruises. I've never commented about an opposing manager before, but this time I have to speak out. Tony Waddington has got to put his own house in order before he picks on players from other clubs. He seems to have appointed himself judge and jury, not only over opposing players, but the match officials and the FA disciplinary committee.'

The Manchester City boss, in his verbal assault, questioning his Stoke counterpart's conduct, conveniently ignored the high frequency of Waddington and his errant players being hauled up before the FA to be admonished for a string of misdemeanours, perceived or otherwise. Book's tirade appeared over the top after his team had lost 1-0 thanks to a late goal from Greenhoff. They had come up against 'Waddington's Wall', the very final version, but the man himself didn't care. Wembley was in sight.

This time he had nothing but praise for the ecstatic Stoke fans, relishing his team's trademark match of defensive steel and silky attacking flair. 'The crowd were magnificent,' he said. 'If they get behind the lads like that in every game we shall win the Grand National as well as the league and the FA Cup.'

Cup fever ensured a near capacity crowd at the Victoria Ground for an eagerly-anticipated fifth-round tie against lower-division opposition. Fans of their opponents, Sunderland, also turned up in droves. As the Durham pits closed, their miners moved to other coalfields including north Staffordshire. Exiled Sunderland supporters made their voices heard along with thousands of their relatives and friends journeying south for the game to the Potteries. This was much to the frustration of Waddington and his players, as at times they out-chanted the restless and increasingly muted home support.

Stoke dominated the game and huffed and puffed but could not score. Overwhelmingly the favourites, they were, in the end, grateful to hold on for a goalless draw. Stoke's disgruntled players were left bemoaning the vociferous nature of the away fans in contrast to the muted reaction of the frustrated home faithful. In the replay at Roker Park, Waddington admitted his team had been 'swamped'. They only lost 2-1 but Sunderland deserved to win by more. Stoke were out of the FA Cup and Waddington had been robbed of his financial lifeline.

As his dejected players trudged off the Roker Park pitch, none realised how grave matters were for their club. Reflecting on the cost of reconstructing the Butler Street Stand, Smith commented, 'Of course we thought it was a really bad thing to have happened but we didn't realise quite how disastrous until little whispers began emerging from the offices into the dressing room that there was a major problem on the horizon.'

He expressed his disappointment that nobody at the club, including Waddington, bothered to sit the players down and tell them of the plan to sell some of them to cover the reconstruction costs. Instead it came out in 'dribs and drabs' in the media. Terry Conroy admitted that he hadn't 'a clue' about the seriousness of the club's financial situation until players began to leave, especially the eventual departure of the captain Greenhoff to Manchester United.

THE ROOF CAVES IN

At first Waddington allowed his younger players to depart, midfielder Sean Haslegrave to Nottingham Forest and Moores to Tottenham Hotspur. Waddington warned Clough that Haslegrave was not his 'type of player' and he would 'kick him up the arse'. Clough, who was bizarrely impressed by Haslegrave's show of petulance and anger at being substituted in Stoke's UEFA Cup tie at Ajax, disagreed. He snapped him up for £50,000 only to offload him to Preston North End a couple of years later.

Moores went to Spurs in August 1976 for £75,000 with Waddington later trying to justify this transfer on footballing grounds. 'Moores never really fulfilled his potential,' explained Waddington. 'He was a local boy who just lacked self-confidence, especially in home games.'

At the time, another couple of promising local boys were pressing for first-team places, winger Kevin Sheldon and striker Garth Crooks, both with top-class potential. The sale of Moores and Haslegrave barely raised the faintest murmur of dissent even from the most critical of Stoke fans. All seemed well at the club. But the bombshell transfer of club captain Greenhoff three months later changed perceptions for good. It could not be justified on footballing grounds and Waddington's Stoke were in a parlous state.

During the summer of 1976 the club posted a profit of £87,873 for the previous season, impressive but making little impact on reducing the overall debt accrued during Waddington's spending spree. This debt was now compounded by the insurers of the Butler Street Stand, the figures revealed, only stumping up £80,000 for repair costs then estimated at £150,000.

As with any large-scale building project, those costs were set to spiral and after a board meeting in August 1976, the Stoke directors admitted the eventual cost was set to rise to an estimated £1m. To appease concerned fans, director Percy Axon boasted, 'This will be one of the finest stands in the land on completion.' This promise never quite materialised.

Additionally, much to Waddington's consternation, the board planned to build a modern stand at the Stoke End of the ground, behind one of the goals. 'My maxim was always to use finances not only to improve facilities for spectators but to improve the entertainment on the field,' Waddington argued. 'The two requirements go hand in hand and too many clubs have found it impossible to cope after major ground redevelopment. I always took the view that team rebuilding was more important than ground development.'

His board, under pressure from the banks to settle the club's massive debt and also struggling to meet new ground safety regulations introduced after the 1971 Ibrox Stadium disaster in Glasgow, disagreed.

'We were under pressure constantly and were getting letters from our bank manager at ever weekly board meeting,' remembered Waddington. 'The implication was that we had to sell a player quickly. The five directors helped by putting £10,000 each into the account and the bank agreed to increase the overdraft by £50,000 for the pressures were still intense.'

Those directors were anxious to secure their loans to the football club and wanted their money back. The easiest way was to sell top players by attracting six-figure sums for them. Remarkably one player they had in mind was the club captain, and they regularly quizzed Waddington at weekly board meetings on whether any offers had been made for Greenhoff.

Much to Waddington's dismay, the Everton chairman had made a direct offer for Greenhoff to his old friend, Albert Henshall. Once Henshall agreed to the sale, Everton's manager Billy Bingham was on the phone to Waddington. The irate Stoke manager tried to fob off his rival, insisting the matter would have to be discussed at a meeting of the club's board. Given that his chairman had already agreed to the sale Waddington must have realised arguing against the sale at any meeting of the Stoke board was futile. Acting, as he put it, in the interests of the player he approached his old club Manchester United to gauge any interest in signing Greenhoff.

'I pointed out his popularity at the club and felt he probably would not leave the club anyway,' Waddington remembered telling his board of directors. 'I was left with little alternative. Everton had offered £100,000 but mentioned to the board that there was only one club Greenhoff would wish to join and that was Manchester United.'

Waddington reasoned that Greenhoff might agree to move to Old Trafford because his brother Brian was already playing there. Manchester United's manager Tommy Docherty offered £130,000, a fee Waddington reluctantly accepted on behalf of his club. He then had what he described as the thankless task of informing Greenhoff.

The bemused player recalled the fateful moment in an interview with the Stoke City fanzine, *Duck Magazine*. 'We were in the social club at the ground for lunch as usual,' remembered Greenhoff. 'We were a close bunch and always ate together. I got a message that the gaffer wanted to see me on the pitch. I found it strange as we didn't have a game. So I walked down the tunnel and there was Waddo in the centre circle, looking up at the Butler Street Stand. I said, "Crikey gaffer, what a mess that is eh." Waddo replied, "Yes it is Jimmy, but it gets worse."'

Waddington then informed him of the emergency board meeting and the directors informing him that the Butler Street Stand was not insured. He had to sell someone to pay for the cost of repairs. That someone was Greenhoff.

The player was stunned. He did not want to go. 'It was probably the most ridiculous transfer of all time,' lamented Waddington in an interview for a Stoke City club video produced in tribute to him some years later. 'He was extremely popular. He was a truly great player. He'd done tremendous service for the club and was still young enough to do it once more and he went for just over £100,000.'

The fee had been reduced thanks to some last-minute haggling directed by Manchester United's former manager, Sir Matt Busby, still a big influence at the club. Indeed his intervention gave Waddington hope of scuppering the deal, especially as Greenhoff was reluctant to go. 'Greenhoff wanted a meeting [with the board] to know where he stood for he did not want any recriminations,' Waddington recalled. 'At that meeting it was accepted that he would be staying with us. Then one director, with the mounting pressure from the bank, said, "There is no way that we can turn down six figures for a player who is 31." Greenhoff said quietly to me, "That's it, boss," and he actually signed for United on lower wages than he was getting at Stoke.'

Greenhoff recalled of the board meeting, 'We were all sat there; the gaffer, me and the directors. I told Waddo and everyone I didn't want to leave. "So what's this all about, Jimmy?" asked someone. "It's about me telling you that I don't want to leave," I replied. After a while someone got up and said, "To be honest, Greenhoff, we think you're past it." I was only 30. They didn't mean it, but it was a way of getting me to go. So I stood up, looked at Waddo and said, "I'm really sorry gaffer, I'm signing for Manchester United." I never wanted to go.'

Denis Smith, the man appointed captain in place of Greenhoff, recalled both his manager and team-mate in tears. 'He [Greenhoff] loved it at the club and cried when he was told by Waddo that he had to go. Waddo cried too.'

Those tears were also shed by fans furious at the sale of one of their all-time favourite players and nothing Waddington or his chairman might say would appease them.

Throughout the Greenhoff transfer saga, Waddington maintained his affable public image. In contrast, his board managed to further infuriate the fans. Members of the board blamed the sale of players on declining revenues from gate money, fans failing to turn up at the Victoria Ground in large enough numbers. Crowds had dropped alarmingly to an average of 16,000. Disenchanted supporters suspected the disappointing gates were not the only reason for Stoke's financial woes. Like Waddington and Greenhoff, they only had to cast their eyes towards the wreckage of the Butler Street Stand.

Just 18 months after watching their side challenging for the league title, Stoke fans feared the spectre of relegation. 'Mr Waddington and the board are now walking a tightrope,' warned one irate fan in a letter to the *Stoke Sentinel*. 'Two or three losing games after the Greenhoff blunder will see crowds of much less than 16,000 and the transfer fee will be small consolation for the threat of Second Division football.'

Another supporter expressed his 'bafflement' at Waddington going to 'great lengths' to say Greenhoff was being transferred because of the club's financial position while his chairman Albert Henshall argued it had nothing to do with finance.

Waddington must have shared that feeling as the sale of Greenhoff was also not enough to solve Stoke's financial problems. 'One hopes the board do not expect the entire £1m estimate [of rebuilding the Butler Street Stand] to come from outgoing transfers,' mused the *Evening Sentinel*'s Stoke City correspondent Peter Hewitt. Otherwise, he warned, 'Manager Tony Waddington has little chance of his ultimate ambitions.'

His optimism, a suggestion of Waddington reinvigorating his side yet again and inspiring them to more trophy success, appeared in the opinion of most fans unwarranted. They feared the sale of more quality players. They feared relegation. They were proved right. The next out of the club was the man Waddington treated as if he were his own son, the enigmatic playmaker Alan Hudson.

Quite remarkably and maybe mischievously the national press speculated that Hudson had fallen out with Waddington. Their relationship had soured, according to the pundits, but that simply wasn't true. Hudson wanted to leave because, in his view, Stoke no longer harboured trophy-winning ambitions. If anything, it was a club in decline.

'I couldn't see Stoke winning anything,' Hudson told reporters after being transferred to Arsenal for a £200,000 fee. 'I wasn't happy with the way things were going.' On speculation that Hudson had fallen out with his manager, the player retorted, 'People have said I had a lot of rows with manager Tony Waddington at Stoke, but that's impossible with that man.'

The deal had been brokered on the insistence of his board. Waddington wanted Hudson to stay, pleaded with him to stay. The night before the deal went through Waddington phoned him at home. 'He was in tears,' revealed Hudson. 'I was really choked. He's such an incredible fella.' In his biography of Waddington, Hudson recalled, 'The night before, Tony would not sanction the move and would sign nothing. He told secretary Bill Williams he wanted nothing to do with it at all and that was the way it was left. My wife Maureen said he cried outside the ground as he pleaded with her to talk me out of going to Arsenal, that the bank manager had changed his mind and the club had some money to pay my wages. I never saw him. I don't know why. It was a blur, it was as if I had never been there before once picking up my boots.'

At the time, Waddington appeared sanguine. He told the *Daily Mail*, 'I had to go into those deals [the sale of Greenhoff and Hudson] against all my managerial instincts. I have lost two tremendous players. Yet unfortunately in this country today the financial climate is such that provincial clubs such as ours have to take advantage of the kind of proposition put to us by Arsenal. A manager in a position like this knows he cannot possibly win.'

Waddington no doubt knew that in blaming the sale of players on the state of the national economy at the time, he was being more than a touch disingenuous. Stoke's financial woes were by and large of the club's own making, spending beyond its means in the transfer market, a bold policy scuppered by the bank calling in its debts. The bank's demand was compounded by being forced, following a dispute with insurers, to take on the bulk of the cost of rebuilding a stand wrecked in a gale.

For all his stoicism, the enforced sale of Greenhoff and Hudson came as a hammer blow for Waddington, one from which he never recovered. His skipper Smith, not just his defensive talisman but a boyhood Stoke supporter, observed, 'Waddo knew he was being forced to sell his best players and when he parted company with Alan Hudson, who had been like a son to him, it was obvious that not only had the heart being ripped out of the side but it had been ripped out of our manager.'

As Waddington found himself being strong-armed into selling his best players, his board offered him a curious vote of confidence. It came in the form of an extended contract. 'Tony will reach the managerial retirement age of 55 in November 1979,' explained chairman Henshall. 'That's the middle of a season so we have extended the contract to May 1980. Mind you, we hope that he'll then consider accepting another contract.'

Waddington, to the day he eventually died, remained stubbornly loyal to his old friend Albert Henshall. This personal loyalty, in the troubled last few months of Waddington's time as manager, was hardly reciprocated by the chairman and his board. Yet just months before Waddington's departure from the club, effectively being given the sack, Henshall crowed to *The Sun*, 'Tony's been with the club so long we look upon him as one of us, the managing director. There is complete trust. Obviously there are troubles. We don't always agree. But we always resolve them [our differences] in a friendly way.'

To reaffirm his confidence in his manager, Henshall added, 'Never in his 16 years as manager has Tony been in danger of the sack. We need our manager. We like him and trust him.'

Those comments led *The Sun*'s columnist John Sadler to hail Waddington as a 'freak' and a football manager 'in no danger of losing his job'. As for Waddington himself, he told Sadler that the admiration between chairman and manager was mutual. 'Football management has to be the most ridiculous way of earning a living. It's crazy,' he explained. 'When I think about it, I can't understand how others do the job without the relationship I have with my board. If you're at odds with them it can't work. It's essential to have a close position of trust.'

But, a bit like the roof of the Victoria Ground's Butler Street Stand, Waddington's professional relationship with his board was about to collapse.

Once Hudson returned to London, Stoke went on a disastrous run of eight games without a win, including five defeats and three draws, with just one goal scored. Waddington seemed powerless to stop the disastrous slide down the league table and his players were simply not good enough.

There were occasional signings of veterans to bolster the side, such as John Tudor from Newcastle United and Alan Suddick from Blackpool. Tudor and Suddick were not, however, of the calibre of veteran players Waddington had picked up in the cut-price transfer window of the 1960s. 'They proved my biggest disappointment in the transfer market', summed up Waddington. 'Both signings simply did not match up with the type of players we had become accustomed to signing.'

Just to compound Waddington's woes, it hardly helped that the curse of injuries to key remaining players struck yet again. Promising winger Kevin Sheldon, an overnight fans' favourite, especially as a local lad from Cheddleton in the Staffordshire Moorlands, broke his leg against Leeds.

It was the tenth time a Stoke City player had broken his leg in six years, a list of casualties beginning with former skipper Peter Dobing and including John Ritchie, Jimmy Robertson, Mike Pejic and, of course, that regular visitor to the casualty department, Denis Smith.

Adding to the injury woes in a relegation season, combative midfielder John Mahoney, an experienced Welsh international and one of Stoke's League Cup winners, spent much of it out with a knee injury.

Another of the boys of 1972, Pejic, who frustratingly enjoyed the briefest of England careers, was also agitating to leave the club he supported as a boy. The sale of Pejic, for Waddington, despite their differences over tactics, served as the final straw. It helped to precipitate his resignation.

Waddington knew Pejic wanted a move and was powerless to stop him from going. At first Pejic made his transfer request to Waddington, making it clear he felt the club, despite at the time being in mid-table, was a prime candidate for relegation. Once Everton's newly appointed manager Gordon Lee, the former Port Vale boss and a man familiar to Pejic, became aware the player was unsettled he put in a bid for the left-back. As a result, Pejic went directly to the chairman telling him he was more than happy to move to Merseyside.

'I was so disillusioned with the club at the time so I didn't hesitate to join Everton,' Pejic told an Evertonian fanzine. Waddington vainly attempted to block the move but failed. 'I could see the writing was on the wall,' Waddington lamented. 'I gave the club an ultimatum that if they sold Mike Pejic I would resign.'

The board ignored him and Pejic was transferred to Everton for £150,000, perfect business sense but for Stoke a poor footballing decision. 'Unnecessary' was Waddington's own verdict. In fairness, the disgruntled player wanted out. In such circumstances it was arguably correct to grant him his wish.

As Waddington had threatened to resign over any transfer of Pejic, the board had effectively called his bluff. They left their manager's door ajar. For the time being Waddington, tied to a new contract from a board publicly insisting he had their support, remained in his post.

He was optimistic he could once again turn around his club's fortunes and stave off relegation, but he wouldn't stay in the job for long. Unbelievably there was a call from the boardroom for a taxi to transport him from Stoke's Victoria Ground.

15

Taxi for 'Waddo'

OFFICIALLY, Tony Waddington resigned as manager of Stoke City Football Club on Monday, 21 March 1976 rather than being sacked. Few fans believed the former scenario to be the case, nor did his shocked players. They concluded that the board had responded to terrace chants of 'Waddington out' by sacking, at the time, the longest-serving manager in English football.

The supporters, incensed by their club's rapid decline in playing fortunes, one brought on by the sale of their favourite players, had vented their fury at the frontman. He was Waddington, who took most of the blame. His departure, as is often the case in football management, was brutal. It was best summed up by Peter Hewitt, the Stoke City correspondent of the *Evening Sentinel*. Hewitt wrote starkly, 'He [Waddington] went home to Crewe, leaving his car. It belonged to the club now. Instead of bowing out in style after giving half his life to a footballing ideal, he had to depart in a taxi.'

Going into a home game against Leicester City on 19 March 1977, Stoke, in an era of two points for a win, were comfortably six points clear of the relegation zone with a third of the season left to play. Waddington had tried and failed to bring in reinforcements for his inexperienced squad, including a bid for Derby County's flamboyant striker Charlie George, but Derby turned him down flat.

Stoke's leading goalscorer at the time was Terry Conroy, a winger rather than a recognised out and out striker, with five goals. Nevertheless, Waddington refused to panic and results eventually became encouraging. The disastrous run over the Christmas and New Year period came to an end with a 2-0 home win over fellow strugglers Coventry City, Conroy scoring both goals. A shock 1-0 away win at title challengers Ipswich Town gave grounds for optimism. There was even speculation that Alan Hudson might return just a few months after leaving.

To put it politely, Hudson enjoyed nowhere near the close relationship with Arsenal's manager Terry Neill as he did with Waddington. 'I would be happy to go back to Stoke if they wanted me,' Hudson revealed. 'Football at Arsenal has become a bit of a joke for me. They cannot be happy with the way I am playing.'

Perhaps with the return of Hudson, a revitalised Stoke would be safe and Waddington able to rebuild his broken team during the summer? Those optimistic thoughts were banished during the course of 90 minutes of football between Stoke and Leicester.

'Inept display underlines Stoke's plight' ranted one edition of the *Sentinel*. Another thundered, 'Dismal fare for City fans'. Those fans numbered a relatively paltry 14,087 with thousands staying away, partly because of those persistent problems of fan violence in and around the Victoria Ground as outlined earlier, and also because of a string of annoyingly inconsistent playing performances.

As Leicester grabbed a late winner, chants of 'Waddington out' rang out loud and clear. Just five brief years earlier the Stoke fans worshipped him. He could do no wrong. Now he was cast as the villain. Football fans are notoriously fickle but the stinging criticism from those who Waddington had once jokingly referred to as his selection committee, clearly hurt him. There was, as he put it, 'pandemonium enveloping the ground'. He went away to consider his future.

Waddington was not to blame for the fire-sale of his best players. Nevertheless, he took the blame. He was also not to blame for a howler from one of his remaining top-class individuals, goalkeeper Peter Shilton. Waddington described Shilton's moment of madness thus, 'We were not playing well, but were within a minute of gaining a valuable point. Then unaccountably, Peter Shilton, who had possession, elected to throw the ball short to [Alan] Bloor when normally he would have punted high up the middle. Bloor was momentarily caught off guard and only pushed the ball out to Leicester's right flank where debutant Winston White's cross fell to the trusty left foot of Frank Worthington who promptly hit his shot into the top corner. We lost 1-0 and that was my last game in charge of a Stoke team.

'After a few words in the dressing room, more in sympathy than anger, I slipped outside the ground listening to the bitter criticism from supporters. I decided there and then that I would hand in my resignation, which I did on the Monday morning.'

His account of his departure, given a decade or so later, was very matter of fact. It was just a simple matter of resigning from the club but he had little choice, and effectively he was sacked. There are clear suspicions that some directors were more than happy to show him the door and usher him into a taxi home, the ultimate humiliation. Others, including his old friend, the outgoing chairman Albert Henshall, appeared keen to keep him at the club, in some capacity or other. Indeed, Henshall briefed Sunday newspaper reporters covering the Stoke v Leicester game to that effect. Waddington would be moving 'upstairs' as general manager according to Henshall. He would not be leaving altogether.

However, in this briefing he quite shockingly and misleadingly blamed his mate for the sale of Jimmy Greenhoff, the biggest bone of contention for Stoke fans. It was not the fault of the board, claimed Henshall. He insisted the Greenhoff transfer was not the result of financial pressure. It was in modern parlance a 'football decision'.

This briefing directly contradicted Henshall's own programme notes a few weeks earlier for a game against Greenhoff's new club, Manchester United. He wrote that Greenhoff's transfer came about 'purely through economic reasons'. What were fans to believe? They were calling for Waddington to go but also wanted to 'sack the board'. Their mood was further darkened by Henshall's intemperate assertion, 'They [the fans] do not deserve First Division football at Stoke.'

By showing his old friend Waddington the door of the manager's office, many in the game of football believed he was about to be granted the sport's equivalent of a death wish. After 14 years of relative success, top-flight football was about to come to an end in the Potteries.

On the morning after the Leicester defeat, Waddington indicated to reporters inquiring about his future that he would not be leaving Stoke any time soon. In his immediate post-match comments he had also appeared upbeat in assessing the looming relegation scrap. 'We shall not go down,' he stubbornly announced. 'If Leicester's form is good enough for sixth place then there is not much wrong with us. But the supporters are fully entitled to criticise.'

Stung by the criticism, the Stoke board held an emergency meeting at the Victoria Ground with Waddington's future, or lack of it, being the only matter on the agenda. The following Monday morning Waddington turned up at the stadium as per usual. He did not storm into the boardroom to hand in his resignation, instead going straight to his office to be debriefed by Frank Mountford on the reserves' Central League game against Bury.

On being contacted by Peter Hewitt about his future, he told him, 'There's nothing to add. I shall make my own decision when to go.'

The pair even sat down to consider what to put in his programme notes for the forthcoming midweek game against Arsenal. There were to be no mischievous comments about the possible return of Hudson to help with the battle against relegation. Instead, Waddington wanted more prosaically to elaborate on remarks he made to the press over the weekend about the considerable cost of meeting the terms of the 1976 Ground Safety Act. As the roof of one of the Victoria Ground's stands had collapsed in a storm at the beginning of 1976, there was little point in moaning about the considerable outlay on stadium improvements. Naturally enough this got little coverage in the national newspapers. Waddington, in or out, was their story in the aftermath of defeat to Leicester.

None of this pattern of events neatly fits a narrative of Waddington automatically handing in his resignation, despite his very own dignified insistence to the contrary. At lunchtime on Monday, 31 March 1977, as his players warmed down in the gym, Waddington was met by chairman Henshall. The pair went into what was described as a 'heated' board meeting. Once the meeting was over, Waddington returned to his office for the final time. As his erstwhile directors called 'a taxi for Mr Waddington', he phoned his captain Denis Smith. According to Smith Waddington 'sounded really cut up'. He told him, 'Denis, the board have called me in and told me they want me to go. They want me to leave. What do you think?' Smith was stunned.

The board had already briefed the national press to the effect of Waddington being to blame for the fire-sale of players rather than Stoke's directors. In fairness, few in the national media believed them. Nor did most fans. Now the club's board was forcing Waddington to resign. 'I thought the board wouldn't want to sack him because Tony was a legend and dismissing him would make them look so bad. But they did,' commented Smith. 'And they'd made out he resigned too. It was a shocking way for the board to treat the manager who had brought so much success and glory to the club.'

At the time it was left to Terry Conroy to pay tribute to him on behalf of the players. 'There have been disagreements between us in the past, as happens in all walks of life, but from a player's point of view he always treated us fairly and for a player like myself allowed us a free rein on the field,' he wrote in the *Evening Sentinel*. 'His strength, I felt, was his persuasive way of talking, reflected, I suppose, by the way he signed up so many star players. We have not had the success he had hoped for and it seems that the League Cup win and three qualifications for Europe was not good enough for the supporters so they have stayed away.'

It was a cheeky dig at absentee fans that only the mercurial and popular Irishman could get away with. More diplomatically, he observed of the circumstances surrounding the departure of Waddington, 'Players are above club affairs generally and keep apart from relations between the board and the manager.'

In his autobiography Conroy was naturally more forthcoming, freed of the obligations of a contracted player. 'There had been a few changes at board level,' Conroy wrote. 'Waddo was now being questioned more than he had been before as the board sought to professionalise things and he didn't like it. He'd spent a lot of money assembling the best squad the club had ever had, but now his lads were being sold from underneath him one by one.'

Given the benefit of hindsight, it was a view accepted these days by Stoke fans once calling for their manager to be sacked. Sadly for Waddington those supporters had blamed him in the spring of 1977 for the slow demise of their football club, the very man who had resurrected it in the first place.

His departure was generally greeted as further evidence of the inexorable decline of the national game, one sullied by feckless owners, in the grip of at best fickle and at worst violent supporters. English football in the 1970s was in a mess. The pile of rubble from the collapse of Stoke's gale-battered roof served as a metaphor for the general state of the game.

A proud man of football had been humiliated by his board of directors. 'Taxi for so and so' is a standing joke among football fans of the Premier League era. In the case of Waddington, Stoke's board of directors made it a sad reality. They had been looked upon as models of propriety, refreshing and honourable owners in contrast to the ruthless owners operating at other clubs.

They were viewed up until the spring of 1977 as 'the best board in the land'. That view was best summed up by *The Sun*'s John Sadler, who wrote just a few weeks before Stoke City's directors sent their manager home in a taxi, 'Football has no feelings for the men who make it work. They use them and abuse them, pay them and slay them without a second thought. Apart from Tony Waddington, of course.'

The distinguished correspondent turned out to be wrong. Stoke's directors were also in the business of 'using, abusing and slaying'.

Attempts to dress up Waddington's exit as a resignation fell on deaf ears in the national tabloid media. They focused on the anger felt by Waddington, noting his refusal to come to the door of his Crewe home with family members insisting he was 'too upset' to talk. Speculation centred on persistent rumours of him being appointed as general manager with the former Northern Ireland international Derek Dougan, then manager of non-league Kettering Town and a popular television pundit of the day, taking over the running of the first team.

Dougan denied that he had been in talks with Stoke and offered sympathy for Waddington. Indeed, in expressing his sadness at the 'resignation', Dougan commented with a strong degree of irritation, 'To put the record straight, I have had no approach from anyone at Stoke City. I hope that categorical statement will be read, marked and thoroughly digested because I have the utmost admiration and respect for Stoke, as I have for Tony Waddington, now their late [former] manager. The suggestion that I have been involved in some kind of cloak and dagger operation leading to my management of the club is ludicrous.'

He added in tribute, 'It must be remembered that Tony Waddington did more for Stoke with limited resources than most other managers would have done.'

Further comments from Dougan about the running of English football clubs would also hardly endear him to Stoke's directors if there was a plan to make him Waddington's replacement. 'I would not want to be a league manager under the prevailing system of hire and fire,' Dougan wrote in a syndicated column for evening newspapers. 'I could not be a lackey for any board of directors.'

Stoke's board turned to Waddington's stunned backroom staff. Assistant manager George Eastham took over first-team duties with long-standing coach Alan A'Court. There was an imminent fixture against Arsenal to fulfil. Quite remarkably, in fraught circumstances, they decided to restore Waddington's son Steve to the first team. He was told he was playing only 24 hours after his dad vacated the manager's office.

Perhaps not surprisingly he ended up being involved in the game's flashpoint, the latest affray in meetings between Stoke and Arsenal, a pattern to be repeated some decades later in the Premier League. Waddington junior took out any feelings of anger and pent-up frustration on Arsenal's playmaker Liam Brady, tackling the Irishman heavily from behind. Brady immediately sprang to his feet and threw a punch at his tormentor, who instantly fell to the ground. In the ensuing fracas, Brady was shown the red card while Waddington was lucky to get away with just a yellow.

Despite having the advantage of playing against ten men for most of the game, Stoke only managed to eke out a frustrating 1-1 draw. In the circumstances, with the loss of a manager so adored, it was arguably a creditable result. From Arsenal's boss Terry Neill, they received fulsome praise. 'Those Stoke players showed a lot of character,' Neill commented. Yet it was another point dropped in the fight against relegation. Ultimately, shorn of the club's most successful manager, Stoke failed to survive in the top flight of English football and won only one of their remaining 12 games.

As it turned out the *News of the World*'s football pundit, a certain former critic of Waddington by the name of Terry McNeill, was present for this midweek game. McNeill offered his observations and revealed how he had bumped into Steve Waddington after the game, no surprise as the man from the *News of the World*'s alter ego just happened to be the Arsenal manager. 'I haven't any grudges against the club,' Waddington junior told McNeill. 'I was shocked about dad, but it hasn't affected how I feel about Stoke City.'

On the departure of Steve's father Tony, McNeill was both sympathetic and scathing. He commented, 'The man is still hurt. But there won't be any mud-heaving when the time comes to pick up the pieces of his life, almost certainly outside football.'

On the latter point, McNeill was wrong and Waddington did eventually return to football as manager of Crewe Alexandra. For the time being McNeill revealed Waddington was 'adamant' that he would 'confine his bitter thoughts to himself'. He was the victim of the vagaries of football economics, all too fragile for ostensibly well-run top-flight clubs even now in the Premier League era.

'Waddington was sucked into the world of high finance,' concluded McNeill in a colourful tribute. 'In the end, he became a victim of the law of diminishing returns. He was ordered to sell his [playing] assets. Local support fell away alarmingly as goals practically dried up and Waddington was trapped. He was squirming in the middle of a financial tug-of-war from the moment a gale blew the lid off the decaying Butler Street Stand.'

Few, at the time or since, disagreed with this analysis. It did though refer to the 'all powerful Safety of Sport Act'. Tragic events at Bradford and Hillsborough, in the decade after the collapse of Stoke's 'decaying' stand, sadly put the lie to such a notion.

For Waddington and Stoke, the roof falling in on the Butler Street Stand led to a financial calamity. It could easily have been a human tragedy with a match due to be played on the day the roof collapsed. Such a disaster was only narrowly averted, by luck rather than judgement. Nobody took any notice of the wider lessons to be learned from the travails at Stoke, whether it be at home at Bradford or abroad at Heysel in Brussels, or for that matter elsewhere.

Reflecting on his departure a decade later, Waddington remained, as already noted, stubbornly loyal to Stoke's board of directors. They had not sacked him, he insisted. He had resigned. 'The die was cast and I said there was no way they could stay in the First Division by selling their best players,' he forlornly commented. 'I said if this is going to continue, anyway, I am just as well away so after 20 odd years I just resigned and that was it.'

During the summer of 1977, Stoke boasted of posting profits of £476,766. That was the good news. The bad news was the books had to be balanced by the sale of first Ian Moores and Sean Haslegrave, then club captain Jimmy Greenhoff, Alan Hudson and Mike Pejic.

The inevitable result was relegation. From the bright lights of performing 'a working man's ballet' on the highest stage, Waddington's old club had descended into the depths of footballing gloom.

16

Legendary Status

FROM hero to villain, then for the notoriously fickle football fan a man to be hailed as a legend. It is a path trodden by many in the beautiful game, not least Tony Waddington. Just five years after tens upon tens of thousands took to the streets of the Potteries to hail him as a conquering hero, the first and only man to bring home a major football prize to the club, a sparse crowd of die-hards stood on the Victoria Ground terraces, chanting 'Waddington out'.

He duly left. Yet within a decade or so he was back in the Victoria Ground directors' box as a man to be applauded and feted. Remarkably, there was even talk of him returning to help in the management of Stoke. All had been forgiven, if not forgotten. To his adoring fans, indeed members of the board with whom he had fallen out, Waddington had achieved legendary status and was a man to be honoured and praised for his achievements rather than demonised as in the spring of 1977.

At the time of his departure, Waddington was still relatively young at the age of 51 but pundits wrote him off. He had, for them, become an elder statesman of the game as England's longest-serving manager. His time had come and gone, cynics concluded.

Waddington felt otherwise. He still had something to offer to the game. Many of his peers felt the same, not least his old friend Brian Clough. As 1978 league champions, Clough's Nottingham Forest side embarked on an ultimately successful European Cup campaign. It was time to repay a debt.

Waddington's phone rang and it was Clough on the other end of the line. 'See you at East Midlands airport,' Clough told Waddington. 'The tickets are in the post. You are travelling with us.' Waddington joined Clough and his assistant Peter Taylor for the trip to AEK Athens. He did the same for the quarter-final against Grasshoppers of Zurich, the semi-final with FC Cologne, and then the final in Munich against Malmo. For the final, the eccentric Forest manager insisted that Waddington sat on the bench alongside himself and Taylor.

Clough felt a debt of gratitude to Waddington for taking him along to Stoke's UEFA Cup clash against Ajax in Amsterdam four seasons earlier. At the time, given his acrimonious departure from Leeds United, Clough, for all his hubris, was made to feel a pariah by his critics. Waddington had invited him, albeit as a one-off gesture, back into the fold of a warm and friendly football club. 'He was direct and honest and it was a pleasure to be in his company,' remembered Waddington. 'He more than repaid that gesture of mine.'

Clough, in turn, was effusive in his praise of Waddington. 'I never understood why Tony and Stoke City split up, the two went together like Gilbert and Sullivan,' commented Clough. 'I wish he'd been allowed to stay there a little longer. He is a very special guy, who when making trips to Nottingham Forest, my club were all the better for him being there.'

Clough had whetted his friend's appetite and Waddington wanted a return to the game. His opportunity soon came at his former club Crewe Alexandra. Twenty-seven years after walking out of Gresty Road to move to near neighbours Stoke, Waddington returned there as manager. He revealed that one unnamed First Division boss had rung him up to ask him why he wanted 'to climb Everest again'.

Waddington enjoyed a challenge, even seemingly impossible tasks but sadly, in the end, it did not work out. He performed minor miracles in his early years at Stoke, although bringing success to Crewe, a club with no history of performing at the highest level, proved impossible.

Waddington ought not to have been surprised. On his return to Crewe, the club had just endured a recent history of consistently battling to stay in the Football League and of the 92 clubs, they finished 92nd in the previous season. They only survived because back then there was no automatic promotion and relegation between the Football League and non-league divisions. Instead, clubs finishing in the bottom four of the old Fourth Division applied for re-election at the Football League's annual general meeting.

Crewe, despite being perennial applicants, always managed to gain a sympathetic hearing from the chairmen of the other Football League clubs but one day, they feared, they might run out of luck, hence the decision to hire Waddington.

Oddly, it meant a return visit to the Victoria Ground at Stoke. Waddington went along to meet Stoke's club secretary Mike Potts, a man he had helped to hire, and sign a release form from the four-year contract he had signed just months before being shown the door. Once the formalities were over, he commented, 'It marks the end of a long association with the club which, I feel, Stoke City cannot feel too displeased about. In truth, I thought it was a relationship which would never end, but that's football.'

Despite the impoverished state of his new club, Waddington confidently pursued his task with vigour, employing familiar managerial tactics; recruit veteran trusted players to supplement talented greenhorn players from the youth ranks. The men to contact? Among them were Jimmy Greenhoff and Alan Hudson, the very players he was forced to let go from Stoke.

The attempt to lure Hudson to Gresty Road bore all the hallmarks of Waddington's keen eye for public relations by creating a stir in the community and focusing interest on the local football club. Recruiting Hudson to this PR cause proved easy but actually managing to recruit him to play for Crewe, a side at the foot of the Football League table, was probably always a non-starter.

Yet Waddington drummed up plenty of publicity, inviting Hudson to sit in the stands to watch the local derby against Port Vale. Crewe lost, leaving them rock bottom of the league table, but that seemed of secondary importance. Would a star player, one being shunned by First Division clubs, run out in a Crewe shirt? Quite possibly, answered Hudson. 'If something can be worked out I would be delighted to join Tony at Crewe,' Hudson insisted. 'I am fit, fitter than for some time, and I feel I could do a good job with a couple of First Division clubs, but even so I feel I would rather play for Tony Waddington.'

The deal failed to materialise. At the time Hudson was contracted to North American league side Seattle Sounders and given the shortage of money at Crewe, Waddington could only afford a loan deal. Football League rules at the time prevented such deals for British players with American clubs. 'Obviously, I am disappointed not to get a player of Alan Hudson's quality at Crewe,' Waddington told local reporters. 'It is also unfortunate that this ruling has made it impossible to go ahead with any other transfers from the United States. It means that I have got to start all over again in a bid to sign players.'

It was yet another sly dig at the footballing authorities, a feature of his career and a characteristic endearing him to fans sharing his seeming contempt for some of those bureaucratic figures running English professional football. Waddington managed eventually to recruit two of his former star players, first Terry Conroy, and then

Jimmy Greenhoff. Hudson did return to playing First Division football, ironically enough for Stoke.

Conroy's deal proved a lot simpler for Waddington to complete. The Irishman had also gone abroad, in his case to play for Hong Kong side Bulova. It turned out to be a disastrous move as within three months he was back after falling out with the club owners. As Conroy flew back to the UK, Waddington was on the phone to the winger's mother-in-law using her as an agent to obtain his signature. Quite how Waddington got word from Hong Kong of Conroy's flight out of the former British colony the player himself never worked out. But he was delighted he did. 'This was great news – my old manager coming to save the day,' Conroy declared in his autobiography.

Waddington, by the time of Conroy's arrival, had also recruited a few more of his former Stoke players, including Ian 'Danny' Bowers and Kevin Lewis. Greenhoff, who lived down the road from Waddington in the south Cheshire village of Alsager, joined them.

After Greenhoff had been dropped by Manchester United, ironically for a game against Stoke, Waddington put in a bid for the player. United accepted. 'If Mr Waddington wants me to sign and goes in with an offer, I will listen to him,' commented Greenhoff. 'If I am going to a lower-division club I would go to Crewe.'

True to form, Waddington had also spotted a talented goalkeeper to help him in the herculean task of trying to lift Crewe Alexandra off the bottom of the Football League table. He was a young Zimbabwean, an eccentric character loved by the Crewe fans, by the name of Bruce Grobbelaar.

Waddington described him as one of the 'outstanding' goalkeepers he'd signed during his career, putting him in the same category as Gordon Banks and Peter Shilton. His signing of Grobbelaar, a loan deal, came about by accident. As he put it, the move came 'out of the blue'. In his quest to find a reliable custodian, preferably on the cheap, he put in a call on the off-chance to an old friend, Tony Walters, himself a former goalkeeper, who had taken over as manager of Vancouver Whitecaps in Canada.

As it turned out, Walters had a youngster on his club's books who he hadn't even seen play, so he suggested that Waddington take him on loan, try him out, and report back. Waddington agreed and eventually did just that. 'Sell him to an English First Division club' was Waddington's impromptu scouting report.

'As soon as I saw Bruce in action I realised his potential, wondering how a goalkeeper with his ability could possibly be left in the wilderness,' Waddington recalled with fondness to the *Stoke Sentinel*. 'His reactions, handling, and timing were tremendous and he was also a superb athlete.'

Waddington quickly recognised that his young goalkeeper was going to be too good to be playing Fourth Division football, and Crewe were also not in a financial position to strike a permanent deal. So as Grobbelaar waited to be given a work permit, Waddington began touting him around to First Division clubs, beginning with Manchester United. He felt a stint with one of his former assistants, Harry Gregg, who had gone back to Old Trafford as goalkeeping coach, would do him good. There was no joy there.

'I just wanted to keep Bruce occupied and I always believed the ideal way to learn was to play with and against better players,' Waddington later explained. 'Bruce had two weeks there, [Manchester United] but nothing further developed. Apparently he was not too happy training at Old Trafford.'

He then sent Grobbelaar to his old mate Brian Clough at Nottingham Forest to train with Peter Shilton, who was by then in the form of his life. Under Waddington at Stoke, Shilton's performances had been, to put it politely, inconsistent; at times brilliant and on other occasions distinctly indifferent. This was not the case in his time with Clough at Forest. Clough, however, did not need a goalkeeper, so Waddington went elsewhere. Fatefully, he picked up the phone to Bob Paisley at Liverpool.

Paisley turned up to visit Waddington at Gresty Road on one of the shortest scouting missions in football history. 'I saw him go up to his seat in the stand, but ten minutes later I saw him again on the point of leaving before our game had kicked off,' remembered Waddington.

He approached the Liverpool boss to ask him, 'What's the matter?' Paisley told him he had seen enough. He then turned around to Waddington to comment, 'He is going to be a great keeper.' Paisley knew that Waddington had not lost his ability to spot a top-class player, especially a goalie.

Grobbelaar, once his work permit came through, made his debut for Crewe alongside Terry Conroy at York City in a 2-2 draw. 'It was obvious Bruce was going to be something special,' recalled Conroy. 'He was funny and eccentric. He would hang on the crossbar while the ball was up the other end during games, or do acrobatic flip flops in his area.'

These antics helped to keep the Crewe fans entertained. Sadly they also saw their side, once again, finish bottom of the Football League table despite their manager's best efforts so they again had to apply for re-election and were yet again successful. Waddington stayed, but it was only to be for another season, while Grobbelaar left to become part of Liverpool folklore.

As Prince Charles was about to walk down the aisle of St Paul's Cathedral with Lady Diana Spencer, Waddington failed to see his own divorce on the cards – his own split from Crewe Alexandra, a club named after a 19th-century Princess of Wales.

Having finished bottom of the table in his first season in charge, Waddington had enjoyed relative success in the following year. With Greenhoff and Conroy in harness together, the crowds were beginning to flock to Gresty Road to see the attacking flair on offer. For the first time in nearly a decade the club's directors did not end up going cap in hand to their Football League peers as re-election was avoided, albeit by a point.

Yet on 27 July 1981, Waddington was sacked by Crewe, just as he was due go back to begin pre-season training. It was every bit as cruel and hurtful as his departure from Stoke. On being given the news, he described himself as 'absolutely shattered'.

In reflecting on his exit, Waddington speculated that the club's board wanted a younger man in charge of team affairs, one able to bring though youth rather than rely on experience. Waddington wanted to do both as he had done so successfully at Stoke. Crewe's directors would eventually get their 'younger manager' in the guise of Dario Gradi but sadly for Waddington they had run out of patience with him, barely giving him a chance to succeed after just two seasons in charge.

Directors of football clubs demand loyalty but rarely display such qualities themselves. As a man who helped to shove his old friend Waddington out of the door at Stoke, Albert Henshall curiously serves as an example. After admitting it was 'a hell of a job' to replace Waddington, he railed at the behaviour of other clubs in trying to lure away his mate's eventual successor at Stoke, Alan Durban. In rather heated language, Henshall moaned, 'It doesn't matter a bugger whether clubs get permission or not any more. There's no such thing as loyalty between clubs. Contracts are supposed to be legally binding but that doesn't seem to deter anyone.'

Waddington's legally binding contracts at Stoke and then Crewe mattered little either.

Yet if there was any lingering bitterness from Waddington over being effectively forced to leave Stoke, it soon disappeared. Stoke did eventually lose Durban to another club and fans, harking back to the glory days of watching Waddington's cavalier style of football, felt it was a case of good riddance. After a dire defeat to Arsenal, Durban had infamously commented, 'Who are we running soccer for?' If fans wanted entertainment, he suggested, 'You could go out and get a bunch of clowns.' Durban's critics immediately and sarcastically pointed out that his predecessor had gathered such 'clowns' as Stanley Matthews, Dennis Viollet, Jimmy McIlroy, George Eastham, Jimmy Greenhoff and Alan Hudson. Waddington might at times have been an arch pragmatist but he wanted his teams to go out, play and entertain. Thanks to Durban's intemperate comments Stoke fans had an early nostalgic reminder of their legendary manager.

Once Durban's successor Richie Barker was sacked, speculation grew that Waddington might even return to Stoke. Bill Asprey, a member of his promotion-winning team playing at right-back behind Matthews, stepped into the manager's dugout. He needed assistance and some wise counselling. The most obvious choice to give Asprey guidance was Waddington, just a few short years after he left the Victoria Ground in a taxi. If such a formal offer was ever made, Waddington politely and sensibly declined it.

Stoke continued to struggle, losing their top-flight status and being left in the wilderness for nearly a quarter of a century until chairman Peter Coates and Tony Pulis revived their fortunes. It was Coates who formally invited Waddington back as an associate director. He clearly did as much as an appreciative fan as chairman of the football club.

'Tony's record was impressive,' the current Stoke chairman told me. 'His place in Stoke City's history is assured. He is judged with great affection.'

Stoke supporters, including fickle fans such as myself yelling 'Waddington out' from the terraces of the Boothen End, looked back at his time in charge with misty-eyed fondness. One of their heroes on the pitch, the late John Ritchie, mused, 'I wonder if people really do remember how much he did for Stoke City.'

His comments were perhaps borne out of frustration at the treatment of Waddington in the late 1970s. Yet his colleagues and fans alike do remember the enormous contribution Waddington made not just to Stoke City, but to the game of football. He had his foibles. He had his faults. Could he have done more to avert the financial disaster at Stoke, notwithstanding the battering the club took from the forces of Mother Nature let alone a deeply unfavourable economic climate? The answer is almost certainly no, though one caveat in hindsight may be the questionable decision to go ahead with a successful world record bid for a goalkeeper.

One of his strengths happened to be the recognition of a need for a top-class keeper, a position in the team too often ignored by some of his managerial peers. Recruiting Irish international Jimmy O'Neill as his first signing was a smart move. Signing the world's best, Banks, quite frankly was stunning. Sadly for even his most ardent supporters, the transfer of Shilton turned out to be a curious mistake.

The money to land Shilton might have been better used to invest in players in other positions, not least in attack. Waddington, much to the surprise of many of his players, failed to trust John Farmer, who was left to articulate his disillusionment in poetry.

Farmer penned this verse entitled *The Reserve Team Goalie's Prayers to Remain Unanswered*:

I pray for silence in the storm,
I pray for speed of thought in times,
When destiny calls,
To take my crown of thorns away.

His colleagues wished that Waddington had heeded Farmer's prayers. Denis Smith recognised that Shilton was a better goalkeeper than Farmer but felt he was, in his view, the 'wrong man' for the Stoke team. 'I firmly believe if Waddo had spent the money on a goalscorer instead of Peter Shilton we could have won the league,' concluded Smith. 'It's odd the Shilts signing didn't work out,' commented Conroy. 'But there it is. It didn't.'

As a judgement call, the signing of Shilton was a rare aberration, one that nobody could foresee. After all, Shilton was one of the finest goalkeepers in the country and he went on to win what was at the time a world record 125 international caps. Fate decreed that Waddington and Stoke lost Banks to injury in the cruellest circumstances, and he turned out to be irreplaceable.

Frankly, in such a scenario there was arguably little more Waddington was able to do. At the time of signing Shilton, no one complained. It seemed the right thing to do, a statement of title-winning intent. Sadly, in hindsight, the decision turned out to be a mystifying mistake. He ought to have gone out and signed a top-class striker, if one was available. Back then, as now, easier said than done. The explanation for his signing Shilton instead lies with his obsession with goalkeepers. As Peter Coates told me, 'The way he looked at a goalkeeper was the same as a striker.'

Waddington's man-management skills did little to assist Shilton as he struggled at Stoke. For other players, even those questioning his level of tactical acumen, his man-management skills were legendary. The late Sir Bobby Robson spoke of his admiration for Waddington's ability to handle players' egos, especially the chiselled veterans such as Stanley Matthews and Jimmy McIlroy in his early years in charge of Stoke.

Sir Bobby said, 'Tony was the first manager to see and employ those who were reaching the end of their careers but who still had two or three years left in the First Division. These kind of players can be very difficult to handle, touchy and very conscious of any suggestion they were over the top, but Tony had a brilliant record with that kind of player, always backing his judgement as to their ability, blending them into teams that kept Stoke City among the challengers for points and publicity for most of his years at the Victoria Ground.'

Waddington's long-time assistant Alan A'Court concurred. 'When I joined up with Tony the first thing that struck me was the skill and ability of the players he had around him,' A'Court recalled. He then went on to list them, 'You think if of the calibre of

Roy Vernon, Maurice Setters, Eddie Clamp, Eddie Stuart, George Eastham, Peter Dobing, Alec Elder, all these players. You could go on. There's a list ad infinitum. All these players that he'd brought had all done it. I think he felt that having those players around him would make for his pure dream of what he'd like to see in football and in general.'

How did he attract this array of fine players over the years? Peter Coates answers, 'He [Waddington] was extremely canny and clever and he had the charm and the skill to do it.'

Alan Hudson arrived at Stoke as a player with a big reputation, yet some of his critics, including the former Chelsea manager Dave Sexton, felt had lost his way. Waddington begged to differ. 'Tony Waddington was a man of great humanity, dignity and standards,' Hudson wrote of his old boss, the man who revived a faltering career. 'He had a wonderful way with you. I could talk to him about anything.'

Hudson had an especially close relationship with his manager, other players less so. Yet even in disputes with him they remember falling for his charm. Conroy often recalls going into his office to make his case for a first-team place. 'As a man, I would say he had lots of charm. You would go steaming into the office, go through the door and brush away the secretary, disregard making appointments. You'd be going in and Tony would be sat there behind the desk and you steam into him and saying what have you left me out for,' Conroy explained.

'It was because he had an ability to sit you down and maybe pour you a drink, if you wanted one, and talk about everything but the reasons why you went in. He'd talk about your family, and how you felt yourself, but football never came into it. He had this ability to be able to turn you away from your way of thinking and divert you away from what your feelings really were and so you'd be going out five or ten minutes later and you'd be apologising for going into his office in the first place.'

As Waddington's time at Stoke came to a close, he introduced a promising young forward from the youth ranks. Garth Crooks remains especially appreciative of not just Waddington's unerring eye for a quality player but those legendary man-management skills. 'I think it's fair to say that Tony Waddington was ahead of his time,' commented Crooks in tribute. 'For a young black lad in the town of Stoke to be given the opportunity that I was given at that time I think was not only brave of him but was typical of the man.'

Crooks came to Waddington's attention in unusual circumstances, living just around the corner from the old Victoria Ground and going to the primary school located behind the towering terraces of the Boothen End. 'Garth was forever dribbling a ball to and from school and hitting it occasionally against my office window,' Waddington noted with amusement. 'When I got the chance Tony took me under his wing,' Crooks commented in gratitude. 'If he hadn't taken me under his wing and protected me to a large degree from some of the more unsavoury aspects of the professional game, then my career might not have been. So, I'm eternally grateful to Waddo.'

Waddington tried to shield his young player from racial abuse, a sickeningly persistent and endemic malady among English football fans of the 1970s and 80s. 'He [Crooks] always had tremendous confidence,' Waddington recalled. 'I left him out of the team initially at Everton because as one of the few black players in the First Division at the time he was coming in for a lot of racial abuse. He came up to me and said, "Boss, I hope you are not leaving me out of the team because of the comments being levelled at me."

'I replied, "I am just trying to protect you. I don't want your confidence affected." Garth said, "I am used to it. I seem to have had abuse all my life and it does not bother me now. If that is the only reason you have dropped me, then I have to tell you that it will not affect my game." Garth went out at Goodison to prove his point.' The admiration between the pair was mutual. Waddington pointed to the eventual sale of Crooks to Tottenham Hotspur as another example of how, in his view, Stoke embarked on a course of self-destruction. Intriguingly, he blamed his successor Alan Durban for the sale rather than the board. To the day he died it seemed he consistently refused to blame his old friends on the board of directors for his football club's demise in the late 1970s and early-to-mid-80s.

In assessing Waddington's managerial skills, it seemed that in the eyes of some of his players he was more to them of a magician than a footballing tactician. He wanted them to perform 'a working man's ballet'; beautiful free-flowing football to delight the watching public. But as the director, he appeared to leave it to them how to go out and do it. He built talented sides. There was no point in telling them how to play. As Alan Dodd put it, 'We played off the cuff.'

Yet there was an element of choreography. For all those twinkle-toed performers offering stylish flourishes, there needed to be support from a few clog-hoppers. As one of Waddington's contradictions his pure dream, as A'Court put it, of playing free-flowing football just happened to be predicated on uncompromising defence.

At first, this was his famed defensive wall of Eddie Clamp and Eddie Stuart, then as Hudson called them the 'barricade' of local players, John Marsh, Mike Pejic, Denis Smith and Alan Bloor, and later Dodd. 'Having played against them I knew how tough they were,' remembered Hudson. 'But in joining them I saw first-hand and got to know the mentality and motivation of such players. Nobody was coming to the Potteries and taking liberties.'

Stoke fans long appreciated these qualities in Waddington's sides, not least those who played for him. In recalling the signings arriving at the football club, Dodd commented, 'The players Tony signed, they could only play one way. They couldn't play defensively. He signed quality players that could only play the skilful way. They played with complete freedom. That's what I will always remember about Waddo.

'I was always a big Stoke supporter so obviously Stoke were my club and to play under Tony Waddington was obviously my ambition. I saw the type of football they played. I think the emphasis was always on the skill side of the game, which was a bonus for me.'

Training sessions were recalled with fondness, especially five-a-side workouts in the gym, not least Waddington's propensity for joining in. On a Monday morning players soon found out if their manager was unhappy with their performance on the previous weekend. Waddington would get his administrative duties out the way in the morning, then go up to the gym at the corner of the ground.

His Welsh international John Mahoney ruefully recalled the ritual. 'He used to love it. You can always tell if you've had a bad game on the Monday. He used to get quite fearsome,' Mahoney commented. 'Everybody got a sweat on. It was a bit feverish and you'd go into a tussle. You'd think, don't whack the boss. But he used to get you. He used to dig you with his elbows. He'd sharpen his elbows. You used to think, "What's going on there?" Then you'd realised. The penny would drop. Maybe he wasn't too happy with your performance on the Saturday because he used to be able to look after himself. He'd give a little niggle there and a littler niggle there.'

As a method of disciplining players for putting in a below-par performance, it was unconventional. There would be no verbal confrontations, or at least any altercations were kept to a minimum.

'He would rather put his arm round you than put his hands around your throat,' Conroy commented. Waddington's League Cup-winning captain Peter Dobing, a player who spectacularly fell out with him by briefly retiring from football, described his boss as 'one of the game's great psychologists'.

When asked to comment on his skipper's observation, Waddington answered, 'Let's just say I'm not neurotic.' In assessing his psychological state, he curiously described himself as a 'Jekyll and Hyde' type of character. 'It's the only way I can be elated and analytical at the same time. I kick every ball. Yet I judge it too,' he explained to *The Sun* just prior to his 1972 Wembley triumph. 'The important thing is to be perceptive. Emotion must not get in the way.'

His calm, dispassionate methods worked, bringing Stoke unprecedented success until on a winter's day the roof quite literally rather than just metaphorically caved in.

As Stoke struggled in the lower divisions in the 1980s and 90s, the club's fans, yearning for a change of fortunes, looked back on the glory days of the Waddington era with fondness. One of those supporters, chairman Peter Coates – in his first stint in charge – invited Waddington officially back into the fold in the role of an associate director. His only problem was trying to physically take his place in the VIP seats. Ill health, not least his dodgy knees, made it difficult for him.

'I remember Stoke having one of the best ever sides under his management,' Coates commented. 'The football club doing well is a plus for any area. He was a plus for Stoke City. In the Potteries, an old industrial area, football means such a lot to people. He delivered one of their best ever periods. You deserve a special place in those circumstances.'

As for Waddington's personal qualities, Coates reiterated a familiar theme, 'He had a certain charm, a nice convivial sort of person.'

Stoke Supporters' Council chair, Angela Smith commented, 'I was lucky enough to meet him on several occasions in and out of the club. He liked a drink, was personable and knowledgeable, but was a football man through and through. He could work wonders when he spoke to players. He sold them the dream of playing in front of a fan base that knew a player and would get behind anyone who gave 100% whilst wearing the red and white stripes of our club.'

Angela, a Stoke fan who fulfilled her own sporting dreams by becoming a world squash champion, concluded, 'More importantly, he knew that he could extract that little bit more from players when others thought they were well past the sell by date and add to that his eye for young talent and we had a recipe for wonderful football that stood the test of time and is looked back on with fond memories. Waddo built a side known for playing good football.'

Anthony Waddington passed away in Leighton Hospital, Crewe, at 5pm on Saturday, 29 January 1994 with his family at his bedside. His grieving son Steve commented that it was 'the end of his match'.

Mourning fans laying tributes to their hero at the Victoria Ground said it was though he was hanging on for the last result. Aside from Waddington's own son Steve, his 'adopted son' Alan Hudson was among those to share his final hours, describing Waddington as his 'manager, mentor and best friend', and his passing as the 'end of a love affair'. He called it a 'privilege' to know Waddington and rather tellingly felt that his former boss had been let down by many people but had not had a bad word to say about anyone.

Mournfully referring to the infamous collapse of the Butler Street Stand roof, Hudson commented, 'The thing that he took with him was never to know why that freak gust of wind blew them away and left him a forlorn, disillusioned and a heartbroken man.'

Gordon Banks, in tribute to Waddington, described his time at Stoke City as the 'best years' of his life. 'I will always savour those years,' he said. 'It was a family club. He was a great man.'

In summing up his father's footballing philosophy, Steve Waddington stressed Tony's desire to produce entertaining sides. Key to his success he believed was an ability to treat players like people. 'He believed in them but above all he loved the game,' Waddington junior commented. 'He loved the adulation [from the fans] but not in a conceited way. He thought of it as a genuine pay-back for the type of football he wanted to play.'

Tony, throughout his time as manager of Stoke, recognised the club's importance to the people of a solidly working-class industrial district, men and women proud of their craft and artistry in the ceramics centre of the world. He ensured the men he sent out in red and white stripes replicated such craft and artistry on the football field.

He simply stated in looking back on his career, 'The Potteries are renowned for their brilliant and traditional craftsmanship and for their warm hearts and friendly faces. I like to think we did our best in my time to ensure that Stoke City enshrined all those qualities.'

By doing his 'best', football's convivial charmer offered Stoke City's fans, the grateful people of the Potteries, living artistry in the guise of sport.

He gave them 'a working man's ballet'.

Select Bibliography

BOOKS:

Banksy, My Autobiography, Gordon Banks, Michael Joseph/Penguin Books (2002)

Just One of Seven, Denis Smith and Simon Lowe, Know the Score Books Ltd (2008)

Potters at War, Simon Lowe, Desert Island Books Ltd (2004, 2009)

Stanley Matthews, The Authorised Biography, David Miller, Pavilion Books Ltd (1989)

The Football League, Bryon Butler, MacDonald Queen Anne Press (1988)

The Football Man, Arthur Hopcraft, Aurum Press (1968, 2006)

The Waddington Years, Alan Hudson, Snide Press (2008)

The Waddington Years DVD, Synergy Studios (2009)

The Way It Was, Stanley Matthews, Headline Book Publishiing (2000)

The Wizard, the Life of Stanley Matthews, Jon Henderson, Yellow Jersey Press (2014)

You Don't Remember Me, Do You? Terry Conroy, Pitch Publishing (2015)

NEWS SOURCES
BBC News
BBC Sport
Burnley Express
Daily Express, London
Daily Mail, London
Daily Mirror, London
Daily Telegraph, London
Duck Magazine, Stoke-on-Trent
Evening Post, Leeds
Evening Sentinel, Stoke-on-Trent
Evening Standard, London
Four Four Two, London
ITV Sport
Lancashire Telegraph, Blackburn
My Story (Evening Sentinel interview series), Tony Waddington with Peter Hewitt, Staffordshire News and Media (1988)
News of the World, London
Sunday Telegraph, London
The Guardian, London
The Observer, London
The Sun, London
The Times, London